"How does one survive the loss of a child? It takes a village. Melissa Monroe's strong, persevering personality and her close network supported her in finding a path through the worst of the pain. Melissa's wise reflections on what was and was not helpful are guideposts for the reader who moves with her through the impact and processing of tragic loss. Eye Movement Desensitization and Reprocessing (EMDR) also supported her in working through the traumatic intrusive images, anxiety, and guilt that compounded her grief. *Mom's Search for Meaning* provides powerful testimony to the strength of the human spirit and our vulnerable, complicated, inspirational ability to heal."

— Kim Cookson, Psy.D., founder of the Trauma and Resiliency Training and Services Program at the Southern California Counseling Center

"Melissa Monroe's "Mom's Search for Meaning" is a book about the unthinkable - and about thinking about the unthinkable. It is not a tale of triumph over adversity, nor is it the story of a descent into heartbreak, though it contains elements of both. Rather, it is a book about how one mother survived a mother's worst possible tragedy. It is the story of how one person found her way – with grief and pain, but also with humor and grace – back to a life that would be forever different but which could not be, and would not be, anything less than purposeful and honest."

— Dan Koeppel, author of *To See Every Bird on Earth, Banana: The Fate of the Fruit That Changed the World*, and *Every Minute is a Day*

"As a study on trauma, *Mom's Search for Meaning* slows down time to the nanosecond. The way Melissa describes the most traumatic moment— the hopelessness, the hope – is not just raw in an emotional sense; it is also technically challenging to put into writing. Somehow, it seems that the EMDR therapy also gave her the ability to get into those moments and describe them to people, which is truly a gift. This book will be profoundly healing to anyone who has undergone a trauma. Melissa does not just say the way out is through; she very much takes us through what that looks like. Moreover, in being so specific, it is universally relatable. The final chapter is 'To Be or Not to Be'- level work. The details are visceral and vivid. It pulls the reader through like a drumbeat or a heartbeat. The rhythm of it echoes the CPR in a way. This is mom-loss Shakespeare."

— Teresa Strasser, author of *Exploiting My Baby*, the upcoming *Making It Home*, and co-host of the syndicated television show, *The List*.

"*Mom's Search for Meaning* is a deep dive into the psyche and a privileged look at the author at her most honest and vulnerable. Melissa invites the reader into her experience profoundly, unlike anything I have read before. Although the circumstances are specific and highly personal, they are also very relatable. This book is a meditation on life, death, and emotional life after child loss by someone who is tragically an expert anthropologist on a topic no one wishes to master. As a non-grieving parent, I found this book incredibly universal and soaked in advice on what is helpful when one is vulnerable and hurting. The explorations of compassion are deep, Melissa's march toward love is inspiring, and the writing is beautiful. It is a book about child loss that — at times — made me laugh out loud. That is weird. And beautiful. And amazing. Just like life. I will never stop thinking about this book. And I am so glad."
    — Liz Friedlander, film and television director

"You have never read anything like this before. Melissa Monroe offers fellow grievers companionship and maybe even a lifeboat by gently inviting us into the deep, intimate details of her journey in *Mom's Search for Meaning*. There is much to marinate over in this pageturner: a wise, intelligent, sad, poignant, and sometimes comical memoir. Melissa's words, crafted together in unforgettable sentences, empty of clichés and platitudes, can help one persevere in unbearable and impossible situations. Her book is a genuine gift of love to grievers but also offers significant insight for us all. Grievers and non-grievers alike will not be able to put this one down. Thank you, Melissa, for giving us a roadmap to get up and make toast again."

— Jo Kaur, Founder of Riaan Research Initiative

"Nothing is more devastating to a parent than the death of their child and the challenge to go on living afterward. In *Mom's Search for Meaning*, Melissa Monroe shares her deeply personal and heartfelt story, demonstrating that child loss grief is a physical, emotional, and spiritual journey unlike any other. For any parent who has lost a child and for those who love and support us, this memoir is a reminder that we are not alone and offers insights and hope for healing after the unimaginable."

— Candace Cahill, author of *Goodbye, Again*

MOM'S SEARCH FOR MEANING

A MEMOIR

MELISSA M. MONROE

FOR GRACE AND ALICE

You give my life meaning
I love you infinity

AUTHOR'S NOTE

In this day and age, I feel I must clarify that the decisions I made for me were for me. My way is not the way in general. When I have verbalized this story to people, I could see on their face the fear I would judge their decisions. Nothing I write here, no decisions made on my part, are a judgment or a declaration about what the reader should do. We all do what we need to do in order to heal. I am writing this not as a guide to grief. It is my guide to grief and I was spitballing, at best. I don't have the time or energy to judge what others do and pray for the same tolerance in return. I do not share this as any kind of mandate. I can only write from my own experience and perspective; I can only report my story. In that spirit, I also do not write about immediate family members who have a more private style of grief. I respected their wishes and left them out of the narrative.

TABLE OF CONTENTS

DAYS

TUESDAY, AUGUST 6, 2013: THE ALLEGED DAY OFF

*T*uesdays are my alleged day off. I say "alleged" because, like most self-employed parents, I am rarely "off." Tuesdays are meant to be my catch-up day. Some Tuesdays I took my two daughters on an adventure for a "special day." Sometimes, I spent them with a sick kid, caretaking and trying to keep myself well. Tuesday, August 6, 2013, was clearly going to be the latter. My youngest, Alice, woke up early with a 99° temperature and a raspy voice. An early riser in a house full of night owls, Alice had recently become more assertive about waking the rest of us. She had celebrated her second birthday just eleven days prior and I was preparing to get her a "big girl" bed to celebrate, but this morning, she had to rely on croakily calling from her crib.

I always wondered if my daughters' sleep schedules were due to their birth times. My eldest daughter, Grace, made an evening entrance three days after her due date. It didn't go as hoped, but I had a healthy baby girl so I didn't give it a second thought. A "late" baby born via emergency C-section was my second lesson in how "kids don't care about your plans and timelines." Scary bits forgotten, the love I felt for her was intoxicating. Grace was teeny-tiny and would not sleep unless she was attached to my body, and even then, it was iffy. I was a newlywed running my new acupuncture clinic while still teaching Pilates clients, working on a doctoral dissertation … with a colicky baby in tow. What I'm trying to say is: I was tired, and this old broad wasn't expecting to find herself expecting within six weeks of discontinuing birth control measures. Grace's conception was the happiest surprise of my life as well as my first lesson in "kids don't give a flip about your plans and timelines."

Two-and-a-half years later, Alice arrived seven hours and thirty-five minutes into her due date after being conceived on spontaneous attempt No. 1, thus proving that occasionally kids do adhere to the expected timeline. Now I had two happiest days of my life. When the lactation nurse handed Alice to me for the first feeding, I thought, "Huh. This one looks *nothing* like the other one," because Alice had chubby cheeks, unlike Grace. Alice then commando-crawled over to my left breast, latched on, and went to town. I did nothing. I did not know newborns could commando-crawl or initiate the first feeding. Then Alice slept in her bassinet next to my bed; I did not have to touch her for her to sleep. She didn't look like Grace; she didn't act like Grace. I knew in one second that Alice would be different than her sister. I was excited to learn what those differences might be.

Although this particular Tuesday was not a day I was having "off," I was grateful, because the previous Saturday, I'd made arrangements to have more private time with Alice. And Alice clearly desired more of me as well. She had recently developed separation anxiety for the first time. The previous morning, she became irritated I was going to leave her at school and thus developed a furrowed brow and a snarl behind her pink binky, while maintaining her usual confident swagger in her rainbow socks, jean skirt, pink top, and brand new, beloved, light-up shoes. The contrast of her attitude, her outfit, and her swagger made me giggle, so I propped her up on the cubby bins and snapped a photo. She wore a look of faraway resignation and cried as I left. I smiled and hugged and kissed her and walked out quickly with tears in my eyes. I hated leaving her like that. I knew I wouldn't see the girls that night because I worked late on Mondays. Alice's separation anxiety was difficult for me as well. I felt guilty that

I couldn't just say, "Screw it. Let's drive back home and I'll cancel work so we can play."

At one point during her birthday party a few days prior, she'd clung to me and tried to shove her head into the womb from whence she'd arrived. I joked that she wanted back inside because she was old enough to know the bankers ruined the entire world economy and no one cared. She laughed, though she could not have possibly understood my joke. Later that day she kept pulling me to sit with her. She patted the place next to her on the blanket and said, "Sit, Mama, sit." I was rushing about hosting and greeting people, but I swear on a stack of Bibles that I felt compelled — pushed down, even — to sit and distinctly recall thinking, "Oh, baby. You are right. It's your party, and I should sit with you a spell." I remember thinking this moment was surreal but I wasn't sure why.

This alleged day off would provide some quality time with Alice — a wonderful silver lining for us both.

I'd figured out a balance of sorts by this point in my working-mother life. It ain't easy. It's first-world problems in the scheme of things, but it ain't easy. Once I had kids, I was surprised to discover I would have preferred to stay home with my kids for a couple of years before returning to work. My generation of women was raised to think "you can have it all" — and you can — but in general, you will likely lose yourself a bit (or a lot) when you "have it all" because, honey, there just ain't enough of you to go around. You can have it all, but you are going to feel like you are dropping all the balls all the time. You can have it all, but you always feel like you should be or could be doing more at home or the office. You will not really have it all, you will have pieces of it all, and it will be frustrating. If you want to work and have a family, it is possible, but you'd better be prepared to feel like a failure much of the time and to be able to talk yourself out of feeling like a failure. I'm just giving it to you straight because I know it's possible that no one else has.

I wasn't in a position to be a stay-at-home mom, however, so — like most parents — I did my best.

Alice was sad to see Grace go to preschool without her on my

3

alleged day off, so we went onto the porch to wave goodbye and blow kisses. A few months prior, Alice had started going to preschool with Grace; both girls were *stoked* and giggled all the way to school. Nineteen months old at the time, Alice had some words but wasn't fully verbal, so it wasn't always easy to discern what she did or did not understand. But on that February day, she clearly understood that she was going to school with Grace, and she clearly thought that this was the best news ever. She beamed as she walked into school and never looked back at me. Though I wished the girls could be home with me more often, I was relieved the girls were so happy at school.

On this particular alleged day off, I noticed an unexpected wave of anxiety as Grace left for school without us. Generally, I felt fine dropping them at school, but after the massacre at Sandy Hook the previous December, I occasionally felt nervous about leaving them. At the time, I wasn't sure how the Sandy Hook parents were going to survive Christmas. Presents under the tree that their child would never open. Family visits that would never be the same. Their attempts at creating beautiful memories for their children were in vain, their history senselessly and violently cut short. I knew that every one of those parents had thought their kids were safe that day. For hours, parents had not been sure if their child was among the living or the dead. My stomach turned.

I could not imagine such hell.

For months, I could not stop thinking about the young children and the teachers at Sandy Hook. Every time I heard of children dying, I thought, "I don't know how any of those parents will ever be able to get up and simply make toast again," and this was no exception. I was sure I would not be able to do so.

The previous Christmas — Alice's first Christmas — a different tragedy had also leveled me. A fire in Stamford, Connecticut, killed all three children as well as the parents of Madonna Badger early Christmas morning. I almost threw up when I heard this. I was an absolute mess and a bit embarrassed I'd become so derailed by a story of people I did not know. I could not imagine a worse hell than surviving the fire that killed all your offspring and both of your parents. I thought, "I don't know how that mother will ever be able to get up and simply make toast again." I thought that if Madonna Badger ever got up and put one foot in front of the other that she would be the strongest human on Earth. I was sure I would die if I were in her shoes.

Both Christmases of Alice's life were preceded by horrific tragedies. Both Christmases, I'd hosted both sides of the family and tried to give my kids and extended family the best possible memories. As a working mom, I didn't often have the opportunity to engage in the types of domestic bliss I envisioned, so I truly cherished every moment. I cooked, entertained, parented, and watched three generations from two sides of family bond through their grandchildren. We even had ubiquitous matching Christmas pajamas. I was happy. I was living my dream and thoroughly enjoyed watching the girls enjoy the dream.

I loved creating the scenes of Christmas for my family and forming the world that would create their memories and inform their traditions. I knew the memories would form their perspective, sense of home, and sense of self — short-term planning of a present that would become the colorful memories of their past in a faraway future. I wanted to form a present that would inform their long-term future in a way that would allow them to relive their past with happiness and to have a sense of continuity and tradition in their life. I always thought of parents as the keepers of time and collectors of stories — the historians — for their children. Parents have many roles, but the role of historian is one I found myself taking quite seriously.

The memories we create for our children, the stories we keep of and for them, how we explain their prehistory and ancestors, all impact the child's sense of self and place in the world. In my opinion, the better we do this, the more well-adjusted the children will be, and the more options they will have. It was, and remains, one of my favorite parts of parenting. I had two boxes of mementos and photos set aside so that I could make their baby books.

I never seemed to have enough time to actually assemble them.

To be a historian for one's child, one must recall the past and be able convey it objectively. You must emphasize the parts where they revealed themselves to you so clearly, they taught you who they are, which in turn taught you how to interact and communicate with them. They will then understand what parts of themselves were present from birth, which parts they picked up from you, and those that they developed on their own. One must also tell the story in a developmentally appropriate manner throughout the years, while maintaining the integrity of the story and the attention of your one-person audience. For instance, I have loved to read for as long as I can remember and my parents have backed this up with stories about hearing four-year-old Melissa talking to someone in the basement, freaking out, and running downstairs only to discover I had learned to read. I was afraid to say "butt" because I thought it was a "bad word." (You will discover I overcame the fear of saying bad words but never lost the joy of reading.) I knew I loved to read, but hearing my parents tell stories about my escapades in my early years solidified this as part of my identity.

It's a big job documenting your child's life. My personal style is to emphasize joy without dismissing the pain. "Grace, honey, I know you have trouble falling asleep sometimes. You have been a pain in the butt to get to sleep since day one. You wouldn't fall asleep unless you were gripping my thumb. I'd have to guess when you were asleep enough to not notice me removing my thumb from your grasp or you would wake up and then I'd have to start the whole thing over! But because you were a terrible sleeper, I was able to have *so much more cuddle time* with you!" Or "Alice! Remember today when the dog barked at you and you laughed and barked back and then the dog looked confused? That was so funny and sweet!"

A parent will, from time to time, have glimpses of their children's future and potential but one mustn't write that; the children must write that for themselves. I was never a parent who planned out my child's future or expected them to live out my unresolved dreams. I am not their sculptor; I am the benefactor who provides the tools for their self-sculpting. I do not write their story; I provide them the pen and keep notes for their reference. The children of today will have their lives documented at levels unmatched by any other era. I attempt to give them a solid sense of home and lovingly document the history they create. I tried — and try — to be the best keeper of their history that I could be.

I didn't take many pictures that Christmas, which bothered me at the time. I realized after the fact that I was so busy hosting and experiencing that I missed the family photo ops again. Don't get me wrong, I'd rather have the experience than the photo, but the girls were little and may not recall the experience later in life. I wanted the photo for them. I felt as if I'd failed my job as historian a bit, but I assured myself that subsequent Christmases would provide plenty of material on which to look back and got on with it. Because I had missed the chance for a great Christmas Day photo, a few days later I staged a photo of the girls in the beautiful Christmas vintage dresses that my friend and client Janet bought them. They looked like little dolls from the nineteenth century.

In the months that followed, my (ancient) phone became full of photos of the girls. I mean literally full. So, as Alice and I sat on the porch to say goodbye to Grace on this alleged day off on August 6, 2013, I began to delete unnecessary apps and videos to make room for new photos and videos. Alice loved "outSIIIIIIDE!" and wanted to run around the yard while we waved goodbye to Grace, but I kept her on my lap so she didn't run up to the car. She happily "helped" me with my phone instead.

We returned inside where I tried, unsuccessfully, to interest her in her breakfast. This was somewhat unusual — she had a healthy appetite for the things she liked — but she was teething and had the low-grade fever, so it wasn't entirely out of the norm. I tried, also unsuccessfully, to get her to cuddle with me on the couch to watch *Sesame Street* and read books. She shimmied off the couch, and began to play. She made the rounds:

• She played with her dolly, arranging the doll's bedding and feeding the baby. I took videos of her doing this for family who lived elsewhere so they could enjoy her as much as I did. I felt a moment of satisfaction for having cleared up space on my phone so I could record new videos.

• She ran toward me and away from me, kissing me on the lips every time she came back to me. I loved it, and did not give one hoot she had a cold. I wanted Alice kisses.

• She pulled out her sister's Ninja Turtles chair in which Grace never allowed Alice to sit. She sat there for a few seconds with a satisfied grin, before returning to the business of playing. She wanted the satisfaction of having sat there, even for a second.

• She took my phone, hid it behind her back, tilted her head and said, "MY pone. MY pone, Mama" with the biggest, sweetest grin you've ever seen. I laughed and said, "Alice, that's not your phone." She laughed and said, "Yes, Mama, MY pone!" And then, with a sweet grin, she handed it back to me, and said, "OK, Mama." I will never, ever forget the expression she held at this moment. She was making baby jokes, and she was proud.

• She played with the toy dinosaurs and balls she'd received for her birthday just a few days prior. The banners from her party were still hanging because neither Alice nor Grace wanted to take them down and I clearly "just work here."

Alice was little. Alice was new. And like all little, new people, she was happy with the simple things. She did not know yet about mass consumerism and greed and malice and murder. She delighted in the sound of my Magic Bullet making a smoothie; it's an awful noise, but she laughed every time. She loved the way her blanket felt on the corner of her eyeball when she was sleepy (an odd, inexplicable habit of hers). Singing. Dancing. Laughing with her family and friends. Seeing dogs. Meeting new people. Riding in her red push car. Eating under the lemon tree. Reading books with us. Singing "Twinkle, Twinkle, Little Star." Preschool. Her caregivers. Going down a slide. She just liked to hang out. She didn't require much to be happy or peaceful: a lesson to us all.

We just hung out that morning. And it was bliss.

She did not look like or act like a sick kid, but she sounded like Kim Carnes and would not even eat blueberries or yogurt, so she was clearly feeling off. I finally got her to eat some watermelon, a food she loved so much that it served as her birthday "cake" when she refused to eat cake for some inexplicable reason.

As it neared naptime, I gave her Tylenol. I normally save the Tylenol for fevers over 102°, but Alice had spiked a 105° fever the previous fall and I didn't want a repeat. I knew she needed her sleep more than anything, so I prepared her for a nap. We sang the ABCs and our rewrite of "Twinkle," which ends with "Twinkle, Twinkle, little Alice, one day you'll live in a palace," which always made the girls laugh. We hung out, Alice on my chest, on the toy bench. I felt our hearts beating together and thought, "How cool is that?"

I hope I told her I loved her.

I placed her in the crib with some trepidation, because in recent weeks she had screamed and thrown her blankies and binkies out of the crib when I left the room. This day, she didn't scream, but she did throw her blankie. I returned to toss it back to her, smiled at her, and left the room. She did not cry again. I was surprised, yet relieved my girl was going to sleep.

The doorbell rang a minute after I left her room. I silently cursed. Our neighborhood is heavily canvassed by Jehovah's Witnesses, which was a major problem in Alice's infancy. Every. Single. Time. I put her down for a nap, the doorbell would ring. I once posted on Facebook, "Every time a Jehovah's Witness rings my doorbell during naptime, an angel gets annoyed on my behalf." I eventually posted a *No Solicitation* sign, which worked like a charm. No Witnesses rang our bell for over a year. Until August 6, 2013.

I opened the door, saw two ladies, and immediately knew they were out to save me. Now, I can respect they are doing what they feel is right. I can respect they had no idea God and I are cool. But I take issue with them ringing the doorbell during naptime. I said, "Oh, ladies. My young one is sick and I *just* this minute got her down for a nap. See, we have this *No Solicitation* sign here to try to prevent folks from ringing the bell during naptime." One of the ladies apologized profusely, saying she was sorry, that they weren't selling anything so thought it would be OK, that she had six kids and knew exactly how I felt, and that I should rest while Alice did.

I thought, "You know, she's right: I should." I was feeling rather borderline. This cold had traveled from Grace to Alice, and though I wasn't sick yet, I could tell I was vulnerable. I could not afford to miss work, so I decided to use this alleged day off to rest, hoping to stave off the cold.

Before I retired, I sent the videos I'd taken of Alice that morning to our relatives and a few friends; I hadn't shared any in a while because of my phone storage situation. I also returned a few calls from patients. During this period of time, I had five separate patients coming to see me specifically for grief, two of whom had lost daughters, so I was extra attentive between sessions. Prior to this, I'd never had more than one patient at a time that came specifically for grief. I thought it odd, even then.

One patient, Rachael, a friend of my friend Pam, had two daughters my daughters' ages. Rachael and her husband had found their 19-month-old dead in her crib. After an autopsy and extensive testing, no cause of death could be determined. Therefore, the death was classified as Sudden Unexplained Death in Childhood (SUDC). Although rare, it is the fifth leading cause of death in toddlers. I sobbed at this news. Though I did not know them well, I could not help but put myself in their shoes; their sweetie was only two days older than mine, after all. The other patient's twenty-year-old daughter had had a fatal seizure. I wondered how either woman could make toast. Or drive a car. Or get out of bed. My heart broke for them.

Although I have never been a great napper, I conked out on August 6, 2013. I woke up at 2:30 p.m. and saw I had a call from Dan, my patient and friend. I recall basically collapsing back down on my left side, almost as if I were pushed. I obviously fell back asleep, because I woke up again at about 4 p.m., clutching the phone to my chest. I thought, "Damn, she has slept a long time again!" Alice had slept that long the previous weekend — I had to eventually wake her up for her own birthday party — so I was not immediately alarmed. I returned the call I intended to make earlier, thinking, "I'd better do it now before I go get her, because I won't have time after she awakens." I was on the phone for about a minute as I walked toward her room. I hung up and immediately opened the door to Alice's room, phone in hand.

Nothing seemed strange at first, other than she was apparently still sleeping, but in retrospect, I know I was aware — in the moment — of moving in slow motion. Haltingly, I went to touch her. She felt cool. My heart raced. I picked her up.

My heart stopped.

TUESDAY: THE DAY OFF

*A*lice's face and hands were blue, and her legs did not move from the tucked position. "Bad, bad, very bad," went through my head as I frantically dialed 911.

"All circuits are busy … all circuits are busy."

I held her and ran as fast as I could to the front door, threw it open and screamed, "Somebody call 911!!!!" as loud as I could. I placed her on the floor and started CPR on my baby. On my dear, sweet, baby. A neighbor we barely knew ran over and sat next to me on the floor. Somehow, 911 finally picked up. I was becoming unhinged. It felt like it took forever to give our address, and my baby needed CPR. Or I hoped she did, anyway, for it did not look good. They directed me back to CPR. I resumed. She began to change color and there were noises from her chest and mouth. "Holy shit, this might work," I thought, "but she is blue so there is no way she won't have brain damage." I continued CPR while breaking down statistics of this sort of thing in my mind. I was very focused and very logical.

Eventually, a very thin, red-tinged watery substance began to dribble out of her mouth and nose. I screamed this to the man on the line. He told me to keep going with the CPR. I counted compressions and debated whether the reddish fluid was the product of decomposition or her watermelon lunch but I had to drop that train of thought in order to keep going. The neighbor began to scream "More is coming out!" to the man. The man said to keep going. I did, to the beat of "Staying Alive," as I had been instructed to do. Whoever had the idea to perform CPR to that song obviously had not performed CPR on their own child, what the hell?! I had these thoughts, but never lost count. I was more focused than I have ever been in my life. The door to the house was still wide open because I didn't want to have to stop CPR to open it for the paramedics.

The firemen arrived and looked noticeably shocked as they ran up the steps. They told me to back away. I found myself standing under the arch between the living and dining room with my toes aligned to the grain of the wood like a child lining up for recess. I stood still, but my limbs, my insides, my mind, all felt like they were running amok through the house. I guess I breathed, because I am still here, but it seemed like all my body functions went on hiatus. I saw them get ready to place an oxygen mask on Alice's face, and thought, "OK, there is hope," but I also clearly saw a nonverbal exchange between the two firemen on the ground. The one touching Alice then looked up at me, and said some version of:

"She's gone. I am so sorry."

I heard an inhuman sound I realized came from me and collapsed on the ground.

My heart was pounding out of my chest. "I should have checked on her all the time! I should not have taken a nap! I should have checked on her all the time! She just had her birthday!" I wailed. A man whose badge read "Captain Trujillo" touched my shoulders, and looked at me in a way that demanded eye contact. He somehow knew she'd died in her sleep. The eye contact made me feel like a shark turned over on its back. I went limp and looked him in the eyes like I have never looked into another human's eyes. This made me aware that before this encounter, my eyes had been darting around like a caged, wild animal though my body was stationary. He said to me, "Ma'am, I have kids. You can't stand there the whole time. Did you check on her any less than you usually do? No, right? There was nothing you could have done. Nothing."

I remember thinking what he said was bullshit, that of course I could have done something, but I also hoped he would not stop telling me it was not my fault. I was hanging by a thread.

The panic hit a fever pitch. What/how was I going to tell the family? Oh, my God, what was I going to say to Grace? Or to the grandparents whose email replies to the video of an alive Alice I'd just sent a few hours ago were arriving in my inbox while she lay dead in my arms? *What the hell just happened?*

I called a family member and started screaming into the phone to come to my house. I continued to scream into the phone — exactly what I do not recall — until the fireman took the phone away from me. He looked me in the eye and said, "You cannot tell locals on the phone. You *cannot.*"

As I waited, it occurred to me no one knew this awful news except me, some firemen, and possibly Alice.

I held Alice and cried. I kept wailing, "But she just had her birthday! All her birthday stuff is still up!" to the police officer at the door, who was clearly assigned to regulate the flow of traffic into the house. I have no idea why I thought her recent birthday should have insured us against the day's events, but I must have, because I kept saying it. The police officer at the door was young and forlorn, and could hardly look at me. The next time I looked up, he was looking down and wearing sunglasses. Seconds later he left the house, and a new officer came in and took his place. I saw a gigantic fireman with his face hidden in the corner of my foyer, shoulders shaking. There were several men in the house, and they all looked gutted. And this fact gutted me further.

I overheard one of the fire captains whisper to an officer: "Can't we get any female officers here? It's all dudes." He came over to me and asked if I would feel more comfortable with a female officer, that the officers were only here to help me, but would I feel more comfortable with a female? Inexplicably, I responded nonchalantly, "Oh, I'm not sexist, it's OK." Why on earth I said that is anyone's guess. What a ridiculous thing to say. It was like another party had taken over command of my body. He said, "I don't care if you are sexist. I want to know if you would like a female officer here."

"I don't want any of you here. I don't want this to be happening at all. I don't care if the officers are male or female," I replied. It had just hit me that officers were there at all. I had seen them and talked to them, but it had not truly registered until this point. They were all very quiet, very respectful, and looked like they had been punched in the stomach. My heart went out to them. How these fine men and women can do this every day without going insane is beyond me.

As I held Alice, rocking back and forth in complete shock, the firemen kept asking me if I had any additional family members nearby that I could call. I finally realized I should call Bubba, my dear friend and my kids' godfather. They returned my phone to me and in the two seconds it took for Bubba to answer, I went from silently rocking Melissa to hysterical Melissa. I can't recall what I said, but Bubba sounded breathless and said he was on his way. I must have said she died because they took my phone again.

The question arose of what to do about Grace. She was at school. I was clearly not going anywhere. I had about an hour to decide. They talked of sending a squad car for her. I became Mama Bear and said, "No way. She will think it is happening because she took her seatbelt off while I was driving one day. She will be scared." They reminded me only certain people could pick her up from school, so there was no choice but to call the school and send a squad car. I informed them that, first of all, Grace could *not* come back here and see this scene. The coroner would be arriving soon. No way did I want Grace to be present for that, nor could I have cared for her if she were, because I was in a bad, bad way. I was literally crippled with guilt and unsure how I was going to survive the feeling I had.

I informed the officers the girls' daycare providers, Teresa and Sal, were on the list as a responsible party, that the girls sometimes spent the night there; therefore, Grace would not be too alarmed if they picked her up. Grace would probably have questions since I had not warned her in advance, but it would not be totally out of the norm. At the time, I didn't realize that the girls had just spent the night there three nights earlier when I had several birthday parties to attend; it seemed like something someone else had done eons ago. The officers finally gave in to me and let me call Teresa. I think I told Teresa what happened but I could tell she did not really get it. My heart sank. She loves my girls as her own, and I knew she was going to be devastated. Teresa agreed to get Grace and have her stay overnight.

Again, they took my phone.

At some point, I realized I was sweating profusely. I mean, I was literally dripping with sweat. It was dripping off my scalp, my back, everywhere. I asked the firemen if they were hot; they said nothing but did turn on the air conditioner. I could not feel it. I could barely feel anything.

I sat there wondering how this could be happening. The odds of such a thing happening at all are very low. The odds of a child over twelve months dying in their sleep are very low, though it had happened to my friend and patient Rachael. The odds of such a thing happening to two kids in the same circle, albeit a wide circle, were probably nearly nonexistent. How could this be? *How could this be?*

I am not sure if I blinked for nearly an hour as I waited for my support people to arrive — the absolute longest hour of my life.

I was on the floor, in front of the door, holding Alice, rocking, wide-eyed and breathless, when loved ones began to arrive.

My head was swimming. I wanted to die. And that is not merely a saying. I really wondered how I was going to find a will to live, because mine left with Alice. I was not scared by this feeling. It was just there, clear and simple.

I cradled Alice for probably an hour, her head above her heart, so she would no longer be blue when others arrived. The rigor was also no longer present by this point, somehow. I did not want anyone else to see her that way. I would not wish it on anyone. Not even the worst person in the world.

My proverbial record seemed to be skipping. I was still wailing variations of:

- *It's all my fault!*
- *I should have checked on her all the time!*
- *I should not have taken a nap!*
- *But she just had her birthday! All her birthday stuff is still up!*
- *What kind of mother does not protect her sleeping child?!*

WHEN I WASN'T CRYING one of those things, I was nearly catatonic. At some point, I was informed the officers were going back to see her room, but only to help us. "Oh, my God, they think I killed her!" I cried. I can't recall what they said to me, only that I felt reassured no one thought I killed her; this was protocol, and the officers were clearly not any happier about it than I was. I was filled with a sensation of horror and paralyzing guilt too large to describe. The guilt I felt was so overpowering that to this day, I don't know how I made it past the first night.

There were still firemen and officers milling about. Quietly. They were giving me a wide berth. They were oh, so respectful.

At some point, I was informed "the child's godfather" was there. Bubba had arrived, but they weren't going to let him in until I'd spoken to the coroner, who had not yet arrived. Around this time, I heard the voices of elderly female neighbors outside my window. They were wailing, "Lord, have mercy! Lord, have mercy on this house and family! Lord, have mercy!" This wailing and the fact that Bubba had arrived reminded me whatever scene was unfolding here, there was a whole additional scene happening outside. This was the beginning of my understanding that this was going to be horrible for more people than just our family unit. I never did look outside. I couldn't.

At some point, I sat on the couch with Alice. I held her, cooed over her, whispered to her, and stared at her for quite a while. We were largely left alone during this interlude. I did not want to let go. We had maybe two hours together before the coroner arrived. I hoped they wouldn't come. I hoped this was a terrible, hideous nightmare from which I would awaken. While whispering to her, I lifted up her eyelids because I wanted to see her eyes, her beautiful little hazel eyes. I wasn't sure if I would be able to do so ever again, and I was correct. Sitting there, that Tuesday night, was the last time I ever saw my baby's eyes. Her signature twinkle was not there. My baby as I knew her was not there. Seeing her eyes stare blankly off was difficult. Gut-wrenching. But it ushered in the fact that *this was real.* In fact, this was perhaps the realest thing that had ever happened to me, and I knew I was forever changed. It was evident, right there, looking at her lifeless eyes, that the old Melissa was gone forever. I did not know this new Melissa, but I was meeting her whether I wanted to or not.

As it turns out, you mourn not only your child, but also the "you" you used to be minutes before who it's no longer possible to be. You mourn for the death of the family unit as you once knew it. You mourn for your daughter, your parents, your siblings, your friends, the first responders, and everyone else you know who will be shattered. You mourn for your best friends who just found out they were pregnant with twins, knowing this will likely result in some (additional) anxiety once their kids arrive. You mourn for every parent who ever lost a child. And you just keep sitting there, rocking your dead baby, mourning for her and for everyone, staring at her lifeless eyes, trying to wrap your head around this giant change in your life.

At some point in this period, I called my parents. I distinctly remember calling them; I know where I sat, what I was wearing, and every visual detail, but I can't remember what I said to them. I think I just blurted it out. I remember my stepdad saying, "What? What? What did you say? What? Let me get your mother." My dad and stepmother had a similar reaction. They had a lot of questions, and I had no answers. Telling the grandparents was a whole new heartbreak. It makes my stomach hurt just typing this. It breaks my heart all over again.

I asked my parents to call my brother and my stepsiblings. I could not go through another phone call. I could not tell my sweet brother. We love each other's kids like our own, and I just could not tell him myself. We had just spent a week together in Flagstaff with my dad and extended family. We visited the Grand Canyon. The cousins, ages two to fifteen, swam and played miniature golf, billiards, and hide-and-seek every night. The concept of hide-and-seek was lost on Alice, but she had a grand time running after my nephews. For the first time, we got a photo of my dad, stepmom, all the siblings, stepsiblings, and their children. Everyone was in the photo. Everyone had a ball.

Sitting there in utter devastation, I noticed I became overwhelmed with gratitude that we were able to make that trip.

At some point, one of the fire captains knelt down next to me in front of the couch and began to speak to me in a very quiet, soothing voice. I have no idea what he said, because I was entranced by his mellifluous voice as well as his appearance. He looked like an Irish priest. He acted like a priest. He was so soothing, it did not matter to me what he said; I just let myself stare and be soothed for a moment. As he was wrapping up, I began to hear his words: "… if there is anything you need at all, anything you need at all, do not hesitate to call. My name is Captain Morgan, and we are all here for you." I looked at his badge and confirmed that it read "Captain Morgan."

Some female detectives arrived. I was introduced, and then they went to look in the girls' room. They came back rather quickly and quietly sat at my dining table. I was told they would sit in on my interview with the coroner so I did not have to verbalize the story more than once, which was unbelievably thoughtful.

To this day, I don't mind sharing the information at all, not even the slightest bit. But I generally don't feel like I have enough breath to tell the story. So, I write instead.

The coroner, a wonderful woman named Denise, finally arrived. Denise attends any case involving a child. Denise deserves a medal — what a gut-wrenching job. I can't even imagine. She gave Alice a cursory look, and then she and one of the two female detectives sat in chairs in front of us on the couch to get the interview started. The other detective sat at the piano, and often had to turn to look out of the window. Denise conducted the interview. She asked what medication I'd given Alice and asked to take it with her so they could test it for possible contamination. This set off a whole new attack of guilt. Had I accidentally given her too much? Was it tainted? Should I have waited until her fever exceeded 102°? And then, back to the original: I should not have taken a nap. I should have checked on her more, etc.

The Guilt was a demon, and it was consuming me alive.

Denise then asked about some medical history, and how Alice appeared earlier in the day. It occurred to me Alice had had her annual checkup with her pediatrician just three days earlier, so I conveyed that information. She'd earned a clean bill of health. She was fiftieth percentile for weight and height, but she had a big ol' head. There was nothing unusual found at this visit. No shots. We had a happy, healthy kid. She was on her way to being fully potty-trained, at her own insistence. I couldn't understand how that was only three days ago; it felt like a different lifetime.

It also occurred to me I had those videos of her playing that morning and showed them to the ladies. They watched with interest, and then Denise turned to look me in the eyes and asked, "What do you think they would have done if you took this child to the ER today? Or even just the doctor?"

"They would have sent me home and told me to give her fluids," I responded.

"That's right," said Denise. "They would have sent you home, because this kid was clearly not sick enough to sound any alarms. There is nothing you could have done."

Now, I still thought this was utter bullshit — I was *sure* there was something I could have done — but I did give her some props for knowing I was consumed with guilt. She wanted us to be prepared for the fact that they might not find a cause of death because there were no obvious signs of trauma or injury, she had not appeared especially sick that morning, etc. She told us about SUDC (Sudden Unexplained Death in Childhood) and that she thought Alice might be a rare case. She said she'd only had one other case that year — a family from

Northeast LA. "A family we know," I told her. She looked at us with utter shock and I stared back. The chances of knowing someone else who suffered the horror of SUDC are pretty damn low.

There was going to have to be an autopsy. On my Alice. Alice was going to the coroner's office that night, instead of taking a walk around the corner, as she generally did on Tuesday nights.

I reflected on Rachael, the friend of my friend Pamela whose 19-month-old died of SUDC, and remembered I'd wondered how she could even make toast. Or how she did anything at all, really. And then I realized I was going to have to learn how to make toast again. In a blink of an eye, I had joined a terrible club: the club of parents who outlive their children.

I didn't want to be in this club. This club SUUUUUUUUUCKS. A club sounds fun, gives you that "special secret" feeling of exhilaration, acceptance, and camaraderie. People want what you're having. This "club" has none of that. Absolutely no one wants to accept this club. There is zero exhilaration. The camaraderie ... well, it's a bunch of devastated people who have little in common other than the fact their child went to sleep and never woke up. One should *want* to be in a club. I want to be in the club where I'm on a beach in Tahiti, peaceful as a prayer in my perfectly toned body eating my weight in lemon bars but never gaining a pound, engrossed in a book until I dance over to the waves, dive in, and frolic joyfully before my hot date pulls up to take me to dinner. *That's* the club I want.

That's not the club I got.

I was in a state of utter shock that this event was not only now a part of my life's story, but also very likely *the* pivotal event in my life's story.

I was now a mother who lost a child.

After the interview, they asked me to step into the other room so they could examine her and take pictures. This did not take long but was excruciating, nonetheless. I knew my final moments with Alice were coming to a close — a sickening feeling.

Denise told us the doctor would conduct the autopsy first thing in the morning the next day, Wednesday. She told us "Alice would be ready to be picked up" by a funeral director Wednesday afternoon. I was assured she could stay there for as long as two weeks, if necessary. I can't remember exactly what I said, but I think I made it pretty clear that while I had not the slightest clue what I would be doing, I did not want Alice at the coroner's office one second longer than necessary. Denise told us she was not allowed to make referrals, but after speaking to me, she thought I might explore a "green" funeral director for Alice. I have to hand it to Denise: She was in my house for probably less than an hour, but she had my number.

Later, I found a card for Natural Grace Funerals in the pile of cards from policemen, detectives, firemen, the coroner's office, and grief groups. This would turn out to be one of the beautiful parts of the horrible aftermath.

Bubba and his husband Rey were finally allowed inside. I kept crying that it was all my fault. And they kept assuring me that it was not.

I asked Bubba what time he'd arrived, and he said he'd been outside for maybe two hours. "Oh, my God, then you probably heard me wailing," I cried. He burst into tears and said, "I did! I did! And I wanted to break the door down and come in here to hold you, but they wouldn't let me!"

These are beautiful friends, folks. Bubba was directly beside me on the Tuesday I gave birth to Alice, and he was there holding me the Tuesday she died. Rey came to the hospital with champagne and hugs immediately after she was born, and he was also here to hug me when I had to say goodbye. I am so lucky to have such friends in this life.

Denise walked outside so I could say goodbye to Alice in peace. She suggested I send her with her blankie and other personal items but handed me back one particular blankie: "She died on this blanket. You should keep it." And I did. I will never wash it. I keep it safe in my room and pull it out from time to time when I need to feel close to Alice.

I felt time speed up. I did not want Alice to go; I did not want her to go to the damn LA County Coroner's office. I have been to the LA

County Coroner's office. This is no place you want your baby to go, I assure you.

Denise came back in to tell us "it's time," and that I should step out of the room for a moment. When I returned, Alice was covered in a white sheet, lying on the couch. I became inconsolable. Denise took Alice to the coroner's car, a white sedan. I was discouraged from following. Someone, I do not recall who, tried to get me back in the house. I wanted to go with Alice. I would have sat with her in the morgue if allowed. I would have slept with her in a freezer if allowed. I insisted on at least standing on the porch and watched Denise put my baby in her car. I saw my sweet next-door neighbor Kaye bawling in my yard. I could not believe this was happening.

I saw a box on the porch after the coroner left with Alice. I brought it inside and forgot about it for a week.

They put Alice in a car seat, just like an alive baby. This made me cry, but for some reason gave me some relief. Thank God, they did not put her in a hearse; I would have come unhinged. The officers were leaving now and asked if I wanted to talk to the grief counselors waiting on our lawn, but not before Kaye ran up and gave me the biggest hug you can imagine. She said she had been prepared to wait all night, if necessary, to simply give me a hug. She was sobbing and kept saying she was sorry. She *loves* my girls. She lives next door with her elderly father Joseph — or "Jofess," as Alice said. They had been so excited that Alice had recently begun to say their names. My heart broke again.

The grief counselors were sweet, but I mainly just stared at them. I was shellshocked. I wanted to talk to Rey and Bubba. I wanted to figure out how to get Alice out of the coroner's office ASAP. I wanted to figure out what the hell I was going to tell Grace. Oh, my God, how do you explain this to a four-year-old?

At some point, I began to list people who needed to be called, and Bubba and Rey began making the calls for me. I looked up advice on how to talk to a preschool child about the unexpected death of a sibling. It was all, well, surreal. There is no other word for it, really.

Some of my Pilates clients and acupuncture patients who had

23

become like family were the first to be called. Lynn is like another mother to me, and my kids both went with me to her house for her Pilates lessons before they started preschool. She liked me to bring them, because, well, she is not what you would call my most enthusiastic student. I'd trained members of her family for over fifteen years, so let's face it, the lack of enthusiasm is somewhat of a game, but a game we both clearly enjoyed. My girls adored her, and so do I. She arrived shortly after getting the call. Longtime clients/friends/surrogate-local-grandparents Janet and Mark also came. Jen C, our awesome neighbor and the mother of Alice's beloved buddy Aria, ran over as well. Everyone was trying not to cry in front of me, and I'll tell you what I told them:

I DO NOT WANT you to be "strong" for me. I want you to be real for me. First of all, real strength does not equal no tears. That our society pushes this agenda, especially on young boys, galls me to no end. We teach young kids, especially young boys, to "suck it up," and then wonder why half of cis-marriages end in divorce and why "my husband won't talk to me about his feelings." It's no mystery why this is. Can we just stop this nonsense already? It takes cojones to have your emotions and to deal with them accordingly. Secondly, another person crying, or not crying, has no bearing whatsoever on my likelihood to cry. My daughter died for no apparent reason: I am gonna cry. I would have to be mentally ill not to cry. If you feel like crying about it, too, go for it. You cannot possibly make this worse for me, no matter what you do or do not do. In fact, I find it helpful to see other people cry. It helps me see my daughter's life had value beyond the walls of our house. It helps me see, yes, this really is as terrible as it seems. It helps me feel loved and supported. That said, I also feel loved and supported by people who aren't crying in front of me, so do what you will. I love you all the same whether you cry or not.

SHORTLY AFTER JANET and Mark arrived, Bubba pulled out some vodka left over from a party and asked if I wanted a drink. This had not occurred to me. In fact, it was probably 8:30 or 9 p.m. by this time and it occurred to me I had not eaten, gone to the restroom, drunk water, or honored any other bodily needs since before noon. I was unsure what the drinking protocol was here, or if I even wanted a drink. "Should I?" I asked. Janet and Bubba replied "Yes" in unison, and Mark silently nodded, as is his way. I sipped on a little through the night. Did it help? I don't know. Maybe? My nervous system was pretty fried, so it's hard to tell what helped and what didn't.

Eventually everyone left but Bubba. We discussed the amazing firemen and police officers, and he asked if I remembered the names of the key officers and firemen. I did. There was Captain Trujillo and Captain Morgan. Captain Morgan. Really? I nearly laughed. Someone has to give him a promotion or a name change, because his having the name "Captain Morgan" was really screwing up my "grieving process." There was no room in my traumatized brain for the fact that my fire captain shared a name with a popular brand of rum. Reality had become ridiculous.

I have to put "grieving process" in quotes because, even that night, the idea I was considered to have a "grieving process" made me want to do the Archie Bunker raspberry. I loathe that term. I loathe all catchphrases for intense experiences, probably because they end up getting bandied about by people describing their disappointment over the discontinuation of their preferred mascara or ice cream flavor.

Bubba spent the night, and in doing so, probably saved my life. Eventually he fell asleep, but I knew there was no way I could go to sleep. My eyes were wide open. I went outside, sat on the porch, and marveled at the quiet night.

It occurred to me I needed to tell my friend Pamela myself. Pamela and her family had just been to Alice's birthday party and I knew this was going to be quite a shock. She would surely think it was a horrible joke if she were to hear it from someone else. The chances of toddler crib death happening to two people you know well are probably next to nil. It was late, and Pamela had an infant and a toddler, so I sent her an email and asked her to call me when she woke up to nurse. I hated, hated, hated to have to tell her.

Because of the hour and time difference, I also sent emails to the girls' godmothers. Both ladies had received video clips that day. I could not believe all those folks were probably looking at those clips while the video star lay dead.

I went into the girls' room, lit a candle, and tried to meditate. I tried to feel Alice. My heart rate decreased, but I could not feel her. In fact, the house had never felt so empty. This was probably when it really hit me: She. Is. Gone. And she is not coming back home. I found it extremely challenging to be in her room and not be able to feel her. "If I can't feel her in her room, will I ever feel her again?"

I went outside and paced. Eventually, I thought of what to say to Grace. I thought of who needed to be called. I made mental notes and became overwhelmed. My phone rang several times that night/early morning, but I could not answer for the most part. I just couldn't speak of it again; I couldn't again say she was dead and we didn't know why.

She was playing. And then she was dead. She filled the house with laughter but would never do so again.

Incomprehensible.

I sat in the yard and stared. As I sat there, I began to become aware of my body. It felt bizarre. It felt like my head weighed 700 pounds and was on a stake that went down into where my torso should have been, except now it was hollow. I felt crushed under the weight of my head, yet I couldn't really feel my body. I could see my arms and legs moving but I could not feel them, and they did not feel connected to me. It felt like they were floating away. It was one of the most profoundly peculiar feelings I have ever had.

Suddenly, I felt as if I were in the center of a cone, my feet in the tip, and then sucked to the front of the cone by centrifugal force. I was unsure what was happening or why I felt that way. I closed my eyes and attempted to relax through it. When I did, I had the over-whelming sensation — as well as a hint of vision — of a swarm of ... something ... flying around the cone. I immediately knew it was protective. I did not question my sanity in that moment. I simply had the overwhelming feeling whatever they were, they were loving, protective, and meant to keep me alive.

As I noticed the swarm, I again became aware of the hole in my chest, but now — honest to God — I could feel light surging through that hole. When I closed my eyes, I saw neon lights the colors of Lite-Brite pegs soaring through. "That's love" went through my mind.

These images were all-consuming yet comforting. I didn't judge them. They didn't make me question reality for whatever reason. I just noticed.

I lost my darling, loving daughter that day. I lost my role as a mother of two. I lost Alice's future. I lost my ability to imagine any future whatsoever. I lost my ability to exist in our agreed-upon reality. But somehow, I still felt love. It's all I could feel because I couldn't even feel my own body. I found that fascinating.

I could see the first glimpses of sunlight breaking and realized I had already moved past the day my baby died. I didn't want it to be a different day than the day she was still laughing. I remembered having a similar thought the day after she was born, but that was a much happier occasion. I was *so happy* in the days after Alice was born, but I do remember thinking, "Now it's eight days past one of the two best days of my life." I was literally bursting with love. And now, I still had all that love, but it was mixed up with shock and intense grief. I wanted to grab the sun out of the sky and move it backward so it was still the day Alice was alive. Life felt bizarre enough and I felt strong enough to do it, which was odd, because I also felt utterly destroyed.

I went back inside to face the aftermath that would unfold that morning.

WEDNESDAY: THE AFTERMATH

I knew it was officially morning when Bubba woke up. Alice was still dead. This was my third lesson in "kids don't care about your plans and timelines." This lesson would take a while to process, and frankly I'm not excited to discover lesson four.

The dread of facing a day that would not include a living Alice was all-consuming.

Even if it were yesterday and she was dead, it would still be the day that she had laughed. I wanted it to be the day she still smiled. I was baffled there could be another day after she died. I didn't understand how the world could keep spinning without her. The world around me looked the same, but the totality of the immense change within my home, my family, my brain, and my emotional state was abundantly clear. This juxtaposition was, and remains, extremely disorienting.

The internal juxtaposition was also clear: I felt simultaneously destroyed and capable of anything. I found that interesting.

I felt like I was moving at a glacial speed in a world moving at an entirely different pace. This feeling was so consuming I found myself staring at my surroundings. Was I really moving like a butoh dancer, or did I just *feel* like I was moving like a butoh dancer? I couldn't ascertain which, so I just kept going. I have no idea if others perceived me as moving slowly; I didn't think to ask. Internally, I was completely out of sync time-wise — that was crystal clear.

We made coffee and prioritized our incomprehensible to-do list. All overwhelming. None foreseen. I remember thinking some of these decisions would be easier if we were affiliated with a church. The church would tell you what funeral home to call, options for services, etc. But (long story) I was not affiliated with an organized religion, so I had to wing it. In the end, although it required more decisions, I was relieved we could express our love for Alice in a unique and authentic manner.

I looked at all the lists, stopped breathing, and probably cried. My mind was blank, and I didn't know how to make it un-blank. There was an immense amount of unexpected information to be processed and I was quite obviously unable to process anything at all. Twenty-four short hours before, I was packing lunch bags for two kids, planning my patient load and treatment plans, ordering work supplies, making grocery lists, preparing invoices and meals, booking dance and swim classes, and planning play dates. Now, I was canceling all of that to plan my child's funeral.

My timeline — and my kids' timelines — changed in an instant. Alice's history ended without a warning. The future I'd spent last week planning disappeared in a *poof*. It seemed so real while planning it. But now that future would never unfold. It's difficult to know where to begin with your new timeline, your new history. You make the adjustments and go through the motions, but your mind just keeps asking, "Are you sure this is *real*?"

I was fairly calm that morning, at least on the outside. By calm, I mean I was moving around and not completely hysterical one hundred percent of the time. My insides, however, were a whir. I thought of the passage by Lord Byron in "Childe Harold's Pilgrimage":

I have thought
Too long and darkly, till my brain became,
In its own eddy boiling and o'erwrought,
A whirling gulf of phantasy and flame:

And thus, untaught in youth my heart to tame,
My springs of life were poison'd. 'Tis too late!
Yet am I changed: though still enough the same
In strength to bear what Time cannot abate,
And feed on bitter fruits without accusing Fate.[1]

THE DEATH IS THE TRAGEDY, but there are so many corollary deaths: the death of your family unit, the death of your child's future, the death of your living child's relationship to their sibling, the death of your own imagined future, the death of your faith in tomorrow or in anything else, for that matter. I only had a few hours to reckon with the fact that she died when all the corollary deaths began to rear their ugly heads. So many decisions and calls to make. We had to find a funeral director and begin arrangements. Family would be arriving soon. And we needed to tell Grace.

What would we tell Grace? I sat and tried to sort it out. I normally can multitask with the best of them, but my brain felt stuck. I could not seem to organize information the way I needed to. "That particular function is no longer available," my brain seemed to say. I conveyed this to Bubba. He nodded. He knew what to do, I could tell, so I didn't worry about it anymore.

Telling Grace was the most important thing, and something I had to do myself, so I focused on that. My brain would only do one thing at a time. I didn't know why I could not multitask; therefore, I knew there was no fixing it.

I accepted that and moved on.

What would I say to Grace and how would I say it? What if I said the wrong thing? Would she understand? How would she take it? Well, she probably wasn't going to take it well — how could she — but what brand of bad would it be? All these things passed through my mind; I watched them go by like traffic. I felt no emotional response to these thoughts. I did not grab a thought and ride it to some conclusion, logical or illogical. I simply watched them, noticed I was doing so, and thought, "Huh. That's what the meditation teachers say we should do: simply observe our thoughts." I guess meditation, however sporadic at times, paid off when the shit hit the fan. Thank God.

In retrospect, I realize I was outwardly calm because I was in a state of shock. Also, my brain had something logical to chew on for a spell. Once I could focus, I found it calming. I practiced what to say as I prepared to pick her up. I desperately wanted to try to tell her without crying. Not because I felt any shame in crying over my deceased daughter, but because — though I strongly felt it would be eventually OK to cry in front of Grace — I needed this morning to be about *her* initial response. I needed to be a loving, blank slate that accepted whatever she had to dish out and to do so without judgment or any other negative emotional response. I needed to be a solid crucible into which her emotions could pour forth and transform by whatever alchemy she required. I could let her see me cry another time. Lord knows there would be plenty of opportunities.

I basically followed Fred Rogers' advice in *Talking with Children About Death*:

• *No euphemisms. Lay it out straight. "Alice died." Gut-wrenching. Saying "we lost her" can make a child think we'll find her. Saying "she went to heaven in the sky" can be confusing if you are going to bury the person in the ground. Saying "death is like going to sleep" can cause a child to have sleep issues. Especially if the deceased child actually did die in their sleep.*
• *Use words the child understands when explaining what death is. This seems like it's stating the obvious, but it's tricky to find age-appropriate explanations for death.*
• *Children can be overwhelmed by the sadness and may think it may never go away. Offer opportunities for the child to share in loving, happy memories, so they can see a grieving person can still laugh.*

WHILE DRIVING TO GET GRACE, I felt nervous, as if I was on my way to a new job or a first date. And I suppose I was. I was on my way to start my new job as a mother of one, on my way to my first date with my sister-less daughter.

It felt like I had a knife in my heart. I could barely feel my body, though I could see it moving around and recognized it as "me." I saw my hand pass by my face to adjust the seatbelt, but I had no idea whose hand it was for a second. When I realized it was mine, I wasn't sure how it arrived there: had I sent the signal for it to move? Otherwise, I was strangely quiet and relatively composed.

We went to Teresa's backyard for the talk. I had to do it immediately, because I knew I couldn't keep it together much longer, and Teresa and Sal were clearly destroyed as well. As I suspected, Grace had a thing or two to say about why we didn't tell her she'd be staying with Teresa and Sal. I told her we had an emergency. She asked, "What emergency?" I took a deep breath.

"Honey. Alice died." I let that sink in a second. Let's face it, I needed that second as much as Grace did. Grace's face screwed up into a mix of sadness and confusion. "Alice *died?*" she asked.

"Yes, honey, Alice died yesterday, and we are very, very sad. When a person dies, their body doesn't work anymore. Alice can't run and jump and play anymore. Her heart doesn't beat anymore, and she cannot breathe anymore. But she will always be your sister, and our hearts will always love her."

"Oh, God help me," I thought. This was the single most difficult thing I have ever had to tell someone. And that someone was four measly years old. And that person was my daughter. I pray to God I never have to relay a harder message than I did that day. I prayed I said the right thing, in the right manner, at the right time.

Grace buried her head into me and began to quietly weep. She asked some questions about what dead people can and cannot do. She asked if Alice was still at home. The script no longer worked; by this point, I was winging it. She asked if the doctor could help her. "I'm afraid the doctors cannot help you once you are already dead, honey. The firemen and policemen and the doctor all came to see her, and sometimes they can help, but they couldn't help Alice, and Mama is very, very sad about that," I said.

She asked if we knew Alice was going to die.

"No, honey. No, we did not know Alice was going to die."

I asked her if there were something fun she would like to do while we talked about some things we loved about Alice. She asked for ice cream, which was not a normal request from Grace. Ice cream? At 9:30 a.m.? Sure! Anything to ease this horrific pain. You want some Cheetos and a side of Sour Gummy Worms with that? Seriously, whatever you want right now, kid. Whatever you want. We got in the car and headed down the street for ice cream. Grace asked about Alice's car seat and what we planned to do with it if Alice wasn't coming home. Great question, though devastating. I knew we likely had weeks of things like this on the horizon: What to do with Alice's diapers? Alice's stroller? I had to push these thoughts aside to get through the moment.

We walked down Larchmont Avenue with our ice cream and remembered some of the times we'd walked this street with Alice. It was unusually quiet. We'd been there only days before when it was packed with Sunday brunchers and farmers' market shoppers. I was relieved the street didn't look the same because I didn't feel the same.

Now Alice would never walk that street again. *How can this be?*

My close friends began to arrive at the house to help. I was consumed by guilt. I felt like the guilt alone could kill me, as if poisonous guilt were contained in millions of tiny packets of plutonium slowly bursting open, one by one. One packet was not enough to kill me, but eventually the cumulative effect would be fatal.

My friends all tried to talk me out of these feelings. Again, I didn't really believe them, but I hoped they would not stop trying. I could point to one small part of my brain, a thin sliver on the left side of my brain, that believed Alice's death was not my fault. The rest of my brain thought this was utter horse crap. I needed my friends to keep telling me it was not my fault, hoping the little sliver would eventually grow enough to replace the guilty part.

Everyone, and I mean everyone, who saw me those first days said I should not feel guilty. And I will tell you what I told them:

THE GUILT IS INEVITABLE, I am sure. As parents, we feel guilty if kids skin their knee, don't share with friends, don't eat their vegetables, or act out in public. So, when you find your child dead in their crib, I don't know who wouldn't feel guilty. It seems impossible to completely avoid guilt over an event such as this, but I am trying.

SOON AFTER, the funeral director from Natural Grace Funerals, Shari, arrived to discuss our options. Bubba had contacted her after the coroner left her card. Her empathy was palpable through her angelic face. She spoke directly to me, and I stared back at her, but my brain could not process the words. She sounded like Charlie Brown's teacher to me; I could hear her talking, but I had no idea what she was saying.

I kept looking at Bubba to translate what she said. Bubba basically took everything she said and turned it into bullet points for me, which was a genius move. I could understand bullet points. If there were too many words, I heard nothing. I thought it strange as it happened, but it didn't make me angry, disappointed, embarrassed, or scared. I have no idea why I didn't go to one of those dark places at that time. I suppose the extraordinary clarity with which I recognized the loss of my executive functioning allowed me to simply accept it and learn how to work around it. I didn't try to fight it. I didn't shake my fist at it.

Bubba and Shari were both extremely patient with me and my failing brain. She talked about cremation versus burial. In a green burial, you basically wrap the body in a sheet and place it in the ground. She also spoke about options for a visitation or viewing, which, because Alice would not be embalmed, were essentially endless. She said that in the unexpected death of a toddler, she would

34

not accept a fee other than the cremation or burial fee. Was she an earth angel?

Cremation or burial: *does not compute.* Cremation or burial? For my child? For my joyful little girl? "Um, neither, thank you very much. I do not want this to be happening at all," I thought.

This simple question, cremation or burial, was my first meeting with denial. I would not like to cremate *or* bury my child. *I would not like it in a house, I would not like it with a mouse. I would not like to deal with disposing the remains of my child here or there, I would not like to deal with disposing the remains of my child anywhere.* I know I want to be cremated, but Alice, well, we never had a chance to ask her what she might want. I felt a lot of pressure to do the right thing by her on this issue, far more pressure than all the other issues combined. It was the thing that hung me up for days.

Shari told us we could do the visitation anywhere, even at home. We all looked at each other with wide eyes. It was the perfect idea. It would definitely be better for Grace to be home than at some horrid 1970s funeral home where she would be expected to be "on" and have to behave like a somber adult. It was going to be better for us because it could be a more relaxed atmosphere. This decision took less than a second to make. We would have the visitation at home, old-school style. We would have her in our bedroom, so people could have privacy when they viewed her, while the rest of the house was full of loved ones, food, and drink. We had a small window of time for this viewing to take place because Alice was not going to be embalmed.

Shari planned to pick up Alice when she was released from the coroner's office. Shari promised to be there waiting so Alice would not be there one second longer than necessary. I knew it didn't really matter how long Alice was at the coroner's office because Alice was gone. But I was an illogical grieving mother who did not want my baby there in the first place. I would have gone myself if I thought I could have pulled that off without ending up in an institution.

By this point, it was clear to everyone Bubba was in charge, because I was quite glazed over.

For days, Bubba watched me. When he could tell I was overwhelmed, he became my filter, translating only vitally necessary information into bullet points for me. He became my press secretary, facilitating my communication to the masses because I couldn't. He became my executive function, enacting and delegating the required unfathomable tasks. He became the guard of my safe space, so I did not become more overwhelmed. He made no mistakes in his filtering, translation, synopsis, execution, or guarding. This was, perhaps, the most valuable gift I have received.

Bubba also taught me to say yes to offers of help. He said he told mutual friends Melissa B. and Bob what happened, and they wanted to help with anything that needed to be done, no matter the cost. We had been at a party at their house three days prior, but in that moment, I truly felt I hadn't seen them in years. Bubba grabbed my shoulders and began to speak to me looking straight into my eyes. It was becoming a theme: anyone who needed me to listen seemed to know they had to force eye contact for the words to sink into my failing brain. He held me there and said, "They are devastated. They want to help. Whether you need help paying for the service, or if you need to move out of this house, or fly your brother's family out here, they want to help with whatever you need."

I argued with the offer to help, as was my way. "I couldn't possibly accept ... we don't know them well enough for that ... it is far too generous an offer ..." Bubba strengthened his grip on my shoulders and said something that changed me forever. He said, "Melissa. They can do this. They *want* to do this. You need the help. Say yes."

It's a simple thing, really, this thing he said. But it never sank in until that moment. I ended up saying yes because it became obvious this was a life event too large for the heroics of pride. This was not an inconvenient situation. This was a whopper.

My next priority was to get my brother Steve and his family on a plane to Los Angeles, so they could mourn with the rest of the family: Bubba and our mutual friends began making that happen. This was an immense relief. It brought me a little peace of mind at a time when peace of mind was hard to come by.

This succumbing to "yes" was possibly one of the most life-altering events in the Aftermath, and for that alone, I will forever love Bubba. This was the day, only hours after my baby died, where the horrific tale began to show a tinge of beauty. It was here I began to learn how amazing people can be when given the chance.

My house began to fill with people. I milled about crying and telling funny stories about Alice while simultaneously being tormented by the vision of her blue face and stiff body coming out of the crib. I felt like a zombie, but I felt compelled to tell Alice's stories as much as possible. I was terrified I would forget some of them. How was I walking and talking? Wish I could tell you but I have no idea.

YEARS LATER, while writing this book, I realized the urge to be her historian did not die with her body. I also realized that it all took place under her birthday banner. Once the firemen left, I forgot about the banners until weeks after.

MANY OF THE new arrivals I did not know by name, but they knew us because of the girls — especially Alice, who we joked was "the mayor of Smallsville." She worked our neighborhood like an incumbent seeking re-election. She sang out her pleasantries with a confidence that dispelled any suggestion of desperation. This was her neighborhood: she knew it, she loved it, and she wanted to take care of it.

There were countless people in my house. I could tell people were staring at me. Some trying to be strong, some almost hysterical, some looking at me like deer in headlights. All appropriate responses, by the way. I judged no one, and most importantly, I was not judging myself. I let it all hang out.

Grace was mad at me but could not say why. It was probably because the house was full of hysterical, crying people. She would walk in, huff at me, and walk away like a little tiny teenager. I was mesmerized by this behavior. I didn't have the energy to do anything about it, so I let her huff at me. It was the least I could do for her.

At some point, I found myself in the entryway to the hall. I could not remember why I needed to enter the hall, so I just stood there. My mind was completely blank. I stared at the wall. I guess I figured if I stood there long enough it would come to me. My mother approached me. I turned to her and blurted out, "How am I going to live the rest of my life feeling this way? I could live another forty, fifty years, which is a lifespan as long as I've already lived. Her presence will be only a beautiful two-year intermezzo in my long life? I don't want her to be a two-year blip in the timeline of my life. I'm not sure I can live another lifespan feeling this way; it feels like guilt alone could literally kill me."

Those words were not in my brain before they shot out of my mouth. My mother shook her head and tried not to cry. I felt badly I'd upset her. I'd had no idea that was going to fly out of my mouth.

I walked back to the living room and realized I needed to go to the bathroom, which is why I had walked through the hallway. I forgot I had to use the bathroom … on my way to the bathroom. Fascinating.

Some relatives called. I talked to my uncle. He kept saying what basically everyone was saying: "I don't know what to say. It does not get worse than this. There is nothing worse than this." I can't count how many people said versions of this to me. I deeply appreciated their empathy, but though I knew they were probably right, the idea of it made me squeamish. We had experienced several difficulties in the previous five years, and I didn't want to invite more trouble. I begged people not to say that. I said to every one of them:

PLEASE DO NOT THROW up challenges to the heavens on my behalf. I can think of worse things. I can. This is horrific, but at least she died peacefully, and not cowered in paralyzing fear in the corner of her classroom because some maniac went on a shooting spree. At least I knew where she was, unlike parents of kidnapped children. At least she did not suffer a long illness.

This is big. But it could be worse and thank God it wasn't. Thank God Grace wasn't home, for instance. And Alice will never know pain. She will never have her heart broken or break a heart. No one will ever make fun of her. All she knew was love, and blankies, and binkies, and trains, and Elmo, *and songs, and her sister, and her family, and her caretakers. All she knew was love. All she knew was love.*

I DID NOT SUMMON these thoughts. I did not try to think of ways to put my great loss into perspective. These thoughts simply down-loaded into me, for lack of a better word. I have no idea why I found myself thinking of worse things. In retrospect, I firmly believe this line of thinking allowed me to keep moving. Baby steps, to be sure, but it was a start.

These are the words I kept telling myself. But "it could be worse" are not words you should *ever* say to anyone other than yourself. I mean, you can, but you'll sound like a dick. People need to come to these conclusions on their own. You cannot effectively tell another person where to search for solace, how to find their silver lining, or suggest ways to gain perspective. If you do, the freshly bereaved will more than likely immediately shut down for they will — rightfully — feel you are downplaying the intensity of their experience because, despite your best intentions, you will be. It may be true that "it could be worse," but telling them that is not supportive. It conveys that you do not understand the depth of their pain and that you do not wish to witness their pain. You don't have to bear witness to someone else's pain if it is too painful for you, but you should never attempt to convince the bereaved to cut short their necessary feelings so that you can feel better.

These things I told myself to get through a day were my realiza-tions and no one else could have successfully forced the issue.

Around this time, the coroner called with the initial findings. Someone else took the call. I was still terrified her death was somehow preventable, leaving me at fault. The coroner had found nothing, however. Not. One. Single. Thing. Was. Wrong. With. Her.

They were going to run tests. The results could take months to complete, but they did not expect to find anything; they were fairly certain it was SUDC. I was strangely relieved they could not identify a cause. If her death defied explanation, there was nothing I could have done to prevent it.

Near the end of the night, a bunch of us sat around talking. My eyes were so red it looked like someone put food coloring in them. I was so dehydrated my tongue was sore and it hurt to eat. Eventually, my head kind of fell to the side, and I felt like someone let all the air out of my balloon. This must have been visible because everyone immediately became quiet and began to leave. My dear friend Clara spent the night that night. No one said anything to me, but it was clear a sleepover schedule had been arranged. No one trusted me to be alone for a second at this point, which was wise. I put on a decent game face that day, but those in my inner circle knew I was paralyzed with guilt. Still, I knew I had to go on for my darling Grace — and for all the people who were supporting me.

It was my first entire day without Alice. I'd been stripped of one of the two most important people in my life. I'd been stripped of my executive functioning. I'd been drained of a good deal of my water content. I'd been robbed of a future I'd envisioned for my family. I'd been disabused of the idea I had any control in the world, but with Bubba's help I'd accepted help. I was gobsmacked by the amount of support flooding my way; it was incomprehensible.

I tried to sleep. The intrusive images of a deceased Alice ran rampant through my mind and I could not figure out how to stop them. I sobbed. I rocked.

Eventually, I slept.

THURSDAY: THE COLLAPSE

I slept for about four hours — my grand total for the last two days. I returned some of the many texts and emails I'd received while I lay in bed. It had been years since I'd spoken with some of the people who reached out. There are some people you never forget, who truly shape and form your life, but sadly we lose touch with them because life gets, well, life-y. It touched me to the very depths of my soul to receive such kindness from them at that time. It was a relief to learn real friendships pick up right where you left off, as if no time has passed.

Time felt slippery.

In the pre-dawn hours, I spoke with a friend for a while, and I remember hearing myself tell the story calmly, as if it happened to someone else. I was still in shock, I noted.

It was unusually quiet outside; there was not even birdsong. I stayed outside for a while and stared at the yard where my daughters had played just a few days ago. I looked at the garden they planted with me and wondered, "How can she have grown these cucumbers, this lettuce, and not be here herself?" The evidence of Alice's life was everywhere. But she was not. I wanted to die, but I knew I could not.

· · ·

I HAVE Grace to care for. I have Grace to care for. I have Grace to care for. This was my mantra.

I FELT like I had an actual hole in my heart. This hole people speak of is no joke — yet another cliché I found to be true. It was somewhat irritating to find truth in cliché, to be honest, but I tried to stay focused on the wonder. Mostly, I succeeded.

I kept thinking Grace was likely to be an only child now. Never in a million years did I think I would only have one child, even before I had kids. I still see myself with two children, one of whom can no longer be seen, who no longer requires a pint of blueberries a day, who no longer gets up at 5:30 a.m. ... but whose mother does. These thoughts ran in a near constant loop in my head.

Around this time, I realized I was sick. I had caught Alice's cold, which should not have been surprising considering I'd kissed her on the lips, proceeded not to sleep for two days after a great trauma, cried a lot, and was terribly dehydrated from the whole ordeal. This illness was not ideal, for we had a visitation and a service to pull off and we had only Thursday to make all the plans. Whatever adrenaline kept me going all of Tuesday night and Wednesday was no longer present.

I tried to contact my dear friends Meleva, Catie, and a few others, without success. Other people had posted about Alice's death on social media, so I needed to make an announcement soon; I didn't want close friends to hear it on social media from someone we barely knew.

PUBLIC SERVICE ANNOUNCEMENT: Unless one is next of kin, or given permission by next of kin, it isn't one's place to announce deaths on social media.

. . .

I WAITED for an hour or two after I sent the last texts and then posted it on Facebook. And then I cried my eyes out. Soon everyone would know this terrible news. Just thirty-six hours before she died — seventy-six hours prior to that moment — I posted I had no idea Alice could count to ten. And the day she did that, I had no idea she was going to die two days later.

I cried until Grace awakened. I got out of bed and pulled it together, as much as I could, for her.

Someone made coffee. Someone tried to get me to eat, but I doubt I ate much. I was exhausted. I had a 101° fever. I was about to have a house full of people. My mind was a barren wasteland, scattered with occasional tumbleweeds of pain, guilt, and intense grief. I looked like someone had stolen my soul. I suppose, in a way, someone had.

Family and close friends arrived and began working on the incomprehensible list of things to do. We had to find a venue for the service Saturday. We had to choose pictures for a slide show and get some enlarged for the altar at the service. We had to choose readings, readers, an officiant, songs, and musicians or playlists. We had to print programs. We had to figure out where and how to feed people. We had to choose Alice's outfit for the visitation. Oh, my God, what clothes do you choose for your deceased child? I wasn't sure I could do it.

And I was still on the fence about what do with Alice's remains, probably because I could not reckon with "Alice's" now being the possessive of "remains."

No one ever thinks they are going to have to decide what to do with their deceased child's body, or how to dress them. It never crosses your mind. Nor should it. It was a trauma all its own. I can't type it without feeling my stomach churn.

I felt like shit. Oh, was I sick. And I had about a thousand decisions to make. People were coming at me from all sides: "Do you want this or that?" "Should we do this or that?" "The rest of the family arrives today or tomorrow?" "Who should do ... ?" I stood there with my mouth agape, my head swirling, and my eyes glazed over and looked to Bubba for help. I don't know what I thought he could do about it;

they were mostly valid questions, questions only I could answer. But for once in my life, I had no problem delegating. Food? Ask Janet and my parents. Venue? Ask Bubba or Stacy. My health? Ask Clara or Fran, who arrived with the sole purpose of making sure I had what was necessary to treat myself the way I tell my patients to treat themselves.

Some questions only I could answer, but I was well beyond overwhelmed. I could *not* multitask. My brain was broken.

When I recounted this feeling to a male friend, he said, "Well, now you know what it is like to be a man. We are like that all the time." If that is so, then I have a whole new level of empathy for the male gender, because that shit is incapacitating.

I had to choose Alice's outfit, stat. She was being prepared for the visitation and they needed her clothes yesterday. I couldn't do it. I was frozen. My dear friend Dawn grabbed my hand and guided me through it. We selected a fancy dress my wonderful friends Paul and Daniella had brought her from Wales. She was only recently big enough for it to fit, so this would be the first, and only, time she would wear it. It had a matching headband, which was important because she needed something on her head to cover the autopsy scar. This detail made my heart turn inside out. I sat on the floor of her closet and sobbed.

We were also asked to make sure she had something covering her arms. I knew this was because Alice's decay might not be suitable for a sundress, which was a gutting realization. Also, she was completely covered in temporary tattoos Grace had applied the weekend before she died. Would they still be there or were they removed? I had no idea. For her pretty little feet, we selected the light-up shoes Sal and Teresa bought her for her birthday. She *loved* those shoes. She wanted to wear them 24/7 for the glorious ten days she was their owner. She wanted to wear them over her footed pajamas. She wanted to sleep in them, such was the love she had for those shoes.

While sobbing in Alice's closet, I saw the crib. The crib was proving to be dangerous to my mental health. I could not look at it without seeing her blue face as I lifted her out of the crib. I couldn't walk near it without developing tachycardia and breaking into a sweat. I couldn't think of it without falling apart and crying, "How am I ever going to get over seeing her blue face coming up out of that crib? How am I supposed to go on with that image haunting me the rest of my life? The crib is going to have to go. I can't take it."

The three grandpas, I was told, quietly took the crib out to the garage without my knowledge at some point that day. This was a crucial step in my healing process.

Although I was not yet ready to part with anything else Alice had touched, I knew the crib had to go if I were to have any chance at living without intense flashbacks. The crib, more than anything, took me out of time.

Next, I needed to choose pictures, so the enlargements could be printed in time for the service. I *wanted* to do that because I felt compelled to document her history. But I was devastated I was documenting the end of her history. So, in order to focus on pictures, I had to tell everyone: I needed to go to my room, shut the door, lie down, and sort through pictures. If something timely came up, they could ask me a question; otherwise, I needed to focus. I was exhausted. I was sick. I was racked with guilt. I was gutted. No wonder my brain didn't work. I begged Bubba to help me protect my privacy because I desperately needed to "coast" for a while. Bubba understood this incomprehensible request and became my filter.

Every once in a while, Bubba came in to ask me something, concerned he was asking too many questions. He wasn't. It was all important. I could handle it from one person, or two, just not the constant barrage from a room full of people. My mother and father came in occasionally. Fran brought me cold meds and would pop in with new fluids from time to time. But mostly, I was left alone to deal with pictures.

I looked at the pictures as if they belonged to someone else or I couldn't get through it. When I looked at them as if they were my photos, of my daughter, I collapsed into inconsolable tears. If I looked at them as if I were there with her in the scene, I could not breathe. Her entire life was documented on my phone camera; there would never be additional entries. The thought sickened me. It took a long time for me to finish this task. In some ways, I didn't want it to end because it meant her timeline ended — something I knew but didn't want to relive. I don't care how tough or how smart you think you are, realizing your history endures beyond that of your child's is something your brain doesn't process immediately, much less your heart.

At one point, Bubba told me our officiant, Jennifer Jacobson, had arrived to talk to us. Jennifer saw I was in bad shape, so sat at the edge of my bed while I lay there. She explained the manner in which she worked and asked us to tell her about Alice. It felt good to talk about Alice with her, although I still could not believe I was lying in bed, talking to the person who would officiate my daughter's memorial service. I was supposed to be at Lynn's house that day pretending to train her, while she pretended to work out. I laughed and cried while recounting Alice's history. I felt like I was on another planet where time and gravity didn't exist. Jennifer would accept no fee for her service. Again, we'd found another angel, from where I have no idea.

Eventually, I went to the backyard where everyone was working on their various tasks. It looked like the freaking Situation Room. People were huddled over laptops and phones and scribbling on Post-its and transferring finalized data into the master notebook Bubba had purchased so I could keep track of all of the information pouring at me from various directions: coroner's notes, detectives' numbers, fire department info, a list of people who had dropped off things for us, information on printing, venues, funeral homes, officiants, photo enlarging, order of service, etc. There was a dizzying amount of information to be managed.

We still had not heard from Meleva. I was becoming concerned about this and tried to call her myself. I left a voicemail. Bubba sent another email. A short while later, she called back, hysterical. She kept apologizing for not having been there. I thought, "Shit, honey, I am here, and I'm not even *here*, so don't you worry a thing about it." She said she was getting in a car that minute to drive down to LA. She lived outside of Sacramento, so this was no short trip. She asked if it would be helpful for her to bring her nearly five-year-old daughter Famke, who is Grace's friend. That was a terrific idea, bless her awesome heart. Grace was still huffy with me, and clearly needed some kid energy.

My friends Eddie and Kristen picked up Grace at some point Thursday and took her to their house for an overnight stay, which was a godsend. Grace adores their daughter Sophie, and I was thrilled Grace had time with a friend. It enabled me to make all these horrible decisions with my one-track mind. It enabled Grace to be a normal kid for a night, somewhere not surrounded by shellshocked grieving people. They went to the park, made popcorn, did magic shows and just kid stuff, which was what Grace needed.

We chose the readings, finalized the order of service, and gave it to the person in charge of drawing up the program. I had to do this like I was someone else or it would have never happened. This went faster than expected because everyone was helping so much.

We did have a handful of visitors beyond the inner circle and family, but we were trying to discourage this as much as possible because I was so sick and overwhelmed. People wanted to come by, and I wanted them to have their chance to do so, but I was in a bad, bad way and not up to hosting. The folks who came said not to worry about hosting, but it cannot be avoided. I needed to go to bed, but you can't go to bed if someone has arrived to see you.

As I walked around dazed, I saw two friends checking the programs that had recently arrived. They asked me if I wanted to check, so I went over expecting to proofread. I saw:

Alice Marie Ferguson
July 26, 2011 – August 6, 2013

And then I heard myself make an inhuman noise and I doubled over with gut-wrenching pain. I ended up on the floor, which was embarrassing, but I could not get up. I don't know what I was expecting. I guess I wasn't expecting anything, to be honest; I was truly going minute to minute at this point. I knew she died, obviously, but

47

seeing something that could be on a tombstone crushed my entire world into a million pieces. When I look at it today, it barely makes sense. This was not the timeline I had envisioned for her. I would not have agreed to that timeframe. I did not want those dates of her history to be so close together. I did not want the second date to exist while I still breathed.

It was getting late. I was a mess. I needed to clear people out of the house; I was completely overwhelmed. The family left after cleaning up for the visitation the next day, and Bubba, Clara, and Stacy cleared out the rest of the people before leaving themselves. Fran spent the night, doing all the things I would normally do for myself when ill.

Finally, I got in the bath. I sat there nearly comatose for some time. I don't think I'd bathed or showered since Alice died. The water felt so good. I was dry and stuffy from the cold, so I'd steamed up the room before getting in. I sat there pondering how I was now a person who had lost a child. But, as I sat in that bath, these words came to me:

IF GOD HAD COME DOWN and said, "I'll give you a second child. Here she is. (God waves their hand and shows me a God-image of Alice.) She will be amazing and sweet and funny and healthy and happy. But she will only live two years and then will be gone in the snap of my fingers with no explanation whatsoever. Are you in, or are you out?" I would have responded, "I'm in. I am fully in. In fact, if you gave me my choice of all the babies in the world, I would still choose this baby. That is my baby." I knew I would choose her all over again. I knew I would choose her and accept the consequences. I knew this like I know I am a woman.

I IMMEDIATELY SAT up and began to pour water on my arms. When pouring the water over my left arm, I suddenly became transfixed by an overwhelming sense of peace — a peace like no other I have ever felt. I was so peaceful I could not move; I was frozen in mid-motion, wetting my arm. I sat there for minutes, basking in the glow of this peace. It was like a literal blanket of peace came down, wrapped me up, and permeated me. It was the most awe-inspiring moment I have ever had in my life to date. I sat there for a long time, marveling at this sensation.

This sense of peace stayed with me as I got out of the bath and ready for bed. Fran helped me get ready for bed and fed me her magic soup. I returned texts until my eyes would no longer stay open.

And then I drifted effortlessly into sleep.

About three hours later, I woke with a start, because I had a dream of Alice being beaten on a playground and I couldn't get there to save her. I was also so dry, so fevered, so stuffed up, and so hysterical I was having a hard time getting a breath. I became consumed by guilt again. I couldn't stop crying. Fran helped set up a humidifier in my room, brought me hot liquids, and listened without judgment as I unleashed the guilts. She held me and let me cry, fed me fluids and helped me remember the peaceful bath experience. She brought me back to a place of relative peace. And then, I collapsed into sleep again.

I released the crib that day. I released the notion that my child's death date should follow mine. I released more control than I thought was possible. Loss upon loss led me to collapse into the arms of so many of my beautiful friends and family, and for once, I didn't feel guilty about it. I knew it was all I could manage.

FRIDAY: THE VISITATION

I woke up with a pit in my stomach first and the realization Alice was dead second. And then came the sobs. "Three mornings ago, she was alive. Now she isn't," I thought. I managed to get six hours of sleep Thursday night, but I was still mighty sleep-deprived overall.

"I could live forty to fifty more years *feeling like this*. How in the name of God am I supposed to live as long as I have already lived, feeling like I do now?" That cycled through my brain several times. On Wednesday, I wasn't sure if I could live to the end of the day. I wasn't going to kill myself, but I did absolutely, positively feel like the feelings I had were so big, so intense, so overwhelming, and so bad, that the feelings themselves could kill me, unaided by human hands.

After sobbing for a few minutes that Friday morning, the peace I felt the night before returned, out of nowhere. I felt ready to face the day I was to view the remains of my daughter.

Suddenly, I remembered I was sick. How odd is that? I forgot I was sick. Generally being sick is enough to remind you that you are sick.

Although I did not *like* what was about to happen, I began the day thinking, "Today, I can do this. Yesterday, I could not have." Wednesday, I felt ready to accept guests. Thursday, I could not handle guests and needed to hunker down and plan things. Friday, I felt like I could handle seeing my deceased daughter for the first time since the day she died. I felt a little nervous about it, sure. I could tell I was pacing around like I was waiting on a flight. But I felt I could do it without ending up in a heap on the floor. To what I owed the gift of that temporary strength, I have no idea. I suppose it was the source of whatever had given me the feeling of all-encompassing peace in the bath the night prior. I noticed I felt more "in my body." I could feel my arms and legs. I felt a little less like I was slumped over a pole that ran through the center of my body. I felt a little more "here."

I distinctly recall feeling like an observer of my emotions on this day, and the days that preceded it. I felt like someone had dropped a sociologist into my body who was observing the person who is/was me. This sociologist invasion was not uncomfortable in any way. In fact, it was somewhat comforting. I suppose the Buddhists would say this is how we ideally operate all the time. Is this the "right" thing to do? I have no idea. It just happened; I have no idea why. And there are far worse things I could have fallen into, so I made friends with the sociologist.

It was time to prepare the room. I placed a flower arrangement on the trunk at the end of the bed and began to arrange some of Alice's favorite things at the top. If she could indeed see us from where she now resides, I wanted her to know her happiness was still of paramount importance to me. I wanted her to know I would love her until the day I die, and hopefully beyond. I wanted her to know I would never forget her. I wanted her to know she was still my beloved little Alice, and I intended to take care of her in death, as I had in life. And I wanted everyone there to know what Alice loved, so that they could know her.

HERE ARE *Alice's beloved Matchbox cars and trains, most of which she had pilfered from school. She was proprietary about the entire collection of cars at* her school, but she had a white one she especially loved. Every day, upon leaving, she would shove it behind her back, cock her head to the side, and with an expression of deep sincerity say, "My car, Mama. Myyyyyyy car." She had her teachers wrapped around her little finger, and they eventually let her keep the damn car. My brother Steve also loved cars as a kid and had given a few to the girls. Grace also knew Alice loved cars, so one day at the store, not long before Alice passed, Grace suggested we get Alice a pink Matchbox car. It was an act of generosity on Grace's part, so I relented.

HERE IS the green recorder Alice swiped from Teresa and Sal's house. Only two days before she died, she walked up to me confidently producing noise from the recorder. She had never done so before, but you would have never known from looking at her. Alice was one confident kid. She gave me a cursory glance from the corner of her eye while she marched around blowing it, a far cry from the greeting I generally received, when she would run up to me crying, "MAMA!" before motioning me toward her belongings. Alice was showing off that day. God, what I would give to see what she could be showing me right now.

HERE ARE Alice's beloved books. She loved for me to read to her. Dawn Bentley's The Icky Sticky Frog was one of her all-time favorites. As the story goes, the frog slurps down several different bugs (before being devoured by a fish), each time with a hearty "SLURP!" When I hammed up the slurp, Alice fell apart laughing. Once the book ended, she would turn back to her favorite slurp and make me do it again. "A-gain, Mama!" And again. And again. Peggy Rathmann's Good Night, Gorilla was another favorite. A few pages have no words. Alice's favorite pages were the black ones. One has different-sized bubbles saying "Good night! Good night!" etc. The next one is completely black except for the wide-open eyes of the zookeeper's wife. I always read this page with a dramatic "HUH?!" that led Alice to throw back her head laughing. She "forced" me into reading the black pages several times in a row. Alice also loved a box of block-sized books my dad and stepmother gave to her, so that was also placed on the bed as well. I Love You Through and Through, *written by Bernadette Rossetti Shustak and given to her by my friend Alison, was also included. I read it in a certain cadence, and I would often overhear Alice using the cadence to "read" the book to her dolly. A Peekaboo! flap book my mother bought for the girls was also a favorite of Alice's and was included in the mix.*

HERE ARE ALICE'S INSTRUMENTS. *Alice loved music, singing and dancing. When she was a baby, the only toys that could earn me enough time to go to the bathroom were her egg-shaped musical shakers. They were also the impetus for Alice making her first friend. She and a little girl named Evie fell in love at a baby yoga class when Alice was about eight months old. They lit up when they saw each other, as if they were old friends who hadn't seen each other in a while — except they had never met. Evie coveted Alice's shakers, and Alice would sometimes share them. They bonded over those shakers and were friends until Alice died. I gave one of the shakers to Evie's mom to remember Alice by. The other lives on our mantel in front of Alice's picture.*

HERE WAS ALICE'S DOLL. *She had recently started to play "Mama" with some of Grace's dolls; the doll Grace liked least was placed up on the bed. Bella Linda was the one Alice liked best but was also the one Grace liked best — and had been a present to Grace from my mother. I did not want to risk alienating Grace by placing Bella Linda with Alice, so we chose a runner-up. I wasn't in any condition to manage a jealousy issue on the occasion of Alice's wake. I knew Alice would understand.*

HERE WAS *the purse Grace bought for Alice. Alice had filled it with crayons she pilfered from Grace; her beloved balls; an apple ("Ap-o!"); a tangerine (also referred to as "Ap-o!"); and the plastic train that held the candles on her birthday cake only two weeks prior. Oh, God. How could we have gone from such a happy day to the saddest day I will likely ever have, in such a short time? My stomach lurched.*

. . .

HERE WAS Alice's quilt made by my Aunt Polly. Alice was going to be laid atop it. I am sure this was not its intended use, and I hoped Aunt Polly would be honored, rather than horrified.

HERE IS Alice's true love, Elmo. She didn't watch Elmo on TV, but she loved her Elmo doll and the Elmo Facetime application. Our Elmo went missing at the girls' preschool a few weeks before Alice died. When I retrieved the girls that night, Alice's three little boyfriends (Frank, Jake, and Neyson) all scurried around the room helping us look for Alice's lovey. None of these three boys spoke but a few words, but they all knew their girl was missing her lovey. I'll never forget how my heart swelled watching three 18-month-old boys help Alice search for her beloved doll. We never did find our Elmo, but one of the little guys pulled an Elmo doll from the school's toy box and handed it to Alice. That's pure love, folks. That Elmo also sits on our mantel, to this day.

REMEMBERING this love between Alice and her little boyfriends reminded me Alice would never know heartache. She died having only known one hundred percent pure love. Love from her parents, her sister, her grandparents, aunts and uncles, and cousins. Love from her teachers and caretakers. Love from her friends and our neighbors. Love from strangers. Alice would never manipulate love or be manipulated by love. Alice would never find out the boy (or girl) she loved, loved somebody else. Alice was a conduit for pure love, and I feel fortunate to have borne witness to it. I focused on this while I continued to select the toys to be laid beside her.

HERE WAS ALL that was left of Alice — the love she spread around. These items were blessed to have been filled with that love. I laid them out with the care one would extend to the crown jewels.

. . .

ONCE FINISHED, I nervously waited for them to bring Alice to me. I hadn't seen her alive in three days. My mind went blank for a while, which was a great relief. I marveled at that for a moment, which ruined the blankness, but was not unpleasant.

Eventually, Bubba and the funeral director, Shari, walked in with Alice. You could hear a pin drop in the house. It was a moment that took my literal breath away. Time truly stood still. My dear deceased daughter was on a sheet-wrapped plank. She was clutching her second-favorite doll in one hand and a car she stole from school in the other. She had her blankie laid across her shoulder and her binky nearby.

I stared and stared but could not make this scene make sense to me.

There was no box. No coffin. I did not want my toddler in a box under any circumstances. The plank was just big enough for Alice and the items we sent for her. I was so relieved Shari had handled this for me. Having Alice laid out as naturally as possible meant more to me than I can explain.

They laid her in the center of the bed, next to me, before stepping out to give me privacy. I burst into deep sobs. The kind that come from your gut, not your head.

She looked perfect, if not for the fact she was dead. She was not the grey-yellow color you see in embalmed bodies; she was pink, just like she was in life. She smelled like a baby, not formaldehyde. I was absolutely floored by how perfect she looked, three days later, with no embalming. I was immediately relieved we had chosen this option.

She looked like a little doll but was noticeably missing some of the curly locks from the top of her head. I sobbed again, knowing some of her hair had been cut off for the autopsy. I touched her, and stroked her head, and arms. I peeked under the doll to see her fingers. Her fingers were blue, and not as plump as they had been Tuesday morning. This was the only real sign of decay, and for some reason, I found myself realizing this like an emotionally detached scientist. I am not saying scientists are emotionally detached, I am only saying I felt 1) emotionally detached from the decay of my daughter's body, and 2) at this point in the day, I felt like a scientist had joined the sociologist. The real me seemed to have been given some time off for good behavior.

Because Alice was not embalmed, we could hold her, so I did. I picked her up carefully and immediately noticed her center of gravity was different. Her head didn't move much, which struck me as well. Her eyes were sewn shut. Oh, God, her eyes were sewn shut. That fact leveled me. I held her, noticing these things, and whispered sweet things in her little perfect ears. I held her for some time. You can't do this at a regular funeral home, and I am extremely grateful I had the chance to do this. At one point, I realized what I was doing was somewhat unconventional. I did not care. I did not care what people thought. My baby was gone. If they didn't like how I handled it, they could step away.

No one said anything.

The grandparents came in next, two at a time. That was devastating. I have no other words to describe it. The aunts and uncles and godparents followed. I couldn't take it anymore, so I left before most of the aunts, uncles, and godparents had their time with her.

I walked outside. It felt strange to be outside. I knew I had been in the backyard the day before, but it didn't *feel* like I had been. Time was still slippery. I think I talked to people. Maybe I walked around in a daze.

Grace and Famke had hung Barbie dolls from my lemon tree. It was more than a little creepy. Myriads of unrealistically proportioned, blonde, plastic wicker (wo)men dangled by their feet from the tree that once shaded Alice. I can't lie: I was impressed with their funerary artistic expression. I wondered if this was giving our guests the creeps. I quickly decided I didn't care if it did. Four-year-olds have to work through their shock and grief as well. I barely knew how to handle my own and certainly didn't want any advice on how to handle it; who was I to tell children how to handle theirs? Hang your Barbies, children; let your freak dolls fly.

My need for solitude sated, I walked toward the house. I heard

Grace telling guests, "Alice is already died. The doctor can't help you when you are already died. *No one* can help you when you are already died," which was causing people to erupt into tears. I watched. I wondered if I should intervene and immediately decided not to. Grace needed to cope in her own way. I assumed no one thought they'd get through the wake of a two-year-old dry-eyed anyway.

Grace decided she was ready to see Alice. She sat on my lap and asked some basic questions about death. She noticed Alice was not breathing. She asked if she could touch her. I told her that she could, but Alice would not be able to touch her back. She went over and tentatively touched her sister on the head, on the arm, on her tummy, her shoes. She asked, again, "When you are already dead, no one can help you, right, Mama?" "No, honey," I replied. "No one can help her anymore, but she doesn't need our help anymore either."

Grace, who is nothing if not meticulous, checked out the collection of toys on and around Alice. She thought it was a good idea that Alice had her blankie and placed Alice's binky closer to her mouth. She asked to have her picture taken with her sister, so we did that. Grace sat next to Alice, put her arm around her, and gave the most melancholy smile I have ever seen in my life. I don't know where that photo is, but eight years later, I'm finally ready to see it. She came back into my lap, and cried, "I'm so sad Alice is dead, Mama!"

Gutting.

After Grace felt "done," I collapsed on the bed next to Alice. I was still sick, I was exhausted, and I wanted to cuddle with my baby, one last time. Oh, who am I kidding? I rarely got to cuddle on the bed with her while she was alive. She was toooooooooo busy. If you wanted a cuddle you had to 1) stand, 2) put a blankie on your shoulder, and 3) catch her in a sleepy moment. Then, she was all yours. But the conditions had to be perfect for her to relent. Today, she could not wriggle away because the entity that animated her body was elsewhere.

My mom joined me after a while. Never again would Alice light up when we FaceTimed with Grandma and Grandpa Duck (so named by Grace because he liked to make Donald Duck noises at the girls, which made them laugh). Alice would never again try to imitate those duck noises.

Meleva and Bubba came in a little later. We sat around and talked while I cuddled up to my baby girl for the last time. I was still completely racked with guilt. They kept telling me not to be, that I was a great mother, and I kept saying, "I must be the worst mommy in the world to let my baby die alone in her crib." I have cried very little while writing these accounts — I sort of have to go to a place just above myself in order to write these pieces — but I am in tears over this memory.

We told stories of Alice, and what Alice might have grown up to be. It seemed a futile exercise because it was. I had no idea what she would grow up to be when she was alive. Her death did not make her now nonexistent future any clearer.

I WAS NEVER a parent who expected my child to embrace the hobbies I enjoy or those I never had the opportunity to undertake. I never expected my kids to go to a certain school, pursue a certain life path, or even follow a specific religion other than "Do unto others as you would have them do unto you." I felt my job was to observe their natural interests and gifts, encourage those pursuits, and offer opportunities to explore their own interests. I did not — and do not — see myself as the writer of their story, but as their benefactor, historian, and ill-qualified teacher. I believe this approach made a real difference when shit hit the fan because I did not have to suffer the disappointment of Alice not living out my unfinished business. I didn't have to suffer the loss of a particular future; I only had to suffer the loss of her future in general.

Mourning the future you imagine for your children isn't healed in a day or a year or a decade. Even the most laissez-faire parents harbor some expectations of how their child's history will unfold — that it will unfold at all. We don't realize these expectations until they become impossible to fulfill. Sometimes we reckon with the grief resulting from our child's abandoned future, and sometimes the grief or anger of that unfulfilled future levels us. I am grateful I didn't have her whole life planned out in my imagination: I had fewer perceived losses to grieve this way. I was able to focus on the real loss, the loss of Alice.

THE SPECULATION of what Alice might have been when she grew up felt pointless and painful, so eventually I stopped. Something someone said reminded me of Tina Fey's "A Mother's Prayer for Her Daughter," which is hilarious. My mother and Meleva had not heard it, so Bubba fetched and read it. We all shared a tearful laugh as I snuggled what was left of Alice.

About this time, Grace appeared in the doorway, looking shy. I asked her if she wanted to come in, but she scampered off into the hallway. She wanted her friend Famke to come in with her, so someone went to get Meleva to see how she felt about Famke viewing Alice. Soon, Meleva, Grace, and Famke walked into the room. The little girls approached Alice slowly and with reverence, but no discernible fear. They asked if they could touch her. As Meleva wrote to her family:

Famke asked Melissa how she knew Alice was dead.
"Well, honey, she wasn't breathing anymore."
Famke responded, "And her heart wasn't beating?"
"No."
Famke said, "Well, we can all see her again when we go to heaven," and then,
"I just think she's the most beautiful baby in the world."
Famke sighed, and out of the silence said simply:
"I wish ... I wish ... she could just come alive."

SHE SAID what everyone was feeling but was too controlled to say.

Eventually, Shari came in to tell us it was time. The family and a few friends said their final goodbyes.

I held Alice, sang to her, and bawled my eyes out. I felt like someone had removed my heart from my chest like that awful scene in *Braveheart*. I did not want to let go.

But I had to, and so I did.

Bubba and Shari carried Alice out of the house and I followed. The sun hurt my eyes. I stood there in a trance watching them get ready to place my girl in the converted van. At this point, I realized every single person at the viewing had followed us out. They kept a respectful distance, but they all were there, on my steps, silently saying goodbye to my Alice, backlit by the afternoon sun. Seeing all my loved ones silently watching me say goodbye to my daughter is something I will never forget for as long as I live. It was like a scene from a movie — like *The Big Chill* with '70s lighting — a movie you never hoped to see, much less star in.

Someone, I don't recall who, walked me inside after the van left. Someone held me while I cried. Someone brought me tissues. I can't recall who did what, but I am deeply grateful to them all.

I snuck outside, to the side of the house, to be alone for a spell. I needed some time. I needed some space. I needed to need nothing for a moment. I needed to be invisible for a moment.

Bubba found me, and within minutes had me smiling through my tears. Our friend Bob joined us, and we all shared some philosophy and jokes.

At some point later that night, I suddenly thought, "If I don't laugh, I'm going to die." It seemed urgent that I laugh — like my life depended on it. I pulled up some videos I knew were foolproof and watched them with my stepsisters. I was immensely relieved to find that I could still laugh.

Sometime later, our friend Bob asked me to tell him about the pictures in my living room. I was deeply touched he cared to ask, so I told him about each picture he pointed to. He continued into the kitchen, down the hall, to every picture in the house. I thought it was awfully generous of him to take the time to ask. I don't know if he knew how healing it was for me to discuss the pictures with a genuinely interested guest, but it was. I felt myself soften. I hadn't realized how tense I was. He gave me the opportunity to describe her history to caring ears, a gift of immeasurable value.

It was as if I read myself a bedtime story of Alice's life, because soon after I collapsed into my bed, hoping a living Alice would visit my dreams.

But that visitation would not happen for a long time.

SATURDAY: THE MEMORIAL

*S*aturday came too early, but I did manage seven hours of sleep without medication. Once I hit seven hours unaided, I felt like I was in a position to manage sleep *sans* medication, for the most part.

I did, however, wake up with a pit in my stomach. And I did let out a guttural cry when I again realized that it was a new day, but my Alice was still dead. Four days since I tossed her blanket back in her crib and casually walked out. Tears burst from my eyes and covered my face.

Crying alone was my preferred method. It took less time. It was more efficient. I didn't have to feel guilty about other people being made uncomfortable by my emotions. No one had expressed any discomfort, mind you, but I could see their pain and The Guilt was there just the same.

I returned some emails and texts then got out of bed.

It was Alice's Memorial Day. I realized only four days earlier we had been preparing to take the girls camping with my friends Nancy and Mike and their kids. The camping trip seemed like a story outline written thirty years ago, or possibly a story I knew but which did not involve me. I felt completely removed from what had been so real just days prior. I could not make sense of the discrepancy between my experience of the passing of time and what the calendar said about the passing of time.

The memorial meant I had to leave the house. I felt as if I hadn't left the house in years, but it had only been three days. The disorientation was baffling — though I suppose disorientation is never coherent. I would be among people that day, probably a lot of people. This didn't scare me; I simply took note.

Strangely, I felt capable that morning. I felt the calmest I had felt since Alice died, which mystified me. Perhaps it was finally getting some sleep; perhaps I was too emotionally exhausted to host an internal war that morning; perhaps the love of my family and friends pulled me to the other side; or perhaps all of the above was true. In any event, I was feeling relatively normal-ish. Emphasis on the "ish."

Figuring out what to wear to your child's memorial service feels like the most trivial thing on earth. The event was devastating in the first place, and choosing an outfit seemed too insignificant to warrant a decision. Still, I couldn't go in my pajamas. Well, I guess I could have — no one would have dared say a thing, I suppose — but I wanted to show respect for my daughter.

There was a "new" blouse I had purchased at a resale shop the week before Alice's birthday. It had been a long time since I had purchased clothing for myself and I wanted something nice to wear for Alice's birthday party, so I'd bought two blouses that day. The one I did not wear to the party had been lying on my hope chest since the day I bought it. Alice had held it up for me several times in hopes I would wear it. "Dis! Dis, Mama!" she would cry. Mostly, she did this as I was about to go teach Pilates or take a yoga class, so I had to deny her, but one night I put it on, after work, just for her. This is the blouse I decided to wear for the service. I chose a black skirt to match. I let Alice choose my outfit.

Some beautiful soul had gassed up my car and left mineral water and a box of tissues in the cup holders. It was so nice to feel so cared for, and I was touched beyond words. Someone else had removed Alice's car seat. That took the wind out of me. I was frozen for a moment. I thought the car seat would be removed because she became too big for it, not because she became too dead for it.

She was *just* in it one hundred eleven hours ago ... *There are probably still Goldfish cracker crumbs that touched her lips on that seat, but she is not.*

It had to be removed at some point, I suppose, and I was grateful I did not have to be the one to make that call. Maybe I would have left it in there a creepy long time? Maybe I would have sobbed uncontrollably? It would not have been pretty; I knew that, so I sat in gratitude to whoever did it for me. I do not remember crying that morning on the way to the service, however, so I guess this pain remained a silent thump in the chest.

I BREASTFED HER. I made her food from scratch with organic products. I made sure she "ate the rainbow" in fruits and vegetables every day. I bought the "good" car seats. I tended to her boo-boos. I bought her preferred rice milk. I placed locks on the medicine cabinet and cleaning supply cabinet. I attached bumpers to the edges of the furniture. I fastened her seatbelt even in the stroller. I didn't let her hold my cellphone near her developing brain. I held her for long periods every day. I read to her. I laughed with her. I prioritized her comfort, health, and happiness. But none of that mattered because in the end, she went to sleep in a perfectly safe crib and never woke up. I should have let her eat Goldfish crackers and watermelon all day. I should have let her hold my phone longer. I should have quit my job and lived every second with her and Grace. We could have lived on love.

I REALIZED this train of thought wasn't taking me to a healthy station, so I jumped off.

The world outside felt like scenery from a film. I felt like was traveling in a clear tube through the world around me. I could see and hear my surroundings, but the sensory information was muffled. For some reason, I felt I could not touch them, and therefore, was not convinced they were real. This experience reminded me of the movie

The Truman Show. I was Truman, and I was beginning to suspect my surroundings were not real, but a set. Of course, I knew this wasn't true, but the unintentional questioning of my perceived reality was very real, very intense, and all-consuming.

When I arrived, a few people were already there, beyond those who were helping. I immediately realized that, to stay composed through the service, I was going to have to remain in "business mode." This meant I could not hold eye contact, talk, or hug anyone for longer than a split second, or I would dissolve into tears and/or become immobilized. I wished there was a "backstage" area where I could wait until the service started. I didn't care about being perceived as ill-composed; I simply knew I had a long day and needed to ration my emotional stamina. I greeted people as I moved by them. I had to keep moving. My body was on autopilot, going through the motions of being in a crowd. My mind was frozen. My heart was hollow.

Bubba was walking around with a clipboard when we arrived. Nothing says "I am running this damn show" like a calm man walking with a clipboard through crowds of repressed emotional chaos.

I remained composed as I set up the sign-in table. I glanced up to see people staring at me from all parts of the room. There was nothing creepy or malevolent in the stares, and it did not bother me, per se. I was, however, keenly aware of it and had to tune it out. It hadn't occurred to me people might stare at me. I am sure I also would have stared at the temporarily composed, grieving mother arranging her toddler's beloved worldly goods at the sign-in table at her memorial service.

People began to arrive. I felt like I had not seen any of them in years. Some I was certain I had not seen in years and I was shocked they were there. Then I realized the people I *thought* I had not seen in years I had seen just days ago. I was constantly faced with how differently I was experiencing the passage of time.

I noticed the slideshow of Alice's little life playing on the giant screen. I stopped dead in my tracks. I had chosen many of the pictures, but I had nothing to do with arranging the slideshow or with choosing the music to play with it. I think Eric Clapton's "Tears in Heaven" was playing when I first looked up and saw a picture of Alice and me at one of her first swim lessons. Water shot out of my eyes like a cannon. Who would have known on that joyous day of swim class I would be looking at a larger-than-life-sized version of that picture at her memorial service only sixteen months later? I stared and stared at the images onscreen, and the giant photos we had enlarged. I could not believe that I could not reach in there, and pull her out, alive, onto my shoulder.

So many questions, so few answers.

One question I did not ask myself then, and have not to date, was "Why us?" I am not sure why it didn't occur to me; it seems like a natural question. But it just didn't. I only thought of it because so many people asked me if I ever wondered, "Why me?" I suppose I felt like one can't ask a question like that without unintentionally inferring it would be all right if it happened to someone else's family. And I certainly did not feel anyone deserved what had happened to our family.

All I knew was it had happened to my Alice, and that the only way through it, was through it. *The only way through it is through it. The only way through it is through it.* That was/is my mantra. I didn't feel I had the luxury of wasting time asking the unanswerable question "Why me?" Guilt was more my demon, and we were in full-time battle. If anything, I thought, *"Why anyone?"*

Grace, Meleva, and Famke sat with me in the front row. We were supposed to be eating breakfast on the beach in front of our tent with Nancy and Mike's family. Alice was supposed to be following Lenore, and Grace was supposed to be following Julian, and the adults were supposed to be laughing and possibly enjoying the breakfast of champions. Instead, I was at Alice's memorial service. It still did not make sense to me.

I was not angry. I did not blame, beyond the blame-of-self that is guilt. I had not yet experienced those two hallmarks of grief. We had no idea why she died, so there was nothing at which to direct anger or blame, except myself since it had happened on my watch. My great college friend Tommy kindly offered, more than once, to sit on the phone and listen while I yelled and cussed. He lives out of state but wanted to do something to help. But I didn't need to yell and curse her death then, and except for two or three occasions, have not since. Well, that's not true; I have cussed. But not about Alice. Under duress, I like to cuss sometimes — a fact Tommy is well aware of — thus his kind offer. It feels good to pop off on occasion. Sometimes, it feels *really* good. And if you do it right, no one gets hurt.

The service started. I stared. I knew it was happening but at the same time I felt like it was happening to me in another dimension. I don't know how else to describe it. It was happening: I knew that. I was there: I knew that. But "here" did not feel like what I knew of as "here."

I was going through the motions of being a civilized person. I saw my dad read a Bible passage. I heard my friend Ramsay sing "I Saw the Light," as I'd requested. I saw Bubba and my friend J-Do read passages. I heard my friend Jessica play "Twinkle, Twinkle" with a string trio. I saw the officiant give the eulogy.

Why is someone reading a eulogy for Alice? What the hell is happening?

Once the service was over, I turned around, and saw an enormous line of people behind me, queued up to pay their respects. I had not realized how packed the place had become. I was awestruck and touched beyond words.

Most heartbreaking were the teachers, parents, and kids from my girls' school. I mostly held it together until I saw them. Alice's little two-year-old boyfriend Neyson was there with his mama. He looked at me, and simply asked, "Alice?" I lost it. I mean, I totally lost it. My college roommate and dear friend of twenty-six years, Jen, flew in from Chicago. My sweet friend Pamela came with Rachael, my new friend who had also lost her daughter to SUDC. I could *not believe* she managed to come to my baby's service only five months after she had lost her own sweet child. What an amazing woman. The line went on and on, and the love just poured out of every soul. And I soaked up all the love I could get. I remember thinking it was like being at my own funeral. Alice was so young; most of those people were there for me and my family. They were saying to me things they would have said at my funeral. I was living "the Irishman's dream," except the reason I had a chance to do so was a nightmare of epic proportions.

I noticed I had the overwhelming urge to say "Sorry! Sorry! So sorry!" to everyone in turn. I wanted to say, "I'm sorry you have to explain death to your two-year-old child who played with mine." "I'm sorry you have to question your own child's mortality now. And your own, frankly." "I'm just ... *so sorry.*" I felt responsible for the immense amount of grief in the room, in the community, in our extended family.

People were invited back to Janet and Mark's beautiful home for a luncheon afterward. What Janet and Mark did for me that week is immeasurable. I'm sure I am not aware of half of what they did. Feeding hundreds of mourners, in their home, was only the tip of the iceberg, I am sure. I was one of the last to arrive, because I waited until the venue was empty before leaving.

As I entered Janet and Mark's home, I felt like I was moving through molasses inside a rocket ship — as if I was moving my body very slowly inside something traveling at the speed of light.

Somehow, I milled around talking to people. I was so deeply touched by the outpouring of love and support.

Later, I returned to our house with a few friends, and greeted Grace. Grace was clearly overwhelmed by the grieving masses at this point, but I did get a good hug before she went to play on the front porch, as had become her custom that week. Previously, Grace had never played on the porch, but by this point, it had become her sanctuary.

At one point, I overheard her saying, "Poo poo, pee pee, vomit, throw up, fart, trash, stinky," and every other "bad" word she knew in quick succession. I laughed, because it reminded me of the toddler version of George Carlin's "Seven Words You Can Never Say on Television." I laughed because, first, cursing makes me laugh. I don't know why, it just does. Because it makes me laugh, it is the perfect vehicle for taking deep annoyance or frustration and turning it into acceptance and joy. There is nothing like peeling off a string of expletives to turn my mood around in a snap. I feel so good afterward. "Ahhhhhhh."

I also think it's funny we have somewhat randomly designated certain words — which are merely symbols — as "bad." None of those words symbolize something inherently bad, except perhaps "motherfucker." That's fairly tawdry. I enjoy the gentle rebellion in cursing, I suppose. It takes the edge off, doesn't it? I suppose for these reasons, and possibly more, I laughed when I found my four-year-old pulling a George Carlin. I completely understood. She was stressed out, she was four years old, and she was surrounded by stressed-out, devastated adults, half of whom were hysterical and half of whom were obviously repressing all their feelings. She needed a damn minute to let out the frustration. So I walked inside and left her to it.

She did that for several months. I fondly referred to her as "Toddler Carlin" at those moments. Secretly — or now, not so secretly — I was proud of her for finding a release and having the presence of mind to go outside, alone, far from the ears of friends and family who might not find it as funny as Mama did.

At some point during the previous two days, the decision had been made to cremate Alice's remains. I finally decided I didn't want her in the ground should I move away from LA one day. I wanted her with me and Grace. Still, the idea of cremation seemed awfully intense to me. So final. For some reason, it felt more final than burying her. I suppose this is because one can dig up a buried person (should one think that would be helpful and wish to risk arrest). I wanted her remains with me. She was returned to the funeral home too late on Friday for it to happen then, so she was scheduled to be cremated Monday. I felt uneasy about this. I had to divert my thoughts.

I decided not to tell Grace about the cremation: I felt like four years old was way too young to try to comprehend cremation. Other than cremation, we told Grace everything.

Years later, while going through old posts and texts in preparation for writing this book, I noticed I wished people "Happy Birthday" on Facebook the day of Alice's memorial. How in the hell did I do that? I had no recollection of doing so. I think I saw people were afraid when they saw me, and I wanted them to know that though I was grieving, Melissa was still there. I look back on what I was doing and saying at that time, and I don't know how I did it. I guess I was on autopilot for anything requiring human interaction or basic daily tasks while inside I was going through the largest transformation I will likely ever have. It happened to me, I remember it vividly, and even I can't explain it.

It was as if I became two beings: one who had to get shit done despite the tragedy and one who had to experience transformation because of the tragedy. The one who had to get shit done had to go on autopilot because the one processing the tragedy was using all the life force. They knew about each other. There was no jostling for power or decisions about which one was in charge at any time. The transitions were seamless. So seamless, in fact, that I didn't notice the division until I started writing this.

We had presented Alice's entire life history to everyone we knew that day. It would be the last public event of her history. Grace's history would go on but irrevocably changed, which broke my heart further. The cracks in my heart were filled with an outpouring of love from so many people. Shari, the funeral director, told my mother she had never witnessed the level of support I was blessed to receive.

And it made all the difference.

SUNDAY: THE SILENCE

"*A*lice was here five days ago," I thought upon waking, "but now she isn't."

And then I cried.

Sunday was the first day there was no titanic event or decision to conquer. It was the first day my house wasn't packed with people. This allowed the reality of Alice's absence to truly sink in, which was profoundly difficult. In many ways, this day — five days after she died — was harder than the previous days. The size of the hole in that house was so much clearer in the quiet. I had nothing external on which to focus, which left me with the inner stuff, and the inner stuff is in a death spiral when one's toddler dies for no reason.

I recall feeling shellshocked. I recall an aching in my gut like no other I have ever experienced. I recall feeling like someone had yanked a knife out of my heart — and as if I finally inhaled after being underwater too long. I was keenly aware, as I had been a couple of days before, of what felt like an *actual* hole in my heart. I could see why people might feel the need to do something, anything, to fill that hole, or close it down, or cover it up, or to ignore it by any means necessary. There is a strong and immediate desire to make that hole not be a hole anymore. But I knew I was defenseless against this hole.

I knew any effort to fight the hole would be not only futile but exacerbating. So I simply noticed it and went about my day. Still, it was a thing I dealt with all day. For many days. For many weeks. For many years.

I was functioning, but I was preoccupied by the sensation of the hole.

There wasn't anything I could do about the hole in my heart. My precious two-year-old daughter had been yanked off this earth with no warning. In the end, I felt like anything I did to disguise or ignore that hole was a betrayal of her and what had become of her. I did not want to betray her memory. I knew only time would heal that hole — and perhaps even time would not be up for the task. I knew I might very well have that hole for the rest of my life. I felt like it was all I had left of her, to be honest, so I didn't want to muck it up with trivial attempts to hide the pain. I knew, from helping others through grief, that the only way through it is through it. So I committed myself to remain an observer of this feeling and denied the urge to run from it.

Sitting on my back porch, I looked around me and saw so much love, so much support, so many other people hurting, and decided my best bet was to let that hole be, and to allow the light sent by all those loved ones to shine through the gaping hole in my heart. I committed to continuing to say yes to the love and support. "Let's allow all the love directed my way to surge through that hole, and see what a little love can do," I thought. I know this sounds very airy-fairy, but it is the truth. Hand to God, I could feel the love pouring right through, and around, that hole. When I closed my eyes, again I saw those neon lights — the colors of Lite-Brite pegs — soaring through that hole.

Most of my family members were leaving that day. My brother and his family came over to say goodbye. An idea came to me.

I asked my brother's family to come down the hall with me. I opened the linen closet and pulled out one of Alice's precious blankies and gave it to them. I wanted them to have something to remind them of Alice. Adults leave estates, houses, life insurance policies, and sometimes they leave unfinished business. Alice left a mass of broken hearts, but she left no unfinished business, save the business of living what we think of as a full life. Just a child herself, she left no children, and no real possessions. Alice's most precious material (literally) possessions were her arsenal of sixteen muslin blankies. I wanted her loved ones to have something into which she had poured so much innocent love. I selected blankies for the grandparents and other siblings and distributed them with few words.

My inner circle folks had the "day off" and deservedly so. I cannot imagine how tired they must have all been, having done *everything* to make the service possible, not to mention having done everything to keep me and my extended family afloat. I was aware they were also hurting. I distinctly recall thinking, "Crap! *What am I going to do without Bubba today?*" I am sure he was beyond exhausted. I was glad he had the day off from my situation but I won't lie: I had a moment of panic wondering if I could press on without him there.

Meleva made noises about leaving, but I begged her to stay. I needed her. I needed to ease into the new emptiness of the house. I felt unable to go from my normal chaos to unexpected funeral chaos to a quiet house with no Alice.

Meleva stayed. And I am forever grateful.

Sunday was the last day Alice's remains would be whole. The thought haunted me. Shari offered to set up a last visit for me at the funeral home that Sunday, an offer I eagerly accepted. The old me — of just last week — would have hesitated to trouble Shari with this extra visit despite her offer, but the new me heard the voice of Bubba whisper, "Say *yes.*" I had not yet seen the funeral home where Alice had been resting since Wednesday. My parents and Meleva kindly offered to take care of Grace so I could say my very last goodbye to Alice.

Again, it felt weird to be outside my home. I still felt completely out of sync with our agreed-upon reality. The world around me still looked like a set. I felt a little nervous. I felt a little sick to my stomach. This day was so much quieter than any other day that week, so my feelings seemed more intense than they had the previous days. There were no distractions. There was only me, silently riding to see my deceased daughter for the very last time.

. . .

THE MEMORY NAUSEATES me to this day.

IT WAS SUNNY. That pissed me off. I wanted the weather to match my feelings, I suppose. I wanted it to be gray with torrential rains, winds, and thunderstorms. A green sky threatening a tornado would suffice. A tsunami would be perfect. When the outside doesn't match your insides, it is extremely disorienting.

For several days — and weeks — I had the overwhelming feeling the world had shifted exactly ninety degrees below my feet. At times, I felt as if I moved with it, acutely aware I was operating ninety degrees away from normal. At other times, I felt as if I was stationary during the earth shift, leaving me at a right angle to the "normal" world, though still right-side-up in relation to earth. Either way, I occasionally became overwhelmed by the feeling of an exact ninety-degree shift. My proprioception – my ability to sense the location of my body parts and movement as a whole – was haywire, but precise. It didn't bother me: it was more awe-inspiring.

The funeral home was empty. There were no services that day. There was only a receptionist and Shari. It was utterly silent in there. Shari apologized for wearing workout attire, explaining she was moving that day.

This amazing woman could have sent someone else, but she didn't. She never told me she was moving that day, or I would have not gone. She had gone so far and above the call of duty already, I simply could not have asked for more.

Before going in to see Alice laid out in the chapel, I needed to sign some papers. I had hemmed and hawed so long on the cremation versus burial question that there had not been an opportunity to do this. Shari said all kinds of wonderful things to me that day. I cannot remember them verbatim, sadly, but basically, she told me ours was one of the hardest cases she had ever worked on and that I had some of the best people around me that she had ever met. She was genuine, and so very kind. She is one of the most truly kind people I have ever met.

Shari patiently explained each paper, while I sat there wide-eyed and quiet. I was basically signing permission slips for Alice. But instead of permission to go on a field trip, I was signing permission to have her remains cremated.

I burst into tears, big ugly tears, the second my pen hit the paper. I had to stop for a moment because I was visibly and uncontrollably shaking. Shari had to look away, and I could see tears in her eyes. She did this for a living and was crying, though unlike me, it was all very ladylike. I did not look so ladylike. I felt horrible that I had made this über-professional woman cry. So I cried more — head on the desk, shaking and sobbing. It wasn't the most composed moment of my life.

The papers finally signed, I had to put my head down again for a minute. I was overwhelmed with existential dread and profound agony. I wasn't sure how I was going to move my body.

Once I got myself together, Shari walked me down the hall and explained I could take my time, there were no services that day, that she had plenty of work to do there, so not to worry about her. I mean, c'mon. This woman is remarkable. She walked me to the door of the chapel and said to have the receptionist get her when I was done, because she wanted to discuss a couple of things with me.

The chapel was utterly, devastatingly silent and filled with a soft, natural light. The light was noticeably whiter than most natural light, I noted. Why did I note this? No idea. It was different in some way I could not exactly put my finger on.

One enters the chapel from the back right, as you face the front. I could see my Alice, laid out there like a porcelain doll, front and center. She was completely still, in the utter silence. I got chills.

The only other time I'd encountered silence like this was on one of the serious backpacking trips I had done in the Sierras. I was with my friends Michael, Brian, and Jeff, all geologists. We were many miles away from civilization. We hit the ridge, which I considered "the top," when they informed me the actual peak was around the corner and up a few feet. I peered around to look. It was a move for which a sane person would have used ropes. "Um, you fall, you die?" I asked. This was confirmed. "OK, have fun, I'll sit here at *my* top and wait for you, do a little meditation, read my Alan Watts book. See you soon!" The boys took off, and I sat on that ridge with incredible views of two enormous valleys. It was *silent* — literally not one sound except my own breath. I mean, you could hear the wings flap on a dragonfly kind of silent. The chapel was that silent. I felt like I was in a vacuum.

Alice was not exactly known for her silence. She wasn't a fussy kid, or a particularly loud kid, but she certainly was not silent. Alice made her presence known. Looking at her lying completely still in the utter, deafening silence was perhaps the strangest experience I have ever had in my life. It defied explanation. I could *not believe* my precious, funny, little sweetheart would make a sound no more.

My guts churned.

I cried again as I walked toward her. Not an ugly cry, but a still, silent cry where water just pours down the face without effort as if someone turned on the faucet and forgot to turn it off. Like a water- fall. Like gravity nonchalantly pulling water from my face.

I knelt beside her. I hugged her and cried. I think I said, "I'm sorry, Alice, Mama is so sorry" about a hundred times. I was still racked with guilt. I looked her over slowly. I looked at her fingers. Her arm was heavy and limp and not at all how I wanted it to feel. I wanted her to hop up, and say "Hi, Mama! Funny joke!" but I knew this was not going to happen. I looked at her autopsy scars. I had to do it. I realize some folks would never do that in a million years, but I felt compelled to do it from the very marrow of my bones. I had to take in the truth of this moment, and what Alice was now. It did not upset me further; in fact, I was rather stoic during this part of the viewing. How? No idea.

I picked her up. Again, I noticed her center of gravity was differ- ent. Like I had so many times during her life, I put her blankie and her head on my shoulder, swayed, patted her back, and sang to her over and over while I looked up at the altar and stained glass and cried and cried. I realized a passerby might think this behavior was crazy. I didn't care. I felt I *had* to do it, as if I was fulfilling a mission for which

I was destined but had no memory of being assigned. I felt I would regret it the rest of my life if I didn't take this precious time to do exactly whatever I needed to do to say goodbye, to try to make this moment seem real, to try to wrap my head around this profound change in Alice's history and my own. It was my last chance to physically touch my daughter, and I was not going to blow it on acting how I thought I "should" act. I was going to do what I needed to do, dammit.

I meditated and prayed while I held her. And water fell out of my eyes in endless streams.

I did not want to let her go. I did not want this time to end. Part of me wanted to stay with her, even into the incinerator. You might think that sounds crazy, but I am telling you, no mother wants her tiny daughter going anywhere without her, much less into an incinerator or into the ground. There is a primordial mothering instinct that urges you to remain with your child. I had to fight that urge because I had a child still on earth who needed me more than Alice did. Even in my utter devastation, I had no doubt Alice was in a beautiful place. I was simply devastated we were not in the same beautiful place.

I carefully placed her back on the table and arranged all her favorite things around her, as Shari had, because I thought she had done a wonderful job and I wanted Alice to know I tried to get it right, in case she could see me wherever she was now. I felt her chubby thighs one more time. They were cold, but they were still pink. Five days later, she still looked perfect, despite not being embalmed. I kissed her head, which felt different, but I couldn't put my finger on what exactly was different about it. I hugged her. And then I sat beside her in silence and meditated and prayed some more. I tried to feel her presence but could not. I don't think she was there. Or maybe she was, but my grief was too big to allow my sixth sense to operate fully.

Eventually, I felt like I needed to say goodbye, or risk getting to a place where I would have to be physically removed. I thought choosing the moment to leave was going to be difficult, but in the end, I had a little feeling it was time to go and went with it. Look, it was no amusement park, but it was one thing that week that turned out not to be as hard as I imagined.

So maybe she was there after all, silently letting me know it was OK to go, because she wasn't in that body anymore anyway.

Now she was everywhere. Or so I like to believe. This is one thing priests, physicists, and psychics can all agree on so, for now, I am going to go with it: she is everywhere, including within my own being.

I walked out slowly and could not resist the urge to stop and look back one more time. My baby was there, all alone in a big silent chapel, peacefully resting, completely unaware of her mother's complete and utter devastation. I took a mental picture — a "life picture," as one of my friends calls these moments — and walked through the door.

That was the last time I saw Alice as I knew her. The devastation was almost life-threatening.

I collapsed onto the couch. It is possible I had not truly released in days; I had been on high alert since Tuesday. My mind was blank, and I was in emotional pain too large to describe with words. I would never see my little ball of joy again.

Shari came out to discuss the Monday morning cremation. Part of me wanted to scream out and hit something and cry, but the larger part of me could not move, emit a sound, or do anything, really. I saw Shari talking but could not hear the vast majority of what she said. The "Charlie Brown's teacher" effect was happening again. I heard her ask if I wanted her to call as Alice "went in." She explained some people like to know so they can have a moment of silence or pray during the time the body is being transformed. She said that the process would take about fifteen minutes for a person as small as Alice.

Fifteen minutes. That's it. I felt like my guts became a black hole into which the rest of my body became spaghettified by its gravity. Realizing I was discussing the time it takes to turn your child's body to ash is one of the most difficult moments I have ever had in my life.

I pray there are no moments in my future worse than those I had dealt with in quick succession the week after Alice died.

I absolutely did want to know when Alice "went in." Shari said she would call when she was on her way over with Alice, so I could prepare myself and be ready when the moment arrived. She would call again when they arrived at the crematorium, and then again, when it was time.

This all gave me a pit in my stomach, but again, it did not feel like something I could run from. It hurt like hell, it hurt worse than all previous pain I have ever felt in my lifetime combined, but I still needed to know the truth. I still needed to be in the loop. It hurt, but I knew hiding wouldn't heal the hurt.

Shari went on to say we needed to discuss a container for Alice's ashes. She spoke for a while, but I have no idea what she said. I could not hear her, and I could not move; I was blank again. When I came back to "reality," she was saying she had a feeling a traditional urn would perhaps not be the right thing for my particular family. She was imagining a cloth bag — and it hit me.

"Can we make it from the blankie she is holding in there?" I asked. Shari said she thought that would be perfect. She said it might be more cloth than she would need to have the pouch made. I asked if she could use half for the pouch, and then place the other half with Alice when she "went in." She said she could, and she would.

For a moment, I felt better. I loved the idea of Alice being forever wrapped up in her blankie; half would be around her, and half would literally become mixed up with her. I felt like Alice would approve of this. I can never adequately express how grateful I am to Shari for being her forward-thinking, loving, creative, professional self. Every little touch she suggested was perfection, and she was able to perfectly identify our family's needs without knowing us. She is surely an angel.

Shari hugged me. We both had tears in our eyes. My certitude that a traditional funeral would have messed me up in a massive way was strengthened every day. Shari Wolf truly helped set the stage for me to grieve in a way that suited me and to do so without apology. And this, my friends, has made all the difference.

79

The ride home felt silent. A dream. I felt like I was in a horror movie that took place in a busy city on a sunny day, everyone oblivious to my hell though only inches away from me.

Disorienting.

A handful of friends came by that evening. At some point, I received a text from Bubba. I was touched he still checked in despite having a "day off" from me. He said he was sitting quietly in his outdoor space, and the tuned wind chimes we had bought them as a housewarming gift were playing ever so lightly. He felt like it was Alice saying hello.

But, you see, I feel like it was Alice saying, "Thank you, Bubba, for taking such exceptional care of my mama. She needed you, and you were there."

In my mind's eye, I kept seeing my Alice, laid out like a doll, in that silent chapel. The past five days had been a slow stripping away of Alice and her remains. I would never touch her again, alive or dead. My mind could not fathom this was reality. But it was. Time and space were slipperier than ever. Past, present, and future felt interchangeable.

The night was dark and silent, which was a relief, because — unlike the daytime — it matched my insides.

MONDAY: THE RELEASE

Six days. Every day of the week since she died had a different name. The next day would have the same name as the day she died. I didn't want it to be another week. If I was still in the same week, I was still only days away from an alive Alice. I didn't want to have to count the last time I heard her laugh in seconds, much less days or weeks.

Shari called to say she was on her way to the crematorium with Alice. I felt like I was punched in the solar plexus and the heart simultaneously. I noticed I became nervous only because my heart rate noticeably increased. I had no thoughts; my mind was empty. I discovered I was pacing.

I had wanted to plan a fitting meditation to practice during the time she was transformed but hadn't gotten around to it. I felt a little panic about this. "Perhaps I should read from one of the spiritual works that inspires me?" I wondered. I pondered what I could do to honor the profundity of Alice's final transformation. I continued to pace.

I spotted the singing brass bell I brought back from India. You can strike it like a gong or rub the wooden stick around the base to make it sing. When the bell is singing, you can hear the sound whir in circles around the entire room. It is often used before meditation to clear the mind of worldly matters and to dispel stress and tension. My pacing indicated to me that I could use a little stress relief before trying to focus on prayer or meditation. I hadn't played it in a while, but both girls had stopped in their tracks when I did, staring at me wide-eyed and smiling. Alice particularly loved it. I grabbed the bell and took it to my bedroom.

My bedroom décor is inspired by the Far East. I have a Chinese armoire I love, and some beautiful Indian design-based paintings I bought in India. I also have some small statues and candles in the room. I lit some candles. I was starting to feel calmer already. I was not happy, but I was calming down.

Finally, Shari called. In a somber voice, she told me it was time.

My stomach lurched. My eyes welled up with tears. I felt a sickening dread too large to express in words. I grabbed the bell, shut my eyes, and took a few deep breaths before rubbing the wooden stick around the base to make it sing.

The singing bell was soothing, and I found it easier to play than usual. With each circumnavigation of the stick, I felt more and more at ease. Although playing the bell has brought me some peace many times, I was surprised by my unfolding peace that day — I won't lie. I honestly thought I was a lost cause. What followed might sound like malarkey, but I swear on all that is good, it is what I experienced.

I continued playing the singing bell, eyes closed, observing my response. I noticed I was smiling a small smile. I thought, "Oh, that is promising," and continued.

Suddenly, I felt a sense of warmth at the crown of my head that traveled down my body. I then saw — as much as one can see with one's eyes closed — a cone of light above me. I was in the large base; the tip extended some distance above me. I instinctively looked up in my mind's eye and began to feel as if I were effortlessly floating up toward the tip where I saw three shadowed figures: one in the foreground and two smaller figures on either side and slightly behind the central figure. They appeared to be robed. The light behind them was so intense they were in complete shadow. I could make out no features, only outlines. I was in awe but kept playing the bell.

There came a point where I could tell I was not able to float any closer to them. This did not frustrate me, nor was it uncomfortable. In fact, there were no negative feelings at all associated with the inability to get closer to the figures. They seemed friendly enough. I mean, they didn't offer me tea or invite me in, but I was not afraid or frustrated. In fact, I felt simultaneously peaceful and euphoric — two feelings I would have guessed were mutually exclusive before this experience. I also felt warm, loved, and incredibly safe. The feeling of safety was overwhelming. I somehow knew this meant Alice was safe. I somehow knew they were there to receive Alice and to let me know she was in a good place. Suddenly, I saw her grab the robe of the figure in the foreground. She peered out from behind the figure. She was now also in shadow, but I could make out her outline. The beautiful, crazy hair gave it away.

I can't recall how long after that experience I kept the bell going, but it was not long after. I then sat in silence for a spell. I felt peaceful. I even smiled. I daresay I was somewhat happy. I sat — eyes closed — with that feeling for a few minutes.

Eventually, I felt "done" and soon after, Shari called to tell me the process was completed. I expected that call to flatten me — and I won't lie, it hurt — but I still felt peaceful and warm and loved and calm. And deeply hurt. A unique combination of emotions, to be sure.

The last time I had felt so peaceful and calm was after that bath I'd taken on Thursday. And like that Thursday, this peaceful feeling lasted for several hours afterward.

The vision was the first time I surrendered the need to torture myself with the idea that Alice suffered. Was this experience wishful thinking? Was it my subconscious going on autopilot? Was it "real"? I have no idea what sparked that vision but, again, I know for certain it was not wishful thinking because I was not capable of wishful thinking; I had all my eggs in the self-flagellation basket. All I know is I felt immensely better on one of the worst days of my life, so how bad could it be even if it had been wishful thinking?

Another reason I do not think it was wishful thinking is I had not developed a fully formed idea of what I thought, or hoped, happened to Alice. I felt like she was in a better place, certainly; she had done no wrong in this life. I had no doubt she would go to a place of love. But I do not pretend to know what the afterlife looks like or much about the particulars of it. I had always hoped there were mountains and a stream involved, but I know that concept is an earthly one. I had no predetermined notions of who or what would greet her, if anything. I don't know how the newly called are ushered in. So that leaves a subconscious on autopilot, reality, or something I do not understand as possible explanations of my vision.

Was it "real"? You know, it doesn't matter. What matters is the vision changed my feelings, my entire perspective. It helped me stop the negative self-talk for a spell. It felt "right" at a time when absolutely nothing felt right. During the vision, my entire body relaxed, I sighed, and felt giant waves of peace and safety. Afterward, I somehow thought, "It's OK, Melissa; she is fine. She is safe. She is loved. And she doesn't require your self-flagellation." At the worst time of my life, in the throes of not knowing if she had suffered, I was able to know she was well cared for, and in fact, was in a state of perfect bliss. I *knew* it — a deep knowing. I had unflappable confidence she was OK.

I was jealous, truth be told.

In the end, it doesn't matter what sparked that vision. I am going with: "Alice is safe, and it's not my time to join her."

I CAN'T LIE. There are days I wish it were my time to "go and play with Alice." Don't freak out; I am not going to die by suicide. But there are days I wake up and think, "Crap. Sigh. I'm still here." I get over it as the day goes on, with a little help from my friends. No, really. I do. The Beatles were right.

Those sorts of days became more and more spread out over time.

. . .

EVENTUALLY, there was talk of a hike. The day prior, my parents all mentioned they wanted to hike on Monday. Everyone seemed to want to get outside.

I suddenly had the idea we could all hike up to the Baldwin Hills Scenic Overlook and do a balloon release for Alice.

AND YES, I now know that balloon releases are not good for the environment, but I didn't have my best mind then. I was barely getting through the day at that point. I know as soon as some of you read that sentence your first urge was to write me to tell me how wrong I was, because now the world is full of people who read other people's accounts simply to jump on them for some perceived error. The first urge is not to write, "I am so sorry for your loss," it is, "This is how you should have handled your loss," even though most folks cannot handle losing their wallet, much less a child. I did my best and learned as I went along. Thank you.

FAMKE AND GRACE clearly needed a kid-friendly way to express their feelings about the death, and it was the perfect time for such a remembrance. Alice had accompanied me on that hike a few times; it seemed as good a place as any to honor her memory. I did not reason this all out before I had the idea. I had the idea, and then the reasons it was a good one started popping up in my mind.

The bulk of us took off for the trailhead. The girls went with my dad to pick up the balloons because my dad likes having jobs, and the girls seemed like they could use a "job" as well.

We all began to walk up the hill. There was some quiet chitchat as we ascended. It was a beautiful day.

The view: spectacular.

There was a newly built circular area at the top of the hill. It was here we did the release. I think I said a few words. My dad and a few others said a few words. Grace insisted we keep two balloons: one for her and one to remember Alice by. It devastated me to realize she understood all we had left of Alice were memories. The other balloons were released and went basically due east, toward downtown, before heading north. It was a clear day, so we were able to watch them for several minutes. Famke said, "I sure hope God gives those balloons to Alice." I said I thought s/he would. Grace was somewhat reserved during this and hugged me. Eventually, Grace asked, "What is heaven like, Mama?"

Oh, my. Is that all you want to know? I took in a deep breath and hoped I would say the right thing.

"I'm not sure, sweetie, because I haven't been there yet, but I have heard it is very bright and beautiful and everyone is very friendly," I heard myself say. I just spat that out. No thoughts preceded the utterance. Not even I knew I was going to say that.

I didn't want to pretend to know something I do not know, but I also wanted to convey something positive. I hope that sufficed. It seemed to do the trick. Both girls were quiet, but they seemed to be relieved Alice was somewhere friendly. I recall Famke saying what a happy baby Alice was, while Grace hugged me around the legs. There were lots of tears, but quiet tears.

It was a somber walk back down.

Eventually Shari called and said she was ready to come by with Alice's ashes that afternoon.

Now, there is nothing that can prepare you for receiving your child's ashes. Not even preparing to receive your child's ashes can prepare you to receive your child's ashes. But Shari made it as beautiful as one could. She was respectful, reverent, and calm. She made it seem normal. Which, I suppose, it is. We all joke the only things certain in life are death and taxes, but taxes have not always existed. Death, on the other hand ...

We have a story we tell ourselves: We are born, raised by loving parents, released to impose our arrogant stupidity on the world, get our ass kicked a few times before learning to live in the world without imposing our arrogant stupidity upon it, grow old, and die long before our children.

Yet our history doesn't always meet those expectations. We tell ourselves, "It's so rare, it won't happen to my family." Yet here I was, in my dining room, receiving my child's ashes like it was normal. I do not mean to say Shari trivialized this moment in any way. I just mean that there I was, sitting in the home I raised my girls in, the only home Alice ever knew, talking with the funeral director who quietly, respectfully, gave me my child's ashes while the rest of the family enjoyed the backyard. Not a usual Monday, mind you, but still, it did not feel as completely foreign as I imagined.

Alice was in her final resting place all wrapped up in her beloved blankie. The blankie is white muslin and has a pattern of red caterpillars on it.

IN HINDSIGHT, after so many butterfly encounters after Alice passed, I cannot help but believe Alice's ashes are covered with caterpillars, while Alice's soul seems to dance with the butterflies.

IT WAS A HEAVY MOMENT, but the ashes themselves were not heavy, and did not take up much space. My mind could not grasp that my child, who not seven days before was running around the playground at school, following her sister around, and begging for more "gogurt!" was contained in this pouch.

Silent.

Forever.

There are no words for the feelings I experienced at that moment, but the feeling of love was predominant.

When everything we love turns to ash, all we have is love. I began to realize that if I marched toward the love — even on a day when I felt like shit — I would always be guided and surrounded by love. If I cursed the path, I wouldn't see the love that was all around me and would find a cursed path.

When Alice died, it became crystal clear to me that nothing matters but love. That clarity was notable because not one other thing was clear. But more importantly, I began to see that love doesn't die. My love for Alice went nowhere; I just didn't know what to do with

87

all that love when her body was no longer here, when I could not interact with her personality or hug her chubby belly. It was clear to me my love for her survived though her body did not. I could still feel her, though I couldn't see or touch her. Grief is love in the absence of the recipient of the love.

Grief is the phantom limb of love.

This meant I had to learn how to love someone no longer here ... and to do that, I had to focus on the love that *was* here. And there was so much love around me, thank God.

I HAVE LEARNED to love more than I thought was humanly possible in the absence of my daughter. That state of love has kept me going. I am a lucky girl indeed because I am loved by many wonderful people, and I have the opportunity to love them in return. All that love makes one better at loving. Soon, one may find one can love the unlovable, the folks only a mother can love. This is not to say we must accept everyone's love or let everyone close to us. Unconditional love is not unconditional permissiveness; some people need to be loved from afar, so they do not damage us. One cannot annihilate oneself and one's psyche for another person. But I have learned I could love even the unlovable, albeit from afar for my own safety. It's fairly easy to love a living person from afar once you learn how to love someone no longer here at all.

I expected to have more time to love an alive Alice, but are expectations an attempt to craft a guaranteed future and keep our focus on that particular future? None of us are guaranteed a future of any kind, much less a particular kind. We want to manipulate the laws of cause and effect in linear time to obtain our goals. But sometimes inexplicable things happen to people who don't deserve it and sometimes time becomes meaningless. We can become hurt and angry when our expectations are not met.

So, I try to enjoy the love while it's there, cultivate and appreciate and reciprocate it to the best of my ability, enjoy the easy path when it presents itself, and remain grateful for it when the road gets rough. This is my journey. I have no idea what else to do.

. . .

IT WAS A QUIET NIGHT. The grandmas heated up some of the many leftovers. There was so much food and so little room in which to store it. Some of it was going to go bad if not consumed soon, so I sent it with my dad to the firehouse that had responded to Alice's 911 call. I wanted to do something to thank them anyway and figured they could use a giant tray of croissants and several pounds of sandwiches. I wanted to thank them myself, but I knew I couldn't do it without crying and I didn't want to bring them down.

Meleva had to leave. I was sorry to see her go, but I was going to see her soon. Prior to Alice's death, Grace and I had scheduled a twenty-four-hour trip to Sacramento for Famke's birthday in less than two weeks. Still, I cried during our goodbyes.

I had developed an eye spasm — a blepharospasm. It started the day after Alice died, and it was still going strong. It was fairly annoying, but it was the least of my worries. I marveled at it more than I cursed it. It sometimes made it a little difficult to fall asleep, but eventually I would manage slumber. It became worse when I tried to read in bed and after crying. Those two things often happened at the same time, unfortunately.

Before I went to sleep that night, I researched Sudden Unexplained Death in Childhood (SUDC), the suspected cause of Alice's death. It was a colossally stupid idea. The term "suspected cause of death" is doubly ridiculous in this case because SUDC is, by definition, the absence of any identifiable cause of death. I read for only a few seconds before becoming literally paralyzed with agonizing guilt and breathless, heart-pounding regret. I had to stop reading. It was taking me down a spiral I was afraid I would not escape. Had I thought my investigation would have done any good for me, Alice, or my community, I would have soldiered on. But it was pages and pages of suspected causes, all of which whipped up excruciating guilt, followed at the end by the statement "but we aren't sure."

"It could be ... twenty undiagnosable medical conditions to throw you into a life-threatening guilt spiral ... but we aren't sure." It did not seem to be productive for me to read this at that time. I could not sacrifice my mental health for uncertainties.

While I had no doubt I would support SUDC causes one day, that was not the day for me to start. That day, I had to stay focused on maintaining a will to live, and the information on SUDC was not helping me. This is not the fault of SUDC, the SUDC Foundation, or even me. It just wasn't helping me then. Period. I knew one day it might. It may help other parents who recently lost a child, but for some reason, it sent me spiraling down into self-created Darkness, and I could not let that happen. The real Darkness beyond my control was more than enough.

I suppose I felt it futile. It did not appear I was going to know what caused her death anytime soon, and maybe I would never know. I needed to know what happened to her *soul* since no one knew what had happened to her body. I needed to know that whatever and wherever she was now, she was OK.

There was no logic to her death. Spending time digging around into the cause of death felt to me like I was spinning my wheels in a direction that was dangerous for me. When logic leaves the room, that leaves the woo-woo. I've always been a student of science *and* interested in the woo-woo. I have always had an interest in comparative religions. I have always had an interest in the esoteric. I have always had an interest in extrasensory perception, philosophy, psychology, psychics, and all weighty subjects that start with "P."

Logic left the room with Alice's soul. So I began to go way down deep into my woo-woo. I was officially in the largest existential crisis of my life.

This recognition saved me. Hey, it's not for everyone, but it has saved me, this I know. And when you find yourself in an existential crisis, I suppose it helps to just say, "Screw it. I guess I'm about to spend a lot more time on existential fare. Goodbye, gossip. Goodbye, self-criticism. Goodbye, stupid tabloid reading in line at the store. Goodbye, petty dramas. Goodbye, spending time ruminating on minutiae that doesn't matter in the scheme of life." Sure, I still do these things sometimes. But you know what? Not much. And that has been a gift. I have no idea what prompted this realization. It was, perhaps, an act of divine grace.

I hoped it would last. I hoped it was not merely a temporary response to the shock and grief of losing a child. I hoped — and hope — I do not return to letting trivial things consume my day. I hope, like the balloons and Alice's beautiful body and soul, I also released my pettiness that day.

WEEKS

WEEK 2, PART 1: THE "NORMAL" ATTEMPT

*I*t was the same day of the week as Alice died. One week. I woke up too early to begin a second week without Alice. Salt water poured down my face while I stared at the ceiling. I debated whether I should try to go back to sleep or not. I was wide awake yet exhausted. I got out of bed.

The house was noticeably less full, less active. There was a palpable void. Humans try to fill voids at all costs, but the stillness of that morning resonated with the emptiness inside me. It was the only thing that felt real, in fact.

There was a box on the piano. It was the box that had been delivered while Alice lay dead in my arms. I opened it to find a birthday gift from Alice's aunt and uncle. Alice's birthday gifts had arrived at the same time her coroner arrived. I stared at it hoping the deeper meaning of this macabre coincidence would reveal itself to me.

I'M STILL WAITING.

. . .

As THE WEEK BEGAN, I had an overwhelming urge to document Alice's life. I never wanted to forget all the adorable things she did, said, and loved. I knew I might forget some things, for I likely had a long life in front of me. This thought sickened me. The fear one will forget all the little things about one's child is a fear so primal, so intense, so crippling, it defies description. I wanted to get my memories down as fast as possible because I was absolutely paralyzed with fear I would forget.

I wrote for my own pleasure and sanity for years, but I could not yet get pen to paper after Alice's death, and even if I could, the thoughts and memories came bubbling up to my brain so quickly I wasn't sure I could write fast enough. So I borrowed an audio recorder and made recordings. I walked around the house observing the things she'd touched, the spaces she'd filled, and recorded all the stories of Alice I could recall.

It wasn't until years later, while I was writing this book, that I realized I never dropped my role as a historian of Alice's life. Even the days after her death were spent curating photos, telling stories, and assembling her favorite things. The historian role of a parent is so ingrained, so inherent, one still has the urge to record — and make meaning of — the child's life after it has ended.

I AM glad I did this. I am guessing Grace will be glad to be able to hear them one day as well. I had not listened to these recordings until I started writing a blog a few weeks after Alice died (A.A.D., for short). In my mind, I was a wreck at that time and somewhat afraid I would suffer a setback by hearing the horror I knew was in my voice. I remember crying through the stories. But, oddly, I sound somewhat composed in most of the recordings. I did cry, but not as much as I thought I had. I guess I'd turned off the device when a big wave crashed down.

It appears I was in better shape than I thought I was that week. I was coherent and could string a sentence together. I would have never predicted I would be able to do so under the circumstances, and even in my memory, I hadn't.

Sometimes, we are stronger than we imagine we could be. Not that not crying equals strength, mind you, for I believe that to be hogwash. In any event, I wish to God I'd never had to find out I possess this particular brand of strength.

I also watched the videos of her last day a thousand times that week. I had no idea when I took those videos that I was documenting her very last active moments on earth. To this day, I cannot wrap my head around how the little girl playing in those videos would be dead a couple of hours later.

Although I was ready, on one level, to slow down from the relentless pace of the Aftermath, I was not yet ready to be "back to normal," whatever that meant. I suppose I had no idea what normal was anymore. Nothing was normal; therefore, acting as if things were normal seemed, well, crazy. I had no part in creating life as it was now, but I had to go on anyway. No warning. No roadmap. A proverbial gunshot that meant, "Go!"

IN 2013, when I wrote the previous paragraph, I was not aware of the catchphrase "new normal" and I'm glad I wasn't. As I've mentioned, I'm not a fan of using catchphrases to describe traumatic events.

RESUMING "NORMAL" activity meant making plans to go back to work that Friday. I am self-employed so no work equals no pay; therefore, a long sabbatical was out of the question. I had to pull it together and get back to work sooner rather than later.

I love my job. I have never once dreaded going to work since I started my current career. But I was filled with anxiety about going back to work. I wasn't sure how I was going to take care of people and teach them how to take care of themselves. I wasn't sure if I had the energy. I wasn't sure I could make decisions, having spent the last week frozen over choices as basic as "eat or sleep?" and as hideous as "cremation or burial?" At times I honestly could not recall whether I had eaten. Though a compassionate person, I was unsure I could demonstrate compassion for someone's "regular problems" in my current state.

Everyone knew my family was leaving that Tuesday, so close friends started making plans with me. No one thought I should be alone in the house for long periods. At first, I thought this was unnecessary and the old me would have pooh-poohed it. But the new me said yes like a good girl. I was also aware they had all started communicating with each other, despite the fact they were from different friend circles and in some cases had never met until Alice's funeral. I was fully aware my status was being discussed and plans were being made accordingly. It didn't bother me, strangely. I was deeply grateful to them all for managing me during that time and I loved knowing my friends were also all becoming friends.

It was a pretty brave thing for them to do, because they all know I am not one who likes to be managed. I value directness and efficiency. These back-room sessions regarding my emotional state were not direct, but they were quite helpful, because although I knew I needed help with certain things, I was far too overwhelmed to be able to come up with any sort of list. I am normally a list-maker and a taskmaster. I am all about the lists. I make a list my bitch. If I can't make a list, you *know* I am not in optimal shape.

One of the enlarged pictures of Alice had been placed on the mantel, a makeshift altar forming around it. A book she loved placed here, her favorite Matchbox car there, the recorder from Teresa's house placed here, her binky (aka "aga") there. Grace placed a few things up there as well. The altar was not started with much thought — it just happened — but I have maintained it because it seems good for Grace and me to have a designated grieving place.

I NO LONGER LIGHT THE candles every night. This was also unplanned. The first night I realized I had skipped the lighting of the candles, I fell apart. I felt guilty. I felt like I had forgotten my baby. This is all nonsense, of course, but the pull of guilt in those early days and weeks was stronger than me. In the end, I have decided to go easier on myself. I highly doubt Alice gives a rat's ass if I light the candles, for she is surely in a more perfect place. The altar is for me and Grace. It is there every day, to use as we see fit. Some days I simply look at it. Other days, I arrange it, or clean it, or add something, or light the candles. I have tried to not judge myself too harshly these days. I wish I had thought of that sooner, like, oh, decades ago. I found it liberating to stop judging myself so strenuously ... when I remember to stop, that is.

TUESDAY AFTERNOON OF THAT WEEK, I had an episode of intense anxiety. I did not know it then, but it was a panic attack. I had no idea what it was when it happened. I lay down for a while, which seemed to help. Later, I went outside, which possibly helped. I stared at the fence and felt Alice's presence strongly. I could see her, hanging off the fence, face pressed against it, saying "HIIIIIIIIII!" to the passersby. To this day, for whatever reason, I download more memories of her hanging off that fence than I do anywhere else. For whatever reason, I feel her more outside than I do inside. She'd like that, for she loved "OUTsiiiiiiiiiiiide!"

While sitting outside that Tuesday, a large colorful beetle buzzed right by my head. I mean, it missed me by a hair. It dived toward me again. And again. I moved. It followed. It was *loud*. Everyone present thought it was strange how this beetle seemed to be drawn to me. I recalled that, in some spiritual traditions, beetles are considered a symbol of rebirth and regeneration. Aloud, I said, "Alice, if that is you, can you visit as something besides a beetle? It's a little intense for Mama right now." People laughed. The beetle eventually went on its merry way, and several yellow swallowtail butterflies appeared in its place.

Ahhh. That's better, Alice.

This was doubly strange because one of Alice's favorite books, *The Icky Sticky Frog,* is a macabre little tale about the cycle of life as Frog eats his way through a fly, and beetle, and then, right before he consumes a butterfly, is himself consumed by a fish. Alice especially loved the beetle.

And this was triply strange because I had never before seen a beetle anywhere in my yard. Make of it what you will. The little sign helped me that day. I suppose that's all that matters.

Wednesday was eight days after Alice died. I thought I could use some yoga, so off I went. It was the first time I'd personally driven a car since the Monday night before Alice died. It felt incredibly strange to drive the car; I had to think about where my right foot was supposed to go. I couldn't remember if I had to push down on the pedal while I turned the key. I also found it difficult to park. I won't lie; I am an excellent parallel parker (humble, too). But trying to park the car that day felt like the first time I had ever parallel parked in my life. I felt like I had forgotten how to drive. It had been approximately twenty-seven years since I had to consciously run down a checklist to start a car. One thinks one feels "pretty normal" until one tries to do something "normal" outside the cocoon one's friends have built around them. It was an experience that led me to decide, "Yeah, after this, I probably shouldn't drive again for a while."

Driving showed me I was surely not normal.

After the death of his wife, C. S. Lewis wrote, "There is a sort of invisible blanket between the world and me." I concur. I could see, hear, smell, feel, and even taste the world all around me, but the senses felt faint and weren't strong enough to convince me I was *a part* of the world around me. This was not me saying, "No one understands! I'm not like other people now!" It was simply a feeling I noticed. It was the strangest damn thing. I simply did not feel a part of the world around me and did not know why. I say this not to complain or whine; it is simply true.

As I stepped out of the car, I had the overwhelming feeling I was at the vortex of something much larger than myself, larger than the world even. I had no idea what it was, but it felt abundantly powerful, wise, and was whirring all around me as I stood in complete and utter silence in the center. This feeling was omnipresent for weeks. I didn't feel special, mind you; it is not that I felt like this power had sought me out for a special, shitty "lose your child, get a vortex mission" or anything. Perhaps I felt connected to something that had perhaps always been present but I had been too busy and self-absorbed to notice. It was a strange feeling, but at the same time, it felt profoundly natural. I still feel that way from time to time. I have no idea what it is, but it seems to want me to slow down and pay attention.

So I do.

OR AT LEAST I TRY. *I go about things at a much slower pace these days. And the world still spins, dontchaknow.*

WHEN I ARRIVED AT CLASS, my teacher, Pagan George, hugged me when he saw me but instinctively knew I did not want him making a big deal over me. I felt as if I'd missed months of class, but when I counted backward, I realized it had only been nine days. I was clearly not experiencing time the same way I had before Alice died; this was evident and somewhat mesmerizing.

The "Oms" that day felt better than they have perhaps ever felt. I shit you not: I felt like I was plugged into some electrical source by thousands of tiny electrodes. I am completely aware that stating that makes me sound like a nutter or a stereotypical grieving mother grasping for any hope, but I don't care. It's true.

At one point, we did a pose called Salabhasana, or Locust Pose. You begin by lying prone, and then lift your upper body and arms off the floor and then lift your outstretched legs as well, so you are basically in an inverted backbend, balancing your hips. It's harder than it sounds, naysayers. This is considered a chest-opening posture, for obvious reasons, and chest-openers are considered good for grief or broken hearts (again, for obvious reasons). I thought, "Well, we'll see if this shit works."

Pagan stepped quietly behind me and placed one foot gently on my sacrum and strongly pulled my arms back, lifting my upper body much higher off the ground than I was able to do on my own, thus

99

opening my chest an incredible amount. As he did this, he leaned forward and whispered, "Go, Melissa, go. Go, Melissa, go. Go, Melissa, GO!"

I relaxed and felt like a meteor exploded out through my sternum while the rest of my body went limp. It was one of the most profound experiences I have ever had in all the years I have done yoga. A few unexpected tears spilled out of my eyes, but I am not sure you can call it crying; it felt more akin to leaking. Later, in Warrior Pose, I suddenly felt simultaneously melted into the posture and like immense power was emanating from a lightened me. I realized I was in "the zone" I'd heard teachers talk about for years but which had escaped me until now. And then I noticed water dripping from my eyes. I realized I wasn't trying or expecting results. I had surrendered to my fragility and from there came the power.

I felt like sparks were flying out of my sternum for hours after class. Bizarre.

When I walked out of class, I literally felt like I was walking on air. The world around me seemed entirely false. I felt like I was in another dimension. Again, I know this sounds crazy. Again, I don't care — it's true. As I had on my way to the memorial service, I felt like I could see the world around me, but I did not feel like I could touch it, as if I was inside a transparent tube. And after yoga, for some reason, the sound of the world around me seemed un-hearable, despite knowing full well that passing cars produced sound. It was not scary. I had no negative feelings whatsoever about this experience other than noting its strangeness.

My positive experience at yoga class (driving notwithstanding) led me to decide I had to do at least one thing daily for my psycho-spiritual-emotional well-being. I know what has helped me in the past. I have spent years trying different exercise regimes, meditations, therapies, types of bodywork, and researching various religions and philosophies. By this point, I had a fairly good idea of what worked for me, and when, and what didn't work for me. I guess all those years of psycho-spiritual window shopping paid off, because I didn't have time to shop in the wake of Alice's death. I needed safe harbor, *stat*.

So I committed to do at least one hour a day of one or more of the following: yoga, meditation, writing, hiking, dancing, therapy, a long bath, massage/bodywork, reading something inspirational, or seeking spiritual guidance. Additionally, I was laughing and practicing gratitude daily, but I did not have to remind myself to do these. I was overflowing with deep appreciation for the many acts of kindness from so many people, and I had a couple of friends who understood laughing was crucial to my healing and therefore sponsored it.

Some of the aforementioned cost money, so they happen less frequently. But gratitude, yoga, meditation, writing, laughing, and hiking are cost-free. I do attend a yoga class two to three times a week, but at ten dollars a pop, and it is a good investment. For ninety minutes, I get a great workout, release from muscle tension, stress relief, some clarity of mind, and I feel a connection to something larger than myself. For me, it's like going to church, the gym, psychotherapy, and the spa simultaneously. For me, this is most definitely worth ten dollars. I also vowed, once I was on my feet, to do what I could to make the things that helped me more accessible to folks who didn't have access.

NINE YEARS LATER, I can say I have upheld this commitment for the most part, and I believe it has made an enormous difference.

THAT WEEK, I noticed I was making mistakes and forgetting things more often. My mind was not what it used to be, you see. They say this is common in the early stages of grief after a sudden death. They say in those early days and weeks, grief has likely not crept in yet, because what you initially suffer from is shock. I can see, in hindsight, "they" were correct about this. It was crystal clear my cognition was impaired. It bothered me, but not as much as I thought it would, most likely because I did not have enough energy to fight it. I mostly marveled at it.

For three months, we had dinner dropped off at our door every other night. There were always leftovers and folks who came by "off plan," so for three months, I did not have to cook. I love to cook. But, let's face it, I was not back to normal yet, and any task taken off my list was a huge help. Cooking required following steps and timing things and it was evident I was unable to do both. I realized the executive functioning part of my brain was no longer able to even make toast. I'd reflected on my feelings on child loss before Alice died; I had wondered how those parents could even make toast.

Shit. I was going to have to learn how to make toast again.

I sobbed.

Another night, my friend Deanna visited. She asked what she could do to help. My mind went blank, but someone else informed her we had a trash problem. A week of endless streams of people left us far more trash than trashcans. Deanna handled some of the trash problem. That, folks, is truly walking your talk when you say, "If you need anything…"

The largest trash problem, both literally and figuratively, was Alice's crib. The grandpas had removed it from the house because it was torture for me to see it, but it was still in the garage. I was still completely racked with guilt, and nothing whipped up my guilt like seeing that crib. Any thought of the crib directed my mind to the image of me pulling Alice up and out of the crib and seeing her blue face. I still did not know how I was going to survive with that image in my mind. The crib had to go but could not be left on the curb where some unsuspecting person might take it home for their baby. I didn't want any other baby sleeping in that crib. It was doubtful there was anything wrong with the crib, but still, I didn't want to take any chances. It felt wrong to create a situation that might lead to someone unwittingly taking the crib that my baby had died in for their own baby.

I wanted that crib destroyed like I have never wanted to have something destroyed. I wanted to light it on fire and take an ax to it at the same time.

Deanna offered to take it to the proper disposal site — an act of mercy I will never forget.

Many people asked what they could do. My mind almost uniformly went blank. This brings me another chunk of unsolicited advice: when offering help, offer the grieving person specific choices of what you are able to do for them because the bereaved may not be able to articulate their needs.

In those first few days and weeks, I knew I needed help with many things. But I was in a daze. I could barely talk. Honestly, I had to lie down after talking for even an hour. I would occasionally become stuck in space while I tried to sort out my bodily needs as if my body was a foreign land to which I had freshly arrived.

It was extremely helpful when people asked, "Can I bring you dinner/wash your car/take Grace on a play date/organize your kitchen/take you out to dinner/send you for some body work/go to the store for you?" If given choices, I could identify a need. For instance, in the beginning, public places were extremely challenging for me. Having someone offer to go get groceries was a godsend. Although I deeply appreciated all the folks who said, "If there is *anything* I can do, please let me know," I did not have the inner resources to act on it. I still suffer from this to some extent. I also felt strange requesting something from the people who had offered to do "anything" for me. Do they mean babysitting, or a trip to Bali? Do they mean clean my kitchen for me, or send a cleaner? Do they mean do my laundry or take me on a hike? The people who offered me choices took all the awkwardness off the table for me. They allowed me the opportunity to continue to say yes to offers of help, without suffering the indignity of staring blankly at them while I tried, and failed, to assess my needs.

Some people were very good at listening to me talk about my feelings and deciphering my needs from random things I said. Angels, all of them.

I do not think Bubba knew what he started when he encouraged me to drop the strong act and say yes. When a person is so fraught with grief they hope to not wake up in the morning, what they need more than anything is to say yes to life.

I was learning to drop what didn't serve me while walking toward what did, thanks to the incredible amount of support I was granted. I released the crib that week, which reduced the paralyzing flashbacks. I surrendered to the world feeling "fake." I let go of the attempt to hide my emotions in front of others. I surrendered to my less-functioning brain. I committed to doing things that made me feel peaceful and brought relief or succor. I abandoned the expectation to be "normal," which I believe made it possible for me to heal more authentically, effectively, and swiftly.

Normal doesn't seem to cut it when life gets crazy.

WEEK 2, PART 2: THE ANACHRONISMS

*A*t 5:30 a.m., I was awakened by a fly. There had been one buzzing in my room since Alice's visitation. I tried not to think about how it buzzed my head every night as I tried to fall asleep. I tried not to wonder if it was there because Alice's remains had been here. Five-thirty a.m. was Alice's typical "first call." Sometimes, she would go back to sleep until 7:00 or so. In the wake of her death, I would wake up at 5:30 like clockwork, realize she was gone, experience a pit in my stomach and hole in my heart, and then become paralyzed with guilt that I had ever complained about the 5:30 wake-up.

I WOULD GIVE anything to have her wake me up at 5:30 now. I tried not to wonder if Alice sent the fly to get my ass out of bed.

DURING THIS PERIOD, upon awakening, I knew exactly what day it was, what time it was, and how many days it had been since Alice died. But as the day went on, I rarely knew what day it was or what time it was. I discovered I rather liked the feeling of being unbound by time. I seemed to process better when I was unaware of the time. I knew it was a product of shock, but I wondered if I could retain the ability to disregard time after the shock subsided.

The moments I *was* aware of the time, I found myself preoccupied with imagining what Alice would be doing if she were still alive. While I made breakfast, I recalled her routine.

ALICE TRYING TO GET HER *"GOGURT"* and blueberries out of the fridge by herself. I recalled how she laughed when I made my protein shake in the blender, her hand on the device to feel the vibration. She watched with a sense of wonder I will never forget.

Alice entered the school like she owned the place. She greeted me after school with an enthusiastic "MAMA!" At dinner, she'd pat a seat and say, "Sit, MAMA, SIT!" I recalled the feel of her chubby thighs, the weight of her head on my shoulder, the smoothness of her skin.

Alice loved our nighttime routine. And I loved how she laughed at her books and demanded I read the punch-line pages again and again. How she reminded me to turn on her star lamp and sound machine. How she lazily waved at those stars when I sang "Twinkle, Twinkle, Little Star" to her. How she rested her head on the blankie on my shoulder and patted my back ever so lightly while I sang to her. How she put the corner of the blankie in her eye when she was sleepy. How she recently started saying, "Wub you, Mama."

I would give everything I own to hear her say, "I wub you, Mama," just one more time.

I HAD physical memories as well. I knew exactly how the weight of her head felt on my shoulder. I remembered exactly how tall she was and where she came to on my body.

ALL THESE YEARS LATER, I still remember exactly how I had to shift my weight to lift her and to hold her. A mama never forgets. The body never forgets.

. . .

ALTHOUGH HER ABSENCE was painfully obvious in those early days, it was somewhat softened by the extreme changes to our daily routine. In those early days, there was always a guest, a dinner drop-off, or something else that deviated from our regular routine. This was a blessing. But it also inflamed the fear that I would forget what it was to have her in our life on a daily basis. This fear was so deep, so intense, it was difficult to process anything else. Obsessively recalling her routine was a defense against the fear I'd forget what her existence had brought to my life, I suppose.

So I went through my day, imagining what Alice would be doing if Alice were here.

But she wasn't. And she never will be again. I had experienced all the time with her I would ever get. This is officially the worst feeling I have ever felt. There's nothing anyone can do to help this; you must simply endure it.

But there are things you can do to not make it worse.

Countless people asked me that week — and in the years that followed — "What was the worst thing someone said to you?" In the first two weeks A.A.D., I was asked this question more than any other question. I hesitated to answer because honestly, ninety-nine percent of people said or did things that were helpful. I also did not want to shame anyone. No one was intentionally hurtful; they just happened to stumble upon something that didn't work *for me.*

Eventually, it occurred to me people wanted to know so that *they* knew what to say and do, and what not to say and do. They wanted to know so they could better identify what I found helpful, and because they wanted to help me and perhaps better attend to the grief of a friend. It occurred to me people were not asking out of cattiness, but out of respect. It occurred to me that we are so unbelievably inept at grief as a culture, people honestly have no idea what to do in the face of a friend's grief, much less their own. We are not taught some of the fundamental things about life, the most fundamental of which is how to deal with death.

In that spirit, I will share the things I did not find helpful, with some caveats:

. . .

CAVEAT 1: These are things I found difficult or not helpful. I cannot possibly speak for any other grieving person.

CAVEAT 2: The folks that said things I found difficult are not bad people. They are great people who simply did not know what to say in a grim situation. I do not blame them, judge them, or wish them ill.

THE FIRST THING I found difficult was the "angel" talk. People said things like, "Oh, Mama, it's OK; she's an angel now," or "God needed an angel, so He took her," or "She's an angel now; you are OK. You are blessed to have an angel!"

When folks said things like that in those first couple of weeks, I smiled, hugged them, and walked away. It rubbed me the wrong way, I can't lie, but I knew they meant no harm. I knew they wanted to help me, and themselves, deal with the senselessness of it all. I did not feel the need to demonize people for not intuiting what would be helpful to me and what would not. How were they supposed to know? Their words may very well be helpful to someone else.

But when people would say the angel stuff, my thought bubble filled with, "Word on the street is God is omnipotent. If God needs an angel, God can make an angel from scratch. I highly doubt God needs to smite my innocent child to make an angel." And, I don't know, in the immediate shock of losing my child to unknown forces, the human assurance that my child is now an angel I found to be of precious little comfort. I can see how others might, but I didn't see it that way. And I'm going to go out on a limb and predict that no bereaved parent wants to be told, "You are blessed" or "It's OK," because, well, you aren't, and it's not. It is not OK to have a perfectly healthy child not wake up from a nap. I can get to a place where I can live with it — I mean, I *have* to get to a place where I can live with it —

but I guarantee you few parents are going to be there in the first few days after the fact, if ever.

Not to mention I never want to be told how to feel in the first place, but especially not a week after my child has died and especially not from someone who has *no idea* what it feels like, thank you very much.

For reasons unclear to me in retrospect, I attempted a public function for the first time that week, only ten days A.A.D. I was uneasy about it. I still felt out of step with the rest of the world. I still felt like I was moving in another time and dimension; therefore, large groups of people who were operating under "normal" conditions were an extraordinarily disorienting affair. I don't do well in crowds on the best of days, and these were not my best days.

One thing that was difficult for me at that function was when well-meaning people came up to me with a huge smile and said, "HIIII! How are you?! So nice to see you!" I did not know what to do with that. I thought, "Welp. I'm not like *that*." What did they expect me to say? "I'm great, thanks, and you?" Again, they obviously meant well, so I did not hold anything against them, but it was hard for me to respond to a greeting generally used for joyous or neutral occasions. My thought bubble read, "How am I? My kid just died for no apparent reason. Frankly, I'm not that great. Frankly, my therapist friend is impressed I am not in bed with my head under the covers."

But in reality, I smiled, hugged them, and walked away.

I suppose I thought that type of greeting betrayed the greeter's assumption that the greeted should be ready for cheery small talk days after losing a child. I was not ready for superficial party greetings or for pretending nothing was wrong. I did not need to talk about Alice's death 24/7 or to be pitied, mind you, but I wasn't ready for cocktail talk.

Someone else asked me, "How are the grandparents?" I said they were devastated. "Still?" the person asked.

I froze.

"Still? Still? Still devastated ten days after the unexpected, unexplained death of their darling granddaughter? Yes. And you know, I bet they will still be devastated ten years from now as well," read my invisible thought bubble. I also fought the urge to say, "I know. Can you believe these wusses are still upset ten days later?" because I am certain this person meant no harm.

Still, it revealed the fact this person felt there was some timeline to healing, and frankly, their timeline was pretty damn quick. It showed me *they* were over the initial shock — and so imagined my family should be as well. I knew I could not become healthy if I subjected myself to folks who expected me or my family to "be better" in any amount of time, much less ten days later. Nor did I want to judge their reaction in return. They had no idea what to say.

So I smiled, hugged them, and walked away.

I turned directly into another person who asked me how I was doing. I said I was having a hard time but trying to heal. This person then asked me if I had been "helping out at the kids' school" in my "time off."

You know, as if I were on disability for a hangnail.

Shocked, I responded, "In my 'time off' I had to decide whether to bury or cremate my child. I have been trying to figure out a way to handle this in a way that won't screw up Grace for the rest of her life. I have been trying to figure out how to live without being crippled by guilt. I held a wake, a memorial service, received her ashes, hosted hundreds of people on multiple days, and tried to figure out what to do with Alice's belongings. I have tried to figure out how I am supposed to work — on a schedule — taking care of other people when I feel like my innards have been cut out and I barely know what time it is. It hasn't exactly been 'time off' in the usual sense of the term."

I said it nicely, but in retrospect, I wish I had kept my thought bubble inside, hugged this person, smiled, and walked away.

It became clear to me I needed to leave the party before any more thought bubbles became actual speech.

All these people were parents themselves, strangely. I could only guess they wanted me to be "better" because they wanted to think that, in my shoes, they would be "better" quickly. Again, I do not

MOM'S SEARCH FOR MEANING

begrudge these people their reactions. They are good people. But I could not handle that line of questioning.

I decided I wasn't quite ready for "prime time." I wasn't ripe enough for public consumption. I could tell I was going to have to follow my urge to lie low for a while. The pressure of walking around with those cartoon-like thought bubbles I had to consciously translate into something socially acceptable before speaking was profoundly exhausting. I could deal with people one at a time, or a few at a time, but crowds were out of the question for the time being ... and I was *fine with that.* I felt zero guilt about not being able to tolerate crowds.

In retrospect, I do believe it was helpful to me to identify what was not helpful, though I had my reservations about stating it publicly. Learning what/who is not helpful is as important as learning what/who is helpful. I do believe, however, that the unwittingly unhelpful should not be shamed. I am grateful I had the opportunity to identify what was helpful and what was not early in the process. This allowed me to receive what helped, let go of what didn't, and to do so without a painful and lengthy decision-making process or alienating people who meant no harm.

THAT SAME DAY, I had to retrieve Alice's belongings from the preschool. It was impossible not to envision her doing her usual morning walk-in, saying "HIIIII!" to everyone, waiting patiently for her cereal and juice with her toes on the line of the kitchen area (no kids allowed in the kitchen, but she'd get as close as she could), showing the chef her outfit and/or temporary tattoos. That day the big kids all ran up to me asking if Alice had died, the little kids all asked for her by name with quizzical looks on their faces, parents wanted details, and the teachers were all sobbing. I tried to encourage the parents to ask questions once Grace was out of earshot, but to no avail. I was completely surrounded by the big, questioning eyes of so many little children.

And I had no answers.

111

None. Nada. Nothing. Zip.

I went to her cubbyhole like I had so many days before, only this time she wasn't there to help me carry the load. She would never help me empty that cubbyhole again. Things were left there on a Monday, intended to be used on Tuesday, never to be touched by her again. The teachers handed me the art projects she had completed the Monday before she died. That nearly flattened me. How could she have created this piece one day, and be dead less than twenty-four hours later? *How?*

I somehow managed to complete this agonizing task, but partly wished I'd asked someone else to go in my place. I could barely breathe.

Reeling in agony from the party and the school mission, I returned home to find Alice's death certificate in the mail. I didn't expect to be alive to see Alice's death certificate; I'd never thought of Alice's death certificate *at all in any way.* I stared at it for a long time. I guess I thought if I stared at it long enough, the documentation of the end of Alice's history would make sense to me.

This effort was futile. I knew I was going to have to open the envelope. I knew I was going to have to continue experiencing my own history even though my daughter's no longer intersected with mine. I felt as if I could easily evaporate into thin air, probably because I so desperately wanted to do so.

It was a shitty day from start to finish. I felt guilty thinking about days I thought were shitty in the Before Times. Naïve girl. The old version of me had no idea about *shitty.*

Hoping to feel less shitty, I decided to attempt to read one of the several books on grief I'd been gifted. The house was finally quiet enough for me to think of reading something.

I opened the one on top — I do not recall which — and read a couple of pages. I flipped through the book looking at chapter titles and blurbs here and there, and thought, "I can't."

I tried a second.

I tried a third.

I am a studier, but I couldn't get into the books and I had no idea why. It suddenly dawned on me being a studier was the problem. I immediately knew I would read that book like a student and then compare my experience to what the book said, or worse, alter my experience to reflect what the book suggested. I instinctively knew this was going to hinder me, personally. I could see how these books would be helpful to others, and how they would likely be helpful to me in the future, but I *knew* from the very depths of my soul I was going to have to forge my own trail in the beginning of this crisis.

I do not always listen to my intuition without arguing, but when it is that strong, I do, for it is never, ever wrong.

Grief books were abandoned for the time being and remained untouched for years. Meleva, when she heard this, asked if I was on meds. I said I was not. She said, "Ah, you are going to white-knuckle this, I see." I did not feel like I was white-knuckling it, however. I considered it more like freestyling it. I felt I was allowing the emotions that came up to go through me. I know from personal and professional experience that the only way through it is through it. It ain't magic, folks.

White-knuckling it seems to imply one is bracing oneself through "it." I didn't, and still don't, feel that way. I see it more as grabbing a scythe, heading down an incredibly overgrown path, and weed-whacking my way through terrain no one wishes to encounter. Hey, it's not for everyone, but I know with every fiber of my being it is the way for me.

I was not convinced the meds or the books were going to help me allow those emotions to go through me, so I chose not to utilize the books for the time being. If I came to a point where I thought I could benefit, or could tell I was stifling my emotions, or had trouble functioning, I would reconsider.

In hindsight, I felt like, I dunno, I gave in to the grief. It seemed so much bigger than me, I guess I thought, "OK, I get it: I am not in control." I felt like riding the wave of this tragedy was the way to survive it.

I have to do it my own way.

And by my own clock.

And with a purpose and meaning strong enough to drive me forward in time after half of my heart stopped on August 6, 2013.

Since the grief books didn't work, I tried to read about SUDC again. It sent me into an instant nosedive. I was a guilt-riddled, heart-pounding wreck within seconds. It became clearer and clearer my main concern was her *soul,* or the thing that made Alice uniquely Alice. I desperately needed to know what Alice became when she shed her body here on earth. Her earthly mama needed to figure out a way to know if her child was OK in spirit. Your maternal instinct doesn't just shut off when the coroner comes to collect your child. I still harbored every protective instinct I had before she died, after she died. That instinct didn't know Alice's body wasn't here to protect any longer.

I somehow knew this line of inquiry was critical to my mental health and that my ability to do anything else was dependent on my mental health. It became clear to me I needed to search for answers and comfort inside before I looked for answers and comfort outside. I have no doubt — for me — the path leading from tragedy to resiliency was paved by inner work and permitted by the absence of an external focus.

I began to nose around in various religious texts for descriptions of the afterlife. Some were helpful, some were not so helpful, but the pursuit felt meaningful in and of itself, regardless of outcome. The pursuit led me to feel the tiniest bit uplifted instead of leveled, so I continued this approach daily. I continue this practice to this very day. I also decided if I got to a place where it felt like too much, I would step away from the pursuit and just be.

I could *just be.*

Around this time, two different people sent me information about a psychic medium. I never asked for such a referral and these women did not know each other, yet both recommended the same person. I took it as a sign and requested an appointment, which was scheduled three months A.A.D. In the meantime, the medium suggested I read a book called *The Survival of the Soul* by Lisa Williams. She said it would give me some idea of how she worked and possibly answer some of the questions I might have. That was the first book I managed to finish; it turned out to be critical to my healing. Although I still had a lot of healing to do, reading that book left me with confidence Alice's soul was just fine, which erased an immense amount of fear and guilt — for a while, at least.

Is the book true? Who knows? More importantly, who cares? I finished the book convinced Alice was OK and this provided peace. In the end, who gives a rip if it's true if it enabled me to survive finding my healthy daughter dead in her crib?

Coincidentally, most grief support groups do not recommend you start group therapy until three months after the loss of the loved one because you are "too fresh." I found it interesting the psychic and the psychologist were on the exact same page regarding timing. It seemed like for three months, everyone agreed that winging it — with your hand held by family, friends, and private therapy — was the way to go.

Still, I knew I could use some professional support in moving past The Guilt. I was also struggling to simply wrap my head around how Alice's death had so instantly changed my life and family structure. I would occasionally freeze in the middle of some mundane task, completely stunned by the notion that my eldest child was now also my youngest child. I was sickened when I realized that, in the blink of an eye, I no longer had children in diapers. No more naps. No more double school-drops. No need for a stroller. Suddenly, no more baby carriers, no more specially prepared food, no more sippy cups.

I know this all seems obvious, but these particulars did not sink in right away. At first, I had been consumed with simply dealing with her death and memorial service.

Time was not my friend at these moments.

Despite feeling like I was "done" after having Alice, in those early weeks A.A.D., I did wonder if I should try for another baby. Grace asked for another baby almost daily. I guess we were both looking to fill the hole in our family. Clearly, we both felt an immense sense of incompleteness. She asked if I was going to make another baby in my tummy. At one point, she thought I should "make another girl and call her Alice." At another point, she requested a boy. At another point, she

115

recommended adoption "because you don't have to wait for it to come out of your tummy." It broke my heart.

I was no spring chicken, mind you, so the timing of this tragedy was inconvenient. Tragedy cares little for the expected timeline of your life or the age of your ovaries. I was the age where you start to be put out to pasture. But the feeling of incompleteness with regard to my family was so intense, I did consider trying. I made appointments for my first mammogram and to see my OB-GYN. I wasn't sure if I would pursue pregnancy, but I thought I'd better see how my lady parts were faring, just in case.

Other appointments planned before Alice died began to become present-day events; I couldn't understand how this was so. One day, a phone alert told me to enroll Alice in dance class. And for one beautiful moment, I started to call. And then I collapsed into tears on my hallway floor. And then I remembered she was supposed to start swim lessons with Grace that weekend. I knew I couldn't explain why I needed to cancel Alice's classes but not Grace's so my dear friend Chrislie did it for me.

Additionally, Grace was supposed to go to dance class and two birthday parties that weekend. I couldn't. I was still shaken from my first attempt to socialize with groups. The way people looked at me was too much to take in. I could tell I was the living, breathing poster child of everyone's worst nightmare. I could tell people didn't know what to say to me or how to deal with me. And I didn't have the wherewithal to lead them at that time. They couldn't help it. I didn't blame them. It was just too much. We did go swimming at a friend's house, but it was all people who had been there for me from the start, so I was at ease.

The water felt amazing. I melted into it. I went underwater and enjoyed the muffled sounds of life around me while feeling the water caress my skin. I moved around as smoothly as I could. I was dancing, really. There was solitude beneath the water that seemed to merge with my skin. Time did not exist for me underwater, and if time did not exist, then I wasn't moving further away from Alice. I wished I could stay down there in the timelessness.

Instead, I reluctantly came up for air because it wasn't my time to join Alice.

Monday was my first day back to my clinic, and Grace's first day back to her camp. I was dreading this day. I was not certain I could do my job well and I'm not a person who likes to do things half-assed. I wasn't sure I was capable of managing an appointment-based schedule while I still had such a warped experience of time. I wasn't sure I could handle seeing people look at me with a mixture of pity, desperation, fear, and a deep desire to help despite having no idea how to do so. It was only thirteen days after Alice had died. Going back to work meant going back to a "normal" schedule and that felt like a betrayal of Alice somehow. I know, of course, that is absurd but the feeling was there, nonetheless.

On the way to camp, Grace said, "Mama, I am so sad Alice will never be able to go to Spanish Camp with me. I am sorry she will not be able to go to the school we made together with me. I am sad she won't be in the baby class at my school anymore," and on and on. I cried. I said I was very sad about all those things, too. I could see her studying me, and my reaction, intently.

Even Grace knew our family's expected timeline had been obliterated, yet she seemed excited to get to camp. She continued to list all the things she missed about Alice, and things she wished Alice could do with her as we walked in the building. Some parents overheard and cried. Some parents, deep in conversation with each other, stopped mid-sentence when they saw us and regarded me with a look of shock, sadness, and pity. Other parents hugged me silently.

It was grueling.

And then I went off to work. The bills keep coming even when your child dies, and your life is ripped apart and you barely know what day it is — unless that day is Tuesday, and then that's all you can think about.

Once working, I found it refreshing. It was somewhat of a relief to be presented with problems I could solve. "Knee pain? No problem. If you follow my advice, you'll be good as new in no time." "Insomnia? No problem. Neck pain? A breeze." Here was some shit I could solve, and it was a nice change from the overwhelming problem I could never solve.

By the end of my shift, however, I felt a level of exhaustion I did not know could even exist. I could barely move. Simply shutting my eyes seemed like too much exertion, but I did it, because when I was sleeping, I didn't know I was traveling through time away from my dear Alice.

WEEK 3: THE SAVING GRACE

*T*uesday, August 20, was the two-week anniversary of Alice's death. I was beginning my third week as a bereaved parent. Time kept flowing further away from the morning she'd kissed me on the lips. I tried to make sense of it and failed. I cried.

But time marches on, and with it my heart.

My friends Alyssa and Angela came by that Tuesday afternoon to help around the house. This was enormously helpful, as I was still in a deep state of shock, and organizing the house seemed overwhelming. The playroom/office was still set up like a catering room, and I didn't know where to start. I wasn't sure what items belonged to which friends or where to put anything.

Alyssa and Angela went at it with a quiet fury. I was completely exhausted from work the day before, and from recent events in general. They told me to rest, but I puttered around anyway. At one point, I leaned over to pick something up, and inexplicably collapsed in tears. I felt as if I had been hit by a missile. My heart started pounding out of my chest, I broke into a cold sweat, and couldn't catch my breath. I was shaking. I went weak-kneed. I was immediately, instantly consumed by guilt. The guilt was always there at a low hum in those early days, but it was like someone had walked by and turned it up to eleven without my noticing. I could not stop crying. They asked if I was OK, but I could barely talk.

I felt guilty for taking a nap the day she died. I felt guilty for not allowing her to just eat berries and yogurt her whole life like she wanted to because, in the end, it didn't matter. I felt guilty for not hugging her or kissing her one more time before I put her down that day. I felt guilty for putting her down at all that day. I felt guilty for not staying at school longer the last couple of weeks when she suddenly started to cry upon my leaving. I felt guilty she never got to visit her grandparents' house. I felt guilty I ever felt relief once both girls were asleep for the night. I felt guilty for every single second I did not, and would never again, get to spend with her.

As I wrote this part, I cried, not so much out of guilt, but for the part of me so consumed by guilt I was unsure how I could live a full life. I remember that Melissa, and today's Melissa deeply feels for the Melissa that existed in the early days A.A.D. For the first time in my life, I sit here with some compassion for my former self. This is a beautiful thing, but I wish to God I could have learned it in a less drastic way.

So then I felt guilty for not learning the lesson in a less costly way.

GUILT IS a bottomless pit of self-inflicted torture and despair.

I HAD no idea what had brought on that intense episode that day. I forget what I picked up, but it was something completely banal. It wasn't anything of Alice's or anything with heavy meaning. Alyssa walked me to my bedroom and got me to my bed. She brought me chamomile tea. I was still having trouble breathing, and my heart was pounding in my chest so hard I was surprised it was not visible to the naked eye. I rested, but I could not sleep. I lay there, cried, and felt guilty for an hour or so.

Eventually, I realized I'd had another panic attack. By the time I needed pick up Grace from camp, I was feeling somewhat better.

At dinner that Tuesday night, Grace walked over to me with a big smile, and said, "I have a secret, Mama." She then leaned into me, and whispered in my ear, "Maybe we can have a magic trick where Alice can come back alive to our home."

I felt like someone pulled my beating heart out of my chest and showed it to me while the life slowly left my body.

At bedtime that night, she looked up at me with giant, sad eyes and asked, "Is the lady bringing Alice back to the house?"

Oh, shit.

I had decided to wait to tell four-year-old Grace we cremated Alice's remains. I had trouble with the concept at age forty-four. I had also vowed I would not straight-up lie to her about it either. If she asked me in such a way that I could not get around it without lying, I would tell her. But I was hoping for a year or two.

In the end, I decided to answer *exactly* what she asked and not to elaborate beyond that. I explained the lady was not bringing Alice back and fought off tears. Grace cried and hugged me and asked why.

Oh, crap, oh, crap, oh crap.

"When you die, you cannot run and jump and play or breathe anymore. When your body does not breathe anymore, and your heart does not beat anymore, the body starts to fade away. Watching the body of someone you love fade away can be very hard to watch, and very hard to accept, so the lady took care of that for us so we can remember Alice in a way that is happy," I blurted out.

None of those words went through my mind before they shot out of my mouth.

Grace sighed and asked if Alice was happy now. I said I was sure she was, and I meant it with every fiber of my being. And then I sighed, relieved I was not going to have to explain cremation to a four-year-old.

Grace then asked if we could sing "the Alice songs," meaning "Twinkle, Twinkle" and "ABCs." We began to sing together. Grace began to cry through the song and I lost my ability to fight back tears. Eventually, we were both crying through the songs. I stopped a minute, thinking it too much for Grace, but she screamed out, *"Don't stop! Don't stop, Mama!"*

So I pressed on, both of us sobbing through the song.

She asked to sleep with one of Alice's blankies. Of course, I let her do that.

Grace woke up the next morning with a variation of what had become her morning litany. "I am sad Alice is never going to be four-teen, I am sad she cannot go to my Spanish Camp with me, I am sad she cannot play in my kitchen with me," etc. And then, "Mama, I even miss fighting with Alice."

Just stab my heart out, kid, why don't ya?

Out of nowhere, Grace asked for a "neck-o-lace that opens up" — i.e., a locket. "And inside, I want a picture of Alice on one side, and a tiny piece of her blankie on the other." She came up with this one hundred percent on her own. I was astonished. I'd had no idea she was aware of lockets.

AFTER HEARING THIS STORY, my friend Stacy brought her a locket from her personal jewelry stash, but the blankie was too thick for it, sadly, so we put in tiny pictures. I bought her another locket for her Christmas gift that year and arranged it as she desired. How could I not?

IT WAS difficult to go to work that day, though I managed once there. Again, I thought I should add an element of my business that did not depend on my physical presence on an hourly basis, something where I could help many people at once, but from afar. Something that allowed space for the spaciness and timelessness of grief.

I still had the irritating eye spasm, but I guess it didn't bother me enough to do anything about it. I was also receiving so many calls I could not keep up, and my voicemail was nearly always full at this time. I was still having trouble speaking; I could only take one or two calls a day, max. I had also overshot my data plan's text capacity, so I had to upgrade. I remember sitting on my back steps, thinking how stupid it was I had to sit and deal with AT&T when my daughter had just died unexpectedly. I marveled at the ridiculousness of dealing with something so banal when my world had been turned upside down. I suppose this mindset explains why I disregarded the constant blepharospasm.

Dealing with minutiae felt like a betrayal of Alice's importance. And Grace's.

Later that week, my dear friend Elizabeth Flaherty arrived for a visit. Sometime earlier in the week I had realized I had screwed up her visit entirely. I'd told her it was fine to fly in from Baltimore, having completely forgotten I had my twenty-four-hour whirlwind trip to Sacramento that Friday to Saturday. This was definitely not normal for me. She was more than understanding, but I felt rude and stupid. I am generally organized and have managed a crazy schedule for years. Before Alice died, I rarely forgot anything. This was definite proof my mind was still not fully functioning. I realized I was going to have to use alerts on my phone for everything — even basic tasks like paying bills — because I was forgetting so many things.

My other Elizabeth — Elizabeth Christie — also came to visit that day. Elizabeth Christie is the mother of Alice's great friend Darla. No one could ever determine what was so damn funny, but those girls would fall apart laughing when they saw each other. Darla and Alice enjoyed so many shenanigans together we called them Lucy and Ethel. You could plainly see, despite their young age, those two truly loved each other.

But now Lucy was missing her Ethel, which sickened me. They were supposed to take dance lessons, learn to ride bikes, and double-date to prom together, but this was not to be. Darla, who was two years old, asked, "Where is Alice?" I cried and looked to Elizabeth C. I hated the fact she had to determine how to tell her two-year-old about Alice.

Elizabeth C. was absolutely distraught over the loss of Alice, as I would have been if the roles were reversed. No one thinks something like this is going to happen to their child, or their child's friend. Elizabeth C. was also very pregnant at the time. I felt horrible she had to process this loss while pregnant.

Despite her sadness, despite being pregnant, Elizabeth C. was, and continues to be, one of my strongest supporters, and I will be forever indebted to her. She is a member of what I call "my Irish mafia." I have a higher than average number of Irish friends and supporters, all of whom will appear to stop at nothing to ensure I am properly cared for. What I did to deserve such care and love, I will never know, but I thank the heavens every day.

Eventually, we flew to Sacramento. I was anxious about dealing with an airport in the state I was in, but the trip had been planned for months, so off we went. Grace and I had a nice flight, but the airport itself was difficult. Too many people in a hurry. Too many people, period. Some lady in the bathroom was going on and on about how pretty Grace was and how I should have another. I smiled, said nothing, and prepared to walk away, but she was undaunted. She kept pressing on and on about how I should have another. Grace whispered "Alice" to me. And then, it flew out of my mouth: "She had a two-year-old sister, but she died unexpectedly a couple of weeks ago."

The lady stared at me dumbfounded. I stared back. Grace stared her down as well. Eventually she realized I was not kidding and said, "Oh, I am sorry," and walked away in a daze. I am not sure I ruined her day but I am pretty sure I did not do anything to make it better, and I felt somewhat bad about it. But I had shown Grace that I wasn't going to pretend her sister did not exist to make a stranger feel better. Grace was more important. To me, Grace was the only thing that was still important. Everything else felt like complete bullshit.

One of the things that made meeting new people in public so difficult was the high probability I was going to end up in a situation where I had to decide whether to say I had one kid or give them the shocking truth. "Do I deny Alice or speak a truth that will force them to consider the mortality of themselves and their loved ones?" Because when you have one kid, well-intentioned folks everywhere ask you, "Is that your only child? You should have more." My instinct, up to this point, was to absolutely acknowledge Alice's existence. I felt like I had no option but to acknowledge her despite what people would think or feel. So, though I was not eager to pretend Alice did not exist any longer to protect the feelings of others in the first place, this experience in the bathroom showed me that, for Grace's sake, I could not, even if I wanted to do so.

I knew Grace needed to see me acknowledge Alice, so she knew I would not leave *her* unacknowledged, in the horrific event that Grace died. Because young children her age are still necessarily egocentric, I knew every time Grace asked me, out of the blue, "Do you still miss Alice?" what she was really asking was, "If I were dead, would you still miss me? Would you still miss me when you laugh? Would you still miss me when you are busy paying bills? Would you still miss me at work/on vacation/at the store/at bedtime/when you are getting dressed?"

I could truthfully answer yes to all those questions and more. It was painfully apparent to me Grace needed to know.

For months, Grace asked daily, at random times, if I missed Alice. She stared me down to see if I meant it. One day, I did not tear up when she asked this, like I usually did. She put her face inches from mine, tipped up her chin and said, "Cry," like a mobster.

Grace needed to see me cry for her sister.

This was handy, because I could not have fought off tears 24/7 even if you paid me to do so. I needed to cry, and she needed to see me cry. Teamwork makes the nightmare work.

Once we landed in Sacramento, we had a nice evening with Meleva. The girls played and then went to bed with a movie. Meleva and I had a drink and walked around her property atop Barbula Hill, named after her family. Meleva could not look at me without crying. I remember lying in the bed, going in and out of sleep, seeing Meleva kneeling by my bed, staring at me, with giant tears streaming down her face. Meleva is Serbian. She was never a big crier. It was then that I knew this: If Meleva can't stop crying, this is as horrible as it feels.

It would have broken my heart, but it was already broken.

Saturday was Famke's party. The party was difficult for me. I love Famke and wanted to go, and I wanted Grace to have fun with some kids, but I was dreading meeting new people and dealing with the inevitable kid questions. I felt immense pressure around people I did not know. I was also completely drained. I did not realize how profoundly exhausted I was until that day. It hit me at the party. I could barely sit up. I had no appetite. I just wanted to go to sleep.

Eventually I had to go lie down in the car. Meleva was kind enough to watch Grace for me so I could rest.

Grace had a great time, and Meleva and her family were perfect hosts, but it was too much for me right then. I was exhausted for days. This was no one's fault; it was just too much stimulation for my state of mind at that point.

On the way to the airport on Saturday, Grace became sad. I asked her what was wrong. She got tears in her eyes and said, "I am starting to forget what Alice looked like, Mama."

My heart stopped, and I felt the hole in my chest. I felt nauseated. I knew how upsetting that must be for Grace because I was an adult and could barely manage. I asked if she wanted to see some videos of Alice. She did. So I passed my phone to the back seat and let her view at her leisure. She was happy to have the videos, and I was grateful I had them to share with her. I thought about how the most recent photo of Alice was moving further away from my most recent photos. I realized one day I would have to search back through years of pictures to find Alice's most recent photo.

I sobbed.

At another point that week, Grace told me she was "forgetting what it was like to be a sister" and "I do not know how to *not* be a sister, Mama."

This was some pretty deep thinking for a four-year-old, and it broke my heart she had to think this way. She was still asking for a new sibling at this point and offered to be a big sister to Alice's friends Aria and Darla. She was so desperate to fill the hole we all felt.

Walking into Trader Joe's later that week for the first time A.A.D., I found myself looking around and thinking, "None of these people know my Alice was snatched from this earth without warning. None of these people anguishing over parking places know I will never see my child again. To them, life is normal, and I look normal, but I'm not." It was an eerie feeling. Again, I felt like I was in a transparent bubble. I could see the world, but I was not part of it.

I could get through the day of work, but I could not do one extra thing. I look back at my patient charts from that time and think, "Is that my handwriting?" It's unrecognizable as my own. I found that interesting.

Monday morning, I met Elizabeth F. for my yoga class. As we did Warrior posture, I began to feel the nuances of the pose. I felt strong but soft, sturdy yet pliable, intent but not anxious. I then noticed tears were silently streaming down my face. I felt like I'd finally done something right: maintaining the strength to prepare for war without doing anything to cause it while at the same time weeping for all the pain in the world without succumbing to it. It was bliss.

It was also fleeting.

At another point, during the meditation, I felt compelled to cross my arms across my body, close my eyes and roll back on my back.

As I lay there on my back, I felt *exactly* like I did when I held Alice all those hours in the last weeks of her life. I felt her. I *felt her!* I hadn't meant to do so, I wasn't thinking of it: it just happened, which made it all the more special. I wondered if she was sending me a sign that she was still there, with me, on my heart.

It's corny, I know, but I'm going to go with yes, she was there, because the behavior was so unusual for me.

I WISH to God I could feel her every day.

TWO HAS ALWAYS BEEN my favorite age. Even as a little girl, I loved two-year-olds. They are so damn cute: their proportions are all crazy with their giant head, huge eyes, short arms, and wobbly legs. Their ability to get their point across with so few words has always amazed me. Observing their acquisition of language has always fascinated me.

It occurred to me Alice would forever be my favorite age. This thought was both sickening and comforting. Losing a child apparently comes with the ability to feel incongruous feelings simultaneously. In any event, my sweet girl will always be two, in the way we record time here on earth.

I assumed I would spend a lot of time in the months ahead wondering what Alice would be doing if she were still here, as I had for the first two weeks. What new words she would say, what new milestones she would hit, etc. But after those first two weeks, I seemed to stop wondering. The only time I did that was when I saw her friend Aria, who was only four weeks younger than Alice.

In the early days, I would get a sinking feeling in my stomach and heart when I saw Aria. It was not Aria's fault, mind you; it was just that she, more than anyone else, brought to mind what I was missing with my daughter. I could see she had new words, new likes and dislikes, only two-and-a-half weeks later. This gutted me.

WE STILL SEE Aria often and, I now realize, I haven't thought of Alice being her age in years; therefore, it's no longer painful. Alice is still two in my mind, and no amount of mental gymnastics can make me think of her as any older than two. Is this good or bad? Who cares? It just is, and I am committed to dealing with "what is."

She was two. She will never be two years and two weeks old. She will never be three. She will never be forty-four. She will never be one hundred and two.

Two, well, two is all I have to go on.

THE REALIZATION that your life is marching forward, that you are surviving but your child will forever be in the past, is the single most agonizing feeling I have ever felt. I can see why people stay in bed, do drugs, become alcoholics or workaholics, or otherwise unconsciously (or consciously) derail their lives after such a tragedy. The guilt of moving on — which one must do — is so overwhelming it feels like the guilt alone could ruin you. You feel like you are betraying your child by *not* locking yourself in the past.

I knew I needed to figure out how to move on, without allowing guilt to ruin me. I knew learning how to let go of guilt was essential to my mental health. I was getting there, but it was going to be tricky and it was probably going to take a while. I had to accept Alice's last moment was moving further away from my present. Thank God I had another child who needed me here, a child who needed to see me heal, a child who needed to see my real tears and my real triumphs.

She was, and is, my saving Grace.

WEEK 4: THE LEMONADE AND THE TOAST

*T*he overwhelming sense of dread I experienced upon awakening was the only way I knew it was Tuesday. Alice was dead, and I was still alive.

My friend Joy visited that day. She made Grace a photo album full of pictures of Grace and Alice together, the photos in chronological order — a genius gift Grace treasures to this day. I stared and stared at it, trying to understand that Grace would likely have many more pictures in her chronology, but these were the only pictures she'd ever have with her only sibling.

IT STILL DOES NOT COMPUTE, *but I have stopped trying to make it compute.*

WHEN I FOCUSED on the thoughtfulness and foresight required for Joy to create such a special gift, the senselessness of Alice's departure didn't crush me into oblivion.

. . .

DURING JOY'S VISIT, I noticed I still became exhausted by speaking and remembered how this was explained in traditional Chinese medicine. I began to notice the links between the meridians and their associated emotions were perfectly obvious in me, as were the symptoms of imbalance in those meridians—or pathways of energy associated with various organs and systems in the body. In particular, the lung meridian is associated with strength of voice and energy level, as well as being the meridian that processes grief. Fascinating. I thought about this and began taking notes detailing my own symptoms, checking them against my knowledge of Chinese medicine, and noting the similarities and differences. If I had to go through such darkness, I figured I might as well become my own lab rat; maybe then I could better assist other souls in their time of need.

Losing a child is an experience I would not wish on another living soul, but if I had to have such an awful experience, I felt compelled to the very marrow of my bones to try to make lemonade out of the super shitty batch of lemons I had been given. This meant I had to try to find a deeper meaning in this experience. I had to try to become a better person. I had to try to leave the world better than the way I found it. Even before Alice's death, I tried to leave the world better than I found it, but this desire was magnified exponentially after her death. Look, I screw up several times daily like every other human, but I do actively try to find some beauty in this horror.

One night, I heard myself say to the heavens, "Hey, you. Yes, you up there. If I handle this like a trooper, will you please stop killing other people's kids?"

I knew this plea was unlikely to be successful, but I had an intense desire to say it out loud anyway. I felt, and still feel, compelled to try to turn this mess into something beautiful, for Alice's sake. She was a happy, loving kid who saw the world as happy and loving, and I'll be damned if I won't try to make it that way for her.

At some point that Tuesday, I had another panic attack. Again, its onset seemed unrelated to thoughts of Alice, or even to grief in general. I was doing some banal chore when it hit. One second, I was fine; the next, I was shaking and sweating, with my heart pounding and stomach churning, completely consumed by guilt and regret. I got into the bathtub. The water seemed to soothe me enough to make sleep possible that night.

At bedtime, Grace began crying her eyes out: "It's *bad* for babies to die! Why did our baby die?!"

My heart stopped. I froze. I could barely speak, but somehow, I managed to utter it was, indeed, bad for babies to die. Grace could not quite verbalize it, but her endless litany led me to understand she knew very well death had not visited our home in the usual order. It crushed me to know she had to learn this at such a young age. I knew this event would forever change Grace's perspective. Her perspective was going to be very different from most of her peers, for better or for worse.

EVERY SINGLE DAY, Grace says something that reflects a maturity well beyond her years. It no longer automatically makes me sad, but it does cause me to both smile and sigh a lot. It causes me to ponder things more deeply.

I TOLD A FRIEND, "Everything is existential up in this bitch 24/7. There is no more small talk. Ever."

I loathe small talk with the intensity of the Big Bang, so this should have been a welcome change. Instead, it fueled my guilt. "If I hadn't asked for no more small talk, maybe my baby would still be here."

Yes, I am aware that is irrational. I was aware it was irrational as it zipped through my mind. But it zipped through, nonetheless. I noticed this, labeled it "guilt," and once I was aware I was punishing myself with guilt, the guilt popped like a bubble. "Fascinating," I thought.

It started to become clear I could not get around the "negative" emotion by pressing it down, ignoring it, judging it, or condemning oneself for it. The only way through it is through it. It seemed to me that all I could do was try to be aware of my emotion and acknowledge it. Once acknowledged, its strength seemed to diminish. I kept at this practice. Guilt and other negative emotions still appeared, but they did so less frequently.

THE EMOTIONS PASS THROUGH, and I try not to grab them and hang on to them when they do, but it's a work in progress, people.

GRACE CONTINUED CRYING ABOUT "our baby dying." She hadn't cried this hard since Alice died. She wanted to know why the firemen and doctor couldn't help Alice and reiterated her desire to go to the firehouse and police station to thank them. I answered her questions to the best of my ability and fought off tears.

Once Grace fell asleep, I realized I felt like someone had sucked my soul right out of my body. I went outside for some air before going to bed. I had recently realized that I paced. Sometimes I thought and paced, sometimes I was blank and paced, but every night, I paced. I paced from my front steps, down the walk, to the left down the sidewalk to the driveway and back. And again. And again. I am surprised I didn't wear a hole in the ground. I am surprised my neighbors didn't ask what the hell I was doing. Once I realized I was doing it, I was surprised I had done it for several weeks without noticing. Who expends all that energy without noticing?

It seemed as if I had to literally move the unceasing, mercurial thoughts and feelings through my body. I realized I subconsciously knew I was going to have to move my body to allow the perspective shifts, the feelings, the immense downloads of realizations to move through me. I was grateful I honored my unconscious urge to move my body instead of taking to my bed, because it became crystal clear doing so was a key to allowing tough emotions to flow through me instead of taking over me.

As I paced, I suddenly found myself looking down to my right, at hip level. I noticed my heart softened and felt full. I realized that's exactly how tall Alice was before she died. That's where her head was when she walked beside me. I suppose you could say I felt her pacing with me. She would have thought pacing was a hoot. I smiled. And then I teared up. But the love I felt was so all-consuming, the smile remained through the tears.

To this day, every once in a while, I have the all-consuming urge to look down to my right and smile — and then I realize that's space Alice used to inhabit. I hope she knows I still smile for her like I do for her sister.

THE FOLLOWING DAY, I went to my first individual grief counseling session. It went well, and the therapist thought I was doing well, all things considered. That was nice to hear, I suppose. Having never experienced such horror before, I had no idea how I was doing in the scheme of things, and frankly, I didn't care how I measured up to other people. I thought I was doing well, under the circumstances, which was notable only because I was still very invested in self-flagellation. My friends told me I was kicking ass, but I was also aware people thought someone in my position was doing great if they were simply functioning. My friends also said things like, "Don't apologize for crying, I can't believe you aren't under the covers in the fetal position," so it occurred to me folks had a very low bar of expectation for me.

I had never experienced such a low level of expectation. I can't lie: It is super flippin' relaxing. It's a revelation, to be honest. The realization I had such a low bar has been, ironically, a peak experience. I vowed to enjoy the new, low bar. I vowed to ease the pressure I place on myself, and I have had some success with that. Look, the perfectionist runs deep within; I am by no means "cured." I still want to do this "grief thing" right. I still want to learn the lessons I am meant to learn from this, so I do not need to learn them again in a costlier way. And maybe that is not even how it works. Maybe this did not happen strictly to present me with a teaching moment. (It most likely didn't happen to provide me a teaching moment.) I don't want to take any chances, however. My heart can't take it.

Directly after my first therapy session, I had my first mammogram, because what could be more fun than cancer screening twenty-
two days after your child dies? I know how to party. I scheduled this
after she died. I did this on purpose. Why, you ask? Excellent question.
For years, I could not have answered it. I think I was basically puffing
my chest out to the Universe. Or maybe I was flipping the bird to the
Universe, getting in its face and saying, "You want a piece of me? You
want a piece of me?"

Sure, I was overdue to have a mammogram, but it probably could
have waited a little longer. I guess I thought, "If I'm going to get bad
news, it might as well be now, because it would barely register with
the big bad news now headlining in my life." Also, I thought, at this
point in the Aftermath, I might want to try again for another child. I
was forty-four, so time was not my friend and I wanted to make sure
my lady parts were still truckin'. Every day, Grace asked me for
another sister. And every day, I could not believe I only had one child.
I could not believe Grace was going to be an only child. It sickened
me.

My friend Tommy called that day to check on me after my
mammogram. When people check in regularly, it is possible to gauge
your progress by how the conversations go. You have a constant by
which to compare interactions, feelings, etc. Of all the things that
helped, these short but regular check-in conversations were among
the most helpful, because unwittingly, they gave me the benefit of
being able to observe my progress, or lack thereof. They granted me
perspective — something money can't buy.

When I returned home, I began working on Alice's eulogy for our
neighborhood MOMS Club newsletter. They had asked if they could
do their September issue in Alice's honor, which touched me deeply.
They had asked moms who knew Alice to write remembrances of her.
Alice, unfortunately, did not know many of the moms because I was a
working mom and couldn't attend many events. I was terrified no one
knew her well enough to properly eulogize her, so I asked if I could
submit something of my own. I began writing the piece "Thank You,
Alice" that night, twenty-two days after my sweetheart passed.

It started as something I thought I should do, but it soon became something I wanted to do and, in fact, felt compelled to do. I knew I had to write "Thank You, Alice." I knew in the very marrow of my bones.

I found writing that piece healing and surprisingly satisfying, or as satisfying as eulogizing your child can be. I suppose the satisfaction was fueled by the knowledge I would finish it. This was noteworthy because I could barely finish folding the laundry at this point. It was also helpful to learn I could still string a sentence together.

Thursday of that week I scheduled a healing day. I saw a Kabbalah teacher, Gahl, and my friend Erin did a ceremony for me and my dear friend J-Do. Gahl spoke about "soul contracts" as the medium's book had. He postulated it was simply Alice's time and had she not died in her sleep, she would have died another way. "The noblest, most peaceful deaths occur in meditation or during sleep. She was two, so meditation wasn't exactly on option. She died the noblest, most peaceful death she could have."

He asked me if I would feel less guilty had she been awake. "No. I would probably have felt worse because I would have had the mistaken notion I could do something about it." "Exactly," he said. He asked if I would feel better if it had happened on someone else's watch. Nope. I would have felt horrible for that person, knowing they would likely never forgive themselves for being in charge while she died. He looked at me with compassion and said, "You have suffered the greatest loss. There are famous psychologists who say a bereaved mother can be — and should be allowed to be — depressed for the rest of her life. But the guilt is optional, and you must learn to let it go. There is nothing you could have done to change this."

There are zero other people who could have said this to me without pissing me off. But for some reason, when Gahl said it, I felt a great weight lift from my shoulders.

Later, my friend Erin led a beautiful ceremony addressing my deep fear I would forget details about Alice's life. Erin presciently planned the ceremony not knowing I was paralyzed by that fear.

I could write an entire chapter on those two events alone, but if I included every detail of everything and everyone who helped me, this book — like my love for Alice — would never end.

Both of those sessions were incredibly powerful, transformative experiences. I felt close to "it," and I noticed I functioned better when I felt close to "it." I was astounded people I did not know very well were able to target my core issues so accurately and precisely and help me find a way to process them. These two experiences helped me move on to a new level in my A.A.D. life.

Although I got very little work done that Thursday, I made progress in my mission to heal myself and to keep trying to find some beauty in my awful experience. I was beginning to make lemonade and that felt good. It was among the most healing days in my journey thus far.

Later that night, I recalled a strange dream I'd had a few months before Alice died. I don't recall my dreams very often, but every once in a while, I will wake up from one, bolt upright, and think, "Whoa!"

IN THE DREAM, *I was a little old woman on my deathbed. I appeared to be in a hospital or some such facility. It was dark, with a little light peeking in from the hallway through the doorway and window. It was one of those dreams where you are looking at yourself, as if you are in the audience watching, rather than seeing it through your own eyes, as if you are there in the action. Grace was sitting by my side, to my right, between my bed and the door to the hallway. Grace looked to be in her sixties or so. I felt incredibly peaceful. My dream-self suddenly panicked and asked Grace, "Where is Alice?" Grace replied, "Alice is right here, Mama." I told her I couldn't see her, still feeling panicked. Grace turned and pointed over her shoulder, behind her, and said, "Mama, she is right there. See?" Suddenly, I saw Alice. But Alice was a toddler. And Alice was not lit the same as Grace and me. Her dimensions were not the same as ours; she seemed bigger or closer to my eyes, despite being located directly next to Grace. And she was in a strange position, like she was almost floating over the bed next to Grace's head. She was still and silent. It was as if someone had Photoshopped a photo of Alice from another era into the scene and failed to even try to make it look cohesive. In the dream, however, I took no offense to any of that and my dream-self lit up when I saw Alice. Grace lit up when she saw me light up. And the three of us smiled peacefully together.*

I woke up, haunted by the dream. And I thought, "Whoa, what was that all about?" In real life, I definitely thought it was strange that toddler Alice seemed Photoshopped into my deathbed scene where Grace and I were definitely elderly, but I didn't know what to make of it.

THE NIGHT after my "big healing day," my stomach churned for suddenly, out of the blue, I recalled that dream and knew what it meant. I knew that the dream meant Alice would not be at my deathbed, and, in fact, would always be a toddler. It made my heart ache and my head spin. It became another thing to feel guilty about: "I should have known what it meant, and then I could have done something to prevent it."

Bollocks, I know. I was doing much better, but The Guilt still had some claws in me.

Monday, I still woke up sad, but I didn't wake up feeling like I was going to puke and cry simultaneously. It was the first day I would return to teaching Janet — who had hosted the luncheon after Alice's service — at the Pilates studio she preferred.

As I sat waiting for Janet to arrive, one of the other teachers walked up to me, patted my thigh, and said, "Oh, good, you're all better now."

I stared, dumbfounded.

She patted me again, putting her face close to mine. "You're all better, now, right?"

I stammered that I was hanging in there, but not sure if I could be considered "all better." This was less than a month after Alice had died, mind you.

She patted my shoulder then: "But you're all better, right?"

Apparently, she was simply going to insist I was all better until I agreed. I couldn't talk. I just stared.

"You have to be strong, now. You have to move on. You're all better now," she said as she walked away.

As if her words alone could cure me.

I stared at the other teachers, Olivia and Maria, to see what their faces registered. Perhaps I was being too sensitive? The other teachers had tears in their eyes. Olivia came over and hugged me silently. She couldn't talk either. She cried and shook her head.

The "all better" teacher is a parent. I found the entire scenario shocking. Did she honestly think she would be "all better" less than a month after her child died? Really? *Really?*

Another piece of unsolicited advice: Do not tell me how to heal. Do not tell me to be strong. Do not tell me I'm "all better." Do not tell me how to grieve, period. Do not tell me I "have to be strong for Grace." I am strong, dammit. You have no idea how strong I am. Do not tell me how to do anything, frankly. No one can possibly know what this is like unless it has happened to them, and every story, every person is different so even then, people have to heal in their own way. It's beautiful to be concerned. It is wonderful to ask how I am, if I need anything, etc. But if you want me to shut down to you, tell me how you think I should be doing my healing.

As I pondered my internal dialogue after this encounter, I realized I was capable of self-advocacy as well as not engaging in unnecessary drama. This is when I first realized I was going to be OK. So, in a way, I have to thank the "you're all better" teacher. I was not all better, and that was OK, and accepting that I was not all better is, ironically, what would lead me to become better than ever, broken heart and all.

Later that day, I finished "Thank You, Alice" at work between patients. I found that process cathartic and strangely uplifting. Any port in a storm. It had been 102° over the weekend, so naturally our air conditioner went out. (I am not my best self in the heat.) Not wanting to interrupt my flow, I lay on the vintage tile floor in the bathroom, in my underwear, hair in a topknot so it wouldn't touch my shoulders, sweating my brains out while I typed my daughter's memorial piece into my older-than-Methuselah laptop. I wanted nothing to touch me. I wished I could float naked in the air because the thought of one more thing touching me made me feel as if I would suffocate. In the end, neither heat nor emotionally crippled teachers could stop me; I was undaunted. I sweated, and I typed.

To say it is surreal to write your child's memorial piece is the most understated understatement. I sat there, thinking, "I can't believe I am doing this. I cannot believe my life has led me to a place where this is necessary." But I felt compelled to do it. I had to honor my baby.

In the aftermath of losing my child to sudden, unexpected death, reality became very tenuous. The only thing that seemed real was love. And I felt like the best way I could love Alice now was to properly eulogize her.

Writing that first piece was healing, and I wanted to heal. Well, part of me wanted to heal. Another part felt that if I healed, I was abandoning Alice. Luckily, the wiser part of me knew this was nonsense, but there was still a war raging within me. I could observe this war inside me as if I were a foreign correspondent and not the soldiers. How? No idea. I knew the part of me who knew I needed to heal had to win, so I did all I could to facilitate that. I decided to keep writing and to start a blog, so I had somewhere to continue the writing I found healing.

There were other reasons for wanting to write the blog. I wanted to write it for Grace. She was four years old when this happened. What do you remember about being four? Not much, right? I want her to remember her sibling, I want her to know what happened to her family, and I knew before long, I wouldn't remember all the vivid details. I want Grace to have her history available to her when she is old enough to want to know. I want her to know Alice's history, and mine.

Also, I didn't have enough breath with which to verbalize the story in those early days and years. Talking was exhausting. I didn't, and don't, mind sharing the information, but I didn't have enough breath with which to do it. I feel my loved ones, my neighbors, my family, and anyone who cares deserves to know, for they loved Alice — and me — also.

Lastly, I remember sitting across from people in those early days — and in recent days too, truth be told — and seeing their utter shock and horror. I could see "I have no idea what to say" written all over their faces. I could tell they wanted to ask what happened but were not sure if it was OK to ask. I could tell they wanted to know out of a desire to support, not morbid curiosity. I could tell they, in fact, *needed* to know, because they needed to learn to cope with Alice's death also. They needed to know what happened because they needed to know if their two-year-old was going to die for no good reason. They needed to know how I was so that they could best support me; I clearly saw their strong desire to *do something — anything —* to help. The old me would have shunned the help. The new me knew this was too big to do alone.

I wrote for Grace. I wrote to save my breath. I wrote to help myself, and in doing so I have come to realize it has helped some others as well. I figured if I could help even one other person beside myself while honoring Alice and documenting history for Grace, it was something I absolutely must do.

Mothering in Memoriam was selected as the blog title after running a couple of names past my friend Ramsay. It just came to me. I didn't love it at first, but I didn't have anything better and I knew I needed to get going, before I chickened out and didn't share the writing at all. Now, I like the name. It reminds me I am always Alice's mother and Grace's. And though I can still care for Grace's body, mind, and soul, I now can only care for Alice's soul, and maybe not even that. I can, however, take care of her legacy. I can take care of how Grace will relate to the memory of Alice. So I write to care for Alice in the one of the few ways I can think to do so. I write to nurture her legacy and her relationship to her only sibling.

I didn't realize it then, but this was the week where my desire to heal and efforts to do so consumed more time than any self-punishing thoughts. This was the week I truly began to make lemonade as well as the week I began to attempt to make toast. The time spent on what

I found healing belied an inner urge to move forward even though my thoughts tried to tell me doing so abandoned Alice. Healing meant accepting Alice lived in the past. It is not easy to leave your child's life in the past; the maternal instincts fight this tooth and nail. Allowing yourself to focus on healing cannot be taught or rushed: it must happen organically.

I didn't know it then, but this was the week I got my kitchen ready, so to speak. I had all the ingredients, all the tools, and I was beginning to experiment with how to use them to make the best lemonade and toast possible. But the shock prevented me from tasting them, much less enjoying them.

That would come much later.

You can't taste it until you figure out how to make it.

WEEK 5: THE FLOATING

$\mathcal{M}$y sense of time was still experienced through the lens of Tuesdays, though I cried less upon waking and realizing what day it was. Perhaps I was running out of tears?

I DID NOT and have not run out of tears; they fall less frequently and on different occasions.

IN RETROSPECT, I realize this was the week I stopped remembering every single detail of every single day, which was somewhat freeing. I knew it meant I was beginning to emerge from shock just a bit — emphasis on "a bit." I know now I was in some degree of shock for many months. By shock, I mean true psychological and physiological shock, and not the term that gets bandied about when a television series does not end as predicted.

I do know I was still "singing Alice to sleep" many nights at this point, but I became aware I was beginning to do so out of a sense of duty rather than an inner need, so I contemplated letting this night-time habit go. It is incredibly difficult to abandon every daily habit involving your child. I still remembered her walking into my room in the morning, saying, "Up-a, Mama, up-a!" while pressing her open palm toward the ceiling. I still felt like there was an incredible hole in the family because, let's face it, there was.

One day, I came across Alice's favorite shoes — the light-up shoes she received from Teresa and Sal for her birthday days before she passed. I turned them over and saw the dirt stuck in the treads. I sat there, transfixed. How could the dirt from only eleven days of wear be there, but not the wearer of the shoes? How could she just be *gone*, poof? The mind is not equipped to deal with this kind of thing. The heart is even less equipped. You just have to pray your soul and divine providence will pull you through.

I dissolved into tears.

I didn't fight them, however, and then they didn't last long. I'd noticed they only lasted a long time if I fought them. If I tried to reckon with them, or justify them, or stop them, it became difficult to stop the tears. If I let it rip, it didn't take long at all to move past the tears. I was able to be sad without being debilitated when I relaxed, went limp, and let it roll through me like a storm. I could tell I stumbled across a vital tool for myself.

That Tuesday, I was home alone for a spell in the midday and had another panic attack. Again, I was doing some mundane chore when it came on. Again, it dissipated relatively quickly, but was debilitating while active. I was breathless, sweating, unable to focus, and my heart was pounding out of my chest. I drew a bath; the water always helped.

"Thank You, Alice" was published in our local MOMS Club newsletter the following day and I posted the link to my social media pages. I received so many notes of appreciation and support, not only from neighborhood moms and my friends but also from many people I didn't know. In the early weeks, I did feel some guilt on the rare occasion I could get to a place where I celebrated the life she lived rather than grieved the life she lost. But writing "Thank You, Alice" was indeed my very first step toward being able to celebrate her sweet, short life without feeling guilty.

In my writing, as well as in experiencing my feelings, I seemed to be able to shuck aside any notion of what I "should" do or feel. "I should write daily, I should do this faster, I should do it by this method. Or is this method better? I should do more …"

For reasons unknown, I didn't "should" myself during this time. I don't know why. It isn't like me, to be honest. But for once, I allowed things to come out how they came out. This has turned out to be a gift. A gift I wish I would have attained another way, but a gift none-theless.

It feels pretty great to suddenly observe yourself giving yourself a break from the "shoulds."

I wrote when inspiration came. No pressure, no judging myself. Why didn't I do this years ago? And why was I suddenly able to do it at this point? I have no idea. I only know it saves a lot of damn time and energy and I hope I never forget this lesson.

ONCE I AM WRITING, *however, I usually find myself in a sort of flow, and I ride it until it stops. I take a short break. I try it again. Sometimes it flows again. Sometimes it doesn't. When it doesn't, I walk away and don't give it a second thought.*

BY THURSDAY, I was completely exhausted and felt like I had to literally drag my body through life. Grace and I took a train to San Diego to see my awesome stepsister Sarah and her wonderful hubby Jeff. Grace loves taking the train and so do I. But no one loved trains more than Alice. Once we were chugging along, I realized Alice never got to go on a "real" train. The thought sickened me. I tried to console myself: "She will always be with you, and is here with you on this train now." But let's face it, I don't think anyone in the throes of fresh, unexpected, grief believes that or finds it helpful. Maybe they do. I didn't. I imagined her running through the aisles. I cried.

Sarah picked us up from the station and we went to Old Town for lunch. We sat next to a bay window with an elaborate Día de los Muertos diorama. Sarah asked me if it bothered me, and I said it did not. I still did not equate Alice with death at that level, I guess. I knew she was dead but did not think of her as dead. I know that makes no sense, but it is the truth so there it is.

And I took that to mean that yes, I suppose she *was* still with me. I wished to God I could hug her. And truly take her on a train.

Sarah and I spoke of my experience with the beetles and the butterflies. We talked about how other people equate finding bird feathers in the house or on the doorstep as messages from the dead, and how birds in general were thought to portend death in the house. You know, light lunch conversation. She was eager to hear about my session with the Kabbalah teacher. As I began to tell her about it, I felt something above my head, heard a whoosh, and then everyone in the restaurant gasped, including Sarah.

"Oh, my God, Melissa. A bird flew right out of that diorama and right over your head!" Sarah gasped in disbelief.

The bay windows were not open, meaning that bird had sat through my entire conversation about birds and death before flying over me.

"Well, hello, Alice," I said.

The following day was the one-month anniversary of Alice's death. I had to count in months now? I didn't want to count in months; it made me feel hopeless.

One month since she had rested her head on my shoulder. I felt an indescribable heaviness. I was able to get out of bed, but it was a pretty rough way to start the day. Knowing the significance of the day, my friend Tommy texted me early that morning to make sure I was OK. His morning texts were quite helpful, because the mornings were still the hardest and his texts were always sunny. If I was sad, we'd exchange messages about that, but he always started sunny, and by this point in the Aftermath, I found that helpful. He honored my sadness when it was there, but he always gave me a chance to be happy first, without ever judging me if I was not able to be sunny in return.

When you are in an abyss, one of the kindest things a person can do for you is sit on the lip of the abyss, shine a light down for you, see

146

if you can get out by your own steam, and speak to you kindly while you try to get out. This works most of the time and has the added benefit of building self-confidence, which is often destroyed in the newly bereaved. For me, it is not as helpful for someone to dive right in after me because then we are both stuck, and I feel guilty for sucking someone else down.

THIS HAS TAUGHT *me not to jump in the abyss for friends who are suffering. Sometimes, I catch myself starting to do this before correcting course.*

MY FRIEND'S sunny texts were like a light reminding me of the way out, without judging or instructing me how to get there. He was simply being himself, and this helped remind me who I was in return.

In my texts to Tommy that morning, I said the grief came in waves, just as "they" said it would. There are also moments of anguishing guilt and regret. There were also moments where water gushed out of my tear ducts with no sobbing, mainly because there was no energy with which to cry; all I could do was make water, it seemed. But there were also waves of immense peace, some of the most peaceful moments of my life. I felt slow and reflective and like I had profoundly changed — a baseline emotional description that seems to always be there to this day. I told him, and so many others, that I knew the "grieving process" (still hate that term; insert Archie Bunker raspberry here) is a lifelong thing, mainly because I knew Grace would process it differently over the years. She was still so little.

In any event, Tommy — a lieutenant colonel and a federal agent — said my feelings of peace, coupled with the waves of anxiety I had experienced, reminded him of a conversation he had with a colleague who had PTSD (post-traumatic stress disorder).

PTSD? I hadn't thought of that. I guess I thought it was reserved for people who had seen villages annihilated, gone to war, had endured torture, etc. But when Tommy mentioned his friend, my brain began to connect some dots. I was familiar with PTSD because of my job. I recalled "intrusive images" of the traumatic event were a hallmark of PTSD, and I definitely had trouble with that: check. I recalled executive functioning is diminished in PTSD: check. I recalled anxiety, insomnia, and hyper-vigilance are associated with PTSD: check. And I recalled overwhelming guilt and/or shame are often found in folks with PTSD: check.

"Shit!" I thought. "I have PTSD. I don't have time for PTSD." Later, when discussing this with a therapist after being evaluated, I said I was surprised I had PTSD. I thought it took something worse than what I had gone through to develop PTSD. The therapist looked at me with caring eyes and said, "Oh, Melissa. I think finding your beloved child dead in her crib, performing CPR on her knowing she is probably already gone, is more than enough trauma to spark PTSD." I relayed this to Tommy. He empathetically replied, "I know guys who have seen horrific acts of war and all of them would say what happened to you was worse."

Shit. This was not a contest I wanted to win. Maybe Tommy was only trying to make me feel better about my crumbling psyche, but he's not one for bullshit.

I did not love the idea of having PTSD. It made me feel like a weakling. I know it does not make one a weakling, but it made me feel like one, and I knew I could not raise Grace the way I wanted to raise her if I *felt* like a weakling, whether I was or not. I was also aware many people with PTSD felt weak for having PTSD, and I wanted to do my part to change the stigma. This meant I had to address the PTSD within myself.

That evening, I tried to be with Sarah and Jeff and drink craft beer, but I couldn't because it felt like I ate a tray of donuts before I drank one-third of the beer. I mean, damn, that stuff is filling. And the next day was *sad*. Far sadder than most. I realized some sad days were preceded by an obvious prompt and some weren't. I started to piece together that the especially sad days were preceded by the intake of wine or beer. I never had much, mind you, but any amount seemed to activate a down day.

Therefore, I realized I needed to stick to vodka, and even then, no more than two glasses. This was not hard because I didn't — and don't — drink daily anyway. I had enough actual reasons to be sad. I felt it irresponsible to do anything that would knowingly make it worse.

To this day, I rarely drink wine or beer; I can tell they make my next day extra-griefy.

THE TRAIN RIDE home was easier than the train ride there, but home was full of tension during this time. Losing a child brings up so many different conflicting emotions for the affected parties, and it can be hard, if not impossible, to manage them all well.

The loss of a child feels like an internal explosion. I recalled sitting outside the night Alice died, feeling like there were neon meteors soaring through a massive hole in my heart. I felt very still, but like I was exploding open at the same time — as if I was completely stationary while an internal meteor released and ripped me open. I am sure this explosion is too much for some. There is no explaining why the explosion might seem easier for some to manage than others. There are no other life skills that can predict your performance in this area. There is no way to know how'll you do/be/react until you go through it. You may think you know, but you don't, I assure you.

Some dive into the explosion. Some learn to relax through it. Some run from it. Some try to reason with it. Some ignore it. Some try to freeze it out. Some try to dampen the signal through overwork or overeating or drugs or any number of numbing activities. Some try to outwit it or overpower it. These last two groups seem to suffer more than any of the aforementioned, from what I have observed. The suffering may be delayed, but it seems to be more intense. This is simply my observation after talking to many bereaved parents. Maybe it is because this is something so much bigger than you, so much bigger than anything your cocky little brain has ever been prepared to handle, there is no chance you can outwit or overpower the loss.

For me, the loss of Alice immediately seemed like a force I wasn't

149

going to defeat by willpower, cunning, or evasion. I somehow knew I was going to have to dive in, completely surrender, play dead, and slowly reveal myself as alive as I slowly became acquainted with my enemy, until the point at which I could walk away victorious from an enemy unharmed.

That was, and still is, the only path I could see that could get me to a place where I knew I could survive in a world where *this* had become my story: Dive in quick, relax, and let it deal *with me.* It was clear that surrendering was the key to truly being alive and not simply existing. If I had to be alive, I did not want to simply exist — parent, work, consume, clean, rinse, repeat — every day for the rest of my life. If I had to be alive without Alice, I knew I had to do more than exist; I had to become a better me and leave the world a better place. I didn't know what else to do.

I could not then, and still cannot to this day, believe that this is part of my story. No one ever, *ever* expects losing an innocent child to be part of their story, a part of the world in which they have to spend the rest of their life. The loss of a child catapults the entire rest of your life in an entirely different direction, abruptly, with incredible force, and at the speed of light. It is an intense experience thrust upon you, with no warning, and no possible training. It is sink, swim, or float. I had to float, to release into it. I knew that, for me, I wouldn't have a life worth living otherwise.

Sinking has obvious drawbacks. Swimming could work, except I was too stunned to swim, and besides, I had no idea what I was supposed to swim toward. What is the goal in the aftermath of losing a child? Staying alive? Getting out of bed? Remaining sane? Becoming productive? Seriously, what is the goal? I guess it is different for everyone, and I still did not know what my goal was at this point, other than I knew I had to be a good mother for my living child, create a legacy for my deceased daughter, to become a better person, and leave my little corner of the world better than I found it.

This is not to say swimming or sinking are wrong. I am positive many have survived the loss of a child one of the other two ways. I knew I personally had only the float option. It was crystal clear to me, then and now. I knew I had to release into it to eventually rise above it. I had to let go and let it do its thing to move on. *The only way through it is through it. The only way through it is through it.* There is no running around it. No hiding. Float.

There are certainly other people who have fallen in these waters, but no two have ever landed in the exact same patch of sea, so you cannot possibly judge. Or predict. The sea is not the same for different people, nor does it remain the same for any individual.

You may think you know how you would handle it, but you don't. Should you find yourself in the Sea of Child Loss you will realize pretty quickly nothing could have predicted your reaction. You will surprise yourself every minute of every day. It can be tiring. OK, it is completely exhausting, who am I kidding? But it is also an opportunity to gain some insight into yourself, so it seems like you'd better seize the day. I recall thinking, "I have to deal with this *now*, while it is fresh, while I have support, because it will not get easier if I do not deal with it, and by then I will likely not have all of this support."

Most folks say, "I couldn't do it." But you know what? You could. It sucks. It sucks a big fat bag of hair. It is truly awful, but you would do it, because you have no choice. It might take a while — it may take your entire lifetime — but you would.

There is a clarity in those early days of unexpected loss, which is pretty damn surprising. At least it is as close to clarity as I have ever felt. Everything was "yes" or "no." I found myself moving easily and steadily past the few "maybes" that popped up. "The question will pop up again," I reasoned, "and I'll deal with it when I have more information and/or a clear answer."

I had my yeses, my noes, my maybes, and I walked through them all in a daze. For once in my life — for the most part — I did not prolong my decision-making to agonizing lengths.

This occasional pellucid insight and decision-making was a gift of grace, I believe. A consolation gift, I suppose. "Here is a whopper of a tragedy that will make you question your very existence, but here is a remarkable level of clarity with which to process it. Use it wisely," was the message I seemed to be getting.

I still have flashes of that lucidity from time to time, but the depth of clarity amid shock is incomparable. We, as a species, cannot endure it forever, however it seems. It is too much for the brain, I guess. The brain cannot handle what the heart must endure.

It is important to remember the shock is temporary. Should one lose the point of the lesson, one recalls one lost one's two-year-old child for no good reason and the knowledge that all is temporary comes back to slug you square in the face.

I was being burst open upon a raging sea and my brain couldn't catch up. So I tried to allow the rough seas to take me where they may. This can lead one to question reality, and that can be scary. But it was not nearly as scary as I would have guessed. It just *was*. I didn't have the energy to fight it. So I floated.

I AM in a much different place today. I still cry, sure, but the tears are generally short-lived. Every now and then I experience an extended storm. I still have moments where I think, "I cannot believe this happened," but that thought doesn't bring me to my knees. I still have moments where I suddenly feel punched in the gut. But now it feels like a quick, gentle, cleansing storm passing quickly through town, rather than the tsunami it felt like in the early days. I suppose the explosion is complete, and I am here, floating.

WEEK 6: THE PHOENIX

*T*he damn eye spasm awakened me to another Tuesday. I am sure I cried every day at this point, but I wasn't lying in bed sobbing for hours. Mostly I cried while I swept the floor, or made dinner, or drove the car. I was moving and crying. It came in waves.

STILL DOES.

AT THIS POINT, I was actively trying to not feel dead inside by implementing all my self-care routines. I felt drawn to the spiritual, the philosophical, and the religious, but I was — and am — looking for direct experience. I read less in the year A.A.D. than any other year of my life. In retrospect, I didn't listen to music or watch TV either. Maybe you don't need external input when you are very busy sorting out your own personal whopper of an existential crisis. I had, and still have, the urge to be alone a lot. I felt contemplative, reflective, quiet. I pondered. I paced.

Some of my friends helped me with my commitment to laugh every day; they sent funny video clips, told me stories, or were just plain funny. Laughter releases tension. Laughter after tragedy releases immense amounts of tension. But it does more than that; it helps one gain a perspective — one that is likely more positive or lighter — outside of the tragedy, which can otherwise become all-encompassing. The ancient Greeks paired the masks of tragedy and comedy to show the full spectrum of human emotion — living with only one mask is to deny a good deal of our human experience. I say comedy is one of the few consolation gifts of tragedy: I tried to slap it on my face when possible.

Grace had a rough morning that Tuesday. She was acting out. Once she calmed down, she asked, out of the blue, if the balloons we released reached Alice in heaven. I told her I wasn't sure, but I was pretty sure she knew we sent them, and that I was sure it made her happy. Grace sighed and said, "Well, I bet she is always happy now, but we are sad."

And there you have it: *BOOM.* I had no idea where she came up with this stuff. But she was right. This brings up an important topic: balancing one's legitimate grief with the belief your loved one is fine, perhaps even better than fine.

I *knew* Alice was in a better place. I knew it in my bones. And I know it was not wishful thinking, because I was fully self-flagellating myself with guilt.

You can spend your entire life thinking you know what your religious/ philosophical/ spiritual beliefs are, but I am telling you, until something this big happens to you, you are only speculating and/or regurgitating what you've been previously fed. A loss this big shows you immediately what you truly believe. It all comes into laser-like focus, or at least it did for me. Some of the things I thought I believed I found I did, in fact, believe. Some things I came to realize I believed were surprising. Some things I thought I thought, it turns out I didn't. How is that for confusing? It sounds confusing as I write it, but in real life it took no time or effort. It was as if my entire "platform" on life, death, religion, and the afterlife suddenly bubbled to the surface of my consciousness in a pretty little package. "Ta-da!" it seemed to shout.

I had not yet prepared my platform for a four-year-old, however.

Shit, I had barely prepared it for forty-four-year-old me. This was somewhat inconvenient because she had a lot of questions. I was doing a lot of winging it and we were somehow carrying on.

A good chunk of my life since childhood has been spent researching comparative religions, philosophy, mystical traditions, myths, and esoterica. I studied everything from Kabbalah to the Tao Te Ching, from existentialism to nihilism. I did everything from a Great Books course at the University of Chicago to various yoga teacher trainings in LA and India, to a class in Gnosticism at the Philosophical Research Society and meditation classes at the Self-Realization Fellowship in LA, to online courses on everything from the Stoics to feminine embodiment. Some beliefs/tenets/theories seemed "truer" to me than others, but I read and studied other points of view with an open mind. In the past, I never felt like I had a fully formed personal view of religion/theology, and that didn't bother me in the least. I looked at it like a lifetime project — I still do. But in the wake of losing my precious daughter, I have come to know some things that I truly do and do not believe.

There are things you can know in your head, things you know in your heart, and things you know in your gut. The feeling that Alice was in a perfect place, surrounded by love, and completely safe, was something I felt in my head, heart, and gut all at once. That doesn't happen very often, so I take it as truth. And that truth helped set me free.

You can end up feeling pretty damn selfish when you grieve. It becomes pretty clear you are crying for yourself. Alice doesn't need, or likely even want, my tears. That said, I don't think it's healthy to fight them back or pretend to feel other than the way I truly feel. So I relax and let the tears rip when they come and don't judge myself for them, nor do I grab or hold on to them like some kind of macabre trophy I earned for living after loss.

I suppose I knew she was *OK*, and I was stunned to hear Grace say she knew the same because I had not discussed any of this with her.

As I found myself flailing into another panic attack, I remembered it was Tuesday. It seemed like it came out of the blue yet again. I was shaking so badly it looked like I had Parkinson's disease. Tommy called to check in right after it started. This was the first time I ever took a phone call while having a panic attack. I was embarrassed it was happening, but this one was huge, I was alone, and I was scared. He helped me establish a slower breath pattern and asked what had helped in the past. I told him I wasn't sure what helped, that they seemed to go away after an hour or two, but he recalled I had previously told him about the peace in the bathtub I had experienced, so he gently said, "Maybe you could draw yourself a bath and try to relax in the water after we hang up?" Seems obvious, like I should have thought of it myself, but I didn't.

I realized something else that seems obvious now: All the panic attacks happened on Tuesdays around Alice's naptime or the time I found her, and every Wednesday I was drained beyond comprehension but felt peaceful. Before this realization, it all seemed random. But it wasn't.

Ah. Bizarre. My body remembered even when my mind did not. I was experiencing anniversary symptoms.

Our mind needs to do one thing to recover from tragedy, but it seems our body has to do its thing as well. I was having these anniversary reactions around the time Alice died, on the day of the week she died. Even if I wasn't consciously thinking of it, my body went into hyper-vigilance mode as it did when I found her. It took me a few weeks to collect enough data points to sort this out, but there it was.

Not once was I thinking of "the event" when the attack would come on; it seemed to come out of nowhere. I would bend down to get the mail or something, and *instantly* become shaky, sweaty, with my heart pounding and my stomach in knots. And then I realized, it happens when I bend over — at the time and on the day of the week she died — because I was bending over to lift her when I realized she was dead.

.

I WOULD LATER LEARN in Peter Levine's work that shaking is a natural response to trauma and may prevent PTSD. If shaking is impeded at that

*time of the trauma, the likelihood of developing PTSD is increased. I hoped
my shaking was a sign I was processing the grief.*

THAT FRIDAY WAS A HUMDINGER.

As I started the laundry that day, I realized I'd been using the same
bottle of OxiClean spray since before Alice died. My heart fell into my
feet. A bottle of OxiClean barely lasted ten days while Alice roamed
this earth while stuffing her face with blueberries and yogurt, rolling
around in grass, and drawing on her clothes. OxiClean removed all
those stains, but it couldn't remove the pain left in the absence of the
source of all those stains.

Grace had been at her preschool for over two years. Alice had
joined her there the previous February. They had both had many
beautiful days there. We had planned to switch Grace to a different
school before Alice died. But, in the wake of her sister's death, I
wondered if it was a good idea. Maybe another giant change would
not be good for her right now? But maybe a change of scenery would
be good for her? I debated this internally for a while before I decided
to just ask Grace. Little Grace had opinions, so might as well hear
what they were on this issue since my inner jury was hung.

Grace wanted to go to the new school, six weeks after losing her
sister. Grace is indomitable.

The kids at school loved when my girls would bring bouncy
houses on their birthdays, so I sent one to the school for her going-
away party.

I stayed to watch the bouncy house frenzy a little, but we had just
sent one for Alice's birthday and it was too painful to watch for long.
Plus, I had a huge workday. I did always enjoy being there while the
bouncy house company inflated the bouncy house, however. All fifty-
plus kids from the school would come outside to watch, screaming,
laughing, and shaking like teenage girls who'd spotted the Beatles.

Later, I worked. I did my taxes. My executive functioning skills
were basically nonexistent, but I somehow was able to do this.

The coroner called. I was not expecting this. They had said it might be a few months before all the lab results were finished. I panicked. I was doing much better in the guilt department, but this call let me know I was not fine. I went into a tailspin as I listened to the message. I was afraid to hear what they might have to say. I was terrified I could have done something to prevent her death. I was not sure there was anything they could say to make me feel better. I was completely consumed with dread and guilt. And profound sadness. And the emptiness of loss.

I returned the call, shaking and alone.

The coroner said that, so far, they had still found nothing — as she'd suspected would be the case — and that microbiology and neuropathology tests were pending. I sighed a heavy sigh of relief, which may seem odd; I was surprised myself. My family and friends had said they hoped the coroner would have something definitive to offer, thinking this would ease my guilt. But I knew by my reaction there was nothing they could find that would ease my guilt. I knew anything they did find would be used by my brain to whip up the guilt. And I wasn't sure I could live with the amount of guilt I was currently carrying, much less any additional guilt. For me, at that time, not knowing was the least excruciating of all potentialities.

As I have said before, the lack of a logical reason for Alice's death sort of forced me into the spiritual; it felt like this was where I was supposed to go in the wake of her death. I have been a student of science. I was a research tech at a major teaching hospital. I slayed statistics class. I have always enjoyed digging for answers. But when the world offers no answers, and all the potential answers would make one feel like shit, that leaves looking inside.

I went way down deep inside.

That night, I found out we lost a significant source of income. It felt like I was getting hit from all sides. I thought of Madonna Badger, the Sandy Hook parents, Holocaust survivors, and the African moms whose daughters were kidnapped, and soldiered on. But I was so tired. A tired that sleep alone cannot remedy.

Over the weekend, we went to Family Art Day at LACMA.

The featured exhibit was in the religious art section and was truly impressive. We ended up walking through the entire gallery, which was fine by me. I personally love religious art, from any religion. As we entered the Egyptian art area, I spotted what I was reasonably certain was a mummy. It did not occur to me the art museum would have a mummy, but there it was. As I pondered what to do about that — Grace had never viewed a mummy and her sister had just died — Grace walked right up to it. "Here we go," I thought.

"Is this guy died (sic)?" Grace asked.

"Yes, honey."

"Is he very old?"

"Well, I don't think he was very old when he died, but the body is old."

"The body has been here a very long time, after he died? How long?"

"Well, they used to do a special preparation, so the body would not fade away after the person died. The Egyptians were good at that and kept the wrapped bodies in amazing tombs. This body has been like this for about three thousand years! Isn't that amazing? Three thousand! Someone from this museum went to Egypt and brought back a mummy so that kids like you could learn about it."

Grace stared and pondered. Then she waved her hand up and down the glass encasement and asked, "So is this what we are going to do with Alice, Mama?"

I simultaneously teared up, felt my heart break, and stifled a soft laugh.

"No, honey. That is not what we are going to do with Alice."

"But that would sure get some tongues waggin'!" I thought. "That would *really* get the neighbors talkin'."

I silently recited, "Please don't ask me what we did with Alice's body right now, please don't ask me what we did with Alice's body right now."

She did not ask.

Phew.

Then she asked what heaven was like. No easy questions for Mama today!

Sometimes, when I don't know the answer to her question — and nor does anyone else — I like to turn it back on her and ask her what *she* thinks, because ninety-nine percent of the time, it's more interesting than any other theory I have previously heard. "You know, I'm not sure, honey, because if I have been there before, I don't remember it. What do *you* think it's like?" I asked.

She tapped her bottom lip as she stared out the window and said, "Ummmmmm, something like Target, I think."

I laughed. Because, *come on*. Target is sort of like a capitalist heaven.

Later that night, while I lit the candles on Alice's altar on the mantel and cried, I thought about how many great people surrounded me. I closed my eyes for a moment and recalled the massive amounts of support I'd been blessed to receive. When I opened my eyes, I stared at her poster-sized picture: Alice in her pool full of water and balls looking sweetly up at her people, none of whom had a clue she would die ten days later.

I LOOK at the picture all the time, and she looks so real. I can see every detail of her perfect little ear. My brain still can't sort out why I can't reach up and pull her out of there and into a towel in my arms.

THAT MONDAY, Grace started her new school. One of her best friends, Elle, was a student at the school, and Grace seemed excited about going. I knew she'd be shy at first, but if she was excited, I was excited. Grace has always been eager to meet new people and have new experiences, but she approaches them with caution, which is probably wise. As her mother, I find this very relaxing. Alice was not shy. Alice got right in there. But she only allowed a few people to hold her. *Look, laugh, talk, but don't touch* seemed to be Alice's motto.

As I drove to the new school, I remembered I'd been mentally preparing over the summer for a two-school drop-off again, having enjoyed a one-stop drop-off for over six months. I immediately felt guilty about agonizing over such things, because I would give anything to have a two-school drop-off today, and every day.

Once The Guilt starts, it is so difficult to stop. I had to — have to — force myself to change trains of thought.

As we walked in, I realized we knew no one but Elle's family at this school, so no one knew about Alice. I wondered what to do about that. On the one hand, I realized how much easier it was to walk into a room where no one knew what happened. I was treated like everyone else. In the beginning, it was disorienting to me to be in a room where no one knew. As time passed, however, there was some relief in it. Because people who knew stared, looked uncomfortable, and turned to me with eyes that seemed to beg me to tell them what to say and what to do — and being who I am, I then felt obligated to manage the situation. To put them at ease. To be truthful in my feelings but create an environment where they felt comfortable with me. I felt like it was my responsibility to set the tone of the conversation all the time. And, you know, it is probably best for the bereaved to be allowed to set the tone, but it is a responsibility nonetheless, and in the beginning, you feel so very overwhelmed already.

Being on the receiving end of stares of wonder, horror, pity, and confusion all mixed up was a lot to take. I don't blame them. I don't judge them. I'm sure I'd have done the same if the roles were reversed. But I didn't know what to do with it. I felt like my identity, which had taken forty-four years to emerge, had suddenly become reduced to "that poor lady whose two-year-old died in her sleep." It's a very strange experience to realize the way people view you has changed so drastically overnight. And this is nothing compared to realizing the fact your identity *did* change overnight, through no fault of your own — at least, I prayed it was no fault of my own. I no longer had two children running around. I was no longer potty-training a toddler. My daughter no longer had a living sister. I no longer had a "normal" life story.

I wondered if this is what famous people felt like, after they got famous: everyone staring at you, not knowing what to say to you, counting on you to set the tone. Feeling like your *perceived* identity has changed, despite feeling very much like the same person. I always thought fame would be a very strange ride. And if it's anything like my experience A.A.D., yet magnified on a national or international level, then, yikes — it must be quite a head-trip.

I knew I didn't want to only be "the poor lady who'd lost her daughter" the rest of my life. Nor did I want to bypass the real emotions that needed to emerge in order to be transformed. I didn't want to be a victim, but I also knew I could not pretend I was unaffected. I had no idea how I was going to do this; I just made that intention and went on my way.

I thought about this one day as I paced. Tommy called in the middle of this pacing session. He asked if I was OK. I blurted out, "Nope. But I'm going to rise like a phoenix from these mother@#$%ing flames." We were both silenced. I was shocked I'd said that because that thought had never once gone through my brain. Something inside me took over to remind me I had enough ethereal beast in me to survive.

A few minutes later, I heard myself say to him, "I'll tell you what: I am a grown woman now, dammit." I thought I was grown up *before* Alice died, and in some ways, I was, but now I have real, live, big-girl problems. Simultaneously managing the death of a child while raising a living child, financial fragility, running a business while glazed over in paralyzing grief, and marital strain is some grown-up shit. I laughed at myself for thinking I was "grown up" before this.

Because with a thing like child loss, well, you're never the same. The essence of me is the same. But Alice's death polished off the edges. I was softened. I was profoundly vulnerable — maybe the most vulnerable I had ever been in my post-infancy life. It became apparent to me my future strength would not come from the brawn I had used in my youth, but from the vulnerability in my recent adulthood. Realizations like this are at once simple and life-changing. I was no longer a girl. I was a woman. And I *knew* it.

. . .

Look, I can still bring the pain, if I have to survive. And if I'm activated, the brawn returns. But mostly, I feel a strength that comes from surrendering, from being vulnerable. I feel softer but far stronger.

I DECIDED this was all fine by me. They might not allow me to live in LA anymore with this acceptance — embrace, even — of my aging and maturation process, but fuck 'em. I was grown up now whether I liked it or not, because my little girl, she was never growing up. I had to do it for the both of us. And I had to make it good. Really, really good.

Slowly. Softly. Step by step. And with a nap when necessary, because we old vulnerable people like to rest before we burst out of the flames, and we don't see a damn thing wrong with it.

WEEK 7: THE UNSTUCK

*A*lice's ashes lived in my armoire, along with some of Alice's favorite things. Every now and then, I would pull them out. Some days, I'd stare at them in disbelief. Some days, I would hold them on my shoulder, sing "Twinkle, Twinkle" and cry. Some days, I would collapse on the bed, ashes pressed to my heart, and cry for a few minutes. And some days, I would put them near me and go about my business like it was no big deal my daughter's remains were with me. I did what I had to do on any given day and didn't give it a lot of thought, to be honest. On this Tuesday, I held them and cried.

I still didn't care if I was "doing it right." Strike that. At this point, it still had not occurred to me to care if I was "doing it right," or if anyone else thought I was "doing it right." I was focused on remaining sane, functional, and honest in my experience. I was on autopilot and this was a good place for me to be, as it turned out. I wish to God I had learned to operate from this place before and without a precipitating tragedy, but I hadn't. With the benefit of hindsight, I can see I made some good decisions, without haste, while on autopilot.

Who knew?

Later that day, I posted on social media our last Monroe family picture taken at the Grand Canyon at the end of June. I stared at it for a long time. I closed my eyes and tried to go back there. I wanted back in that photo in the worst way. I wanted my dad to call and say we were all going back. The trip had been a great one, but Alice would rarely sleep if she wasn't in an actual bed. So I spent a good portion of that afternoon pushing her around the Grand Canyon, hoping she'd sleep.

She didn't sleep that day and a few weeks later she didn't awaken. The irony cut like a knife dipped in salt and vinegar. But, thanks to my stepsister Mandy, we did get a picture of everyone on my dad's side of the family for the first and last time, so it's a treasure to me. I stared at these photos from only two-and-a-half months prior and wondered how life could change so dramatically in such a short time.

"Thank You, Alice" was published to my newly established blog on this day as well. Though I'd received great support from its publication in the neighborhood newsletter, I was completely bowled over by the response I received after posting it on the blog. I had no idea I would receive that much support, but it helped more than I can explain. Telling my story, and having it heard, is one of the single most healing things I have done since I lost Alice. I knew it was healing me as soon as I started, and I knew I had to keep it up whether I received encouragement or not. *I had to do it.* It was in my bones.

There was another panic attack that Tuesday despite my efforts to outsmart it. It wasn't the worst one I had experienced thus far but it was there, nonetheless.

I'm not sure why I wasn't more proactive about the panic attacks once I realized they were indeed PTSD-induced and that they were cyclical. I was still in shock, so there's that. Also, I suspect I was thinking, "Now that I know they come at the same times, they will stop coming," as if discovering their pattern alone would lessen their power over me. And the panic attack was not as severe that week, which added fuel to my delusional theory.

Grace and I started therapy that night. Grace was fine, but I cried more than I had in days. This made me realize while I had moments where I could press on, grief had not gone anywhere. Grief could pour out and pull me through any open door, my doors being all the practices and supportive people I'd found. So I went through the doors when they opened and let the tears fall. When finished, I walked back through the door and forward down the hallway. It's all I could figure out to do. It seemed to work, so it's a system I uphold to this day.

Like previous Wednesdays, I was exhausted that Wednesday. I went to work anyway. Lying around crying and spending hours wishing things were different didn't seem to make anything different. It was clear to me that going into a "if things were different" rabbit hole did not help, and, in fact, it made things worse. And I'm not sure I needed to lie around crying. I cried in spurts, not long drags. There were many spurts, don't get me wrong.

A lovely mom in our neighborhood, Chaya, took me for Korean massage that week. I vividly remember seeing her in my home the day after Alice died. I remember most of what happened that day, but a few things especially stick out. Seeing Chaya is one of them.

I remember standing in the doorway between the hall and the dining room, about twenty-four hours after Alice died. I was dazed. My eyeballs felt like raw hamburger from crying so much. My tongue hurt, like it had been dragged over gravel. My house was absolutely packed with people.

I looked over my right shoulder and saw Chaya and her husband. Chaya was standing there with her mouth agape, staring at me. I wondered what she was thinking, but not enough to, you know, ask. I stared back for a minute. Eventually I walked over to them. I think we hugged. I am not sure she said anything to me at first. She gave me a baggy full of homeopathic remedies (she is a homeopath, as well as a therapist), in case I was interested. She explained what they were for, and had written down the instructions, which was great, because I was completely incapable of processing lengthy instructions at that time.

I was, in fact, interested in the remedies. I knew immediately after Alice died I wanted to try to do this drug-free, if possible. I wanted pharmaceuticals to be a last resort, not my first stop. Not because I hate Western medicine and definitely not because I think badly of people who need meds. Psychiatric medications have helped many people. I felt like the unexpected death of my child was a legitimate reason to grieve. Grief is a perfectly normal reaction to the death of a child. It wasn't like life was rainbows and bunnies, and I had no idea why I was crying. Grief is not depression. Can it turn into depression? Sure. But Alice's death was fresh. I wanted to see how I did without prescription drugs. They would always be there if I needed support later in my journey. It surprised me how often I had to defend this. There were people in my life, none of whom were medical professionals, who pushed the drugs from day one.

The overwhelming urge to at least try life without the meds was clear. I thought, "If there is ever a time I should be allowed to let my feelings rip, this is the time." I also thought, "If I start on meds from day one, how can I gauge my baseline and my progress, or lack thereof?" It's also generally a bad idea to take meds prescribed by someone who has not earned a medical degree. So, I thought, "Let's try meds last."

As I write that, it sounds like my decision took some time to process. But it didn't. I knew in a flash. Shock, as I've said, makes what is clear for me really effing clear, really effing fast.

In the first few days following an unexpected loss/tragedy, you often don't know how to articulate what you need yet. *You're in shock.* And you know what? No one else knows what's best for you either, so be wary of too much unsolicited advice. The people who have your back give soft suggestions. When I *did* know what I needed, it was something I knew with certainty.

I wanted to feel my feelings. If they became too much, or if I noticed I was becoming nonfunctional, the meds would always be there. For the time being, it seemed that people were willing to let me feel my feelings. I thought, "This is the time to feel whatever I feel. The unmentionable happened. I am entitled to my damn feelings."

And you know what? So are all of you. And if you make different decisions after the unthinkable happens, that is A-OK. What I did, I did *for me*, and what worked for me may not be what works for you. If you want to take meds immediately after the loss of your child, *go for it.* The decisions I made — and make — for myself are not mandated for everyone else. You do you, I'll do me.

(SOME YEARS LATER—IN the middle of a major family health crisis—I did finally try meds. I think they helped?)

IN ANY EVENT, Chaya had given me various homeopathic herbs, but the one I stuck with was a tincture called Star of Bethlehem. It was easy to take. I didn't have to think about it; I just added a couple of drops to my morning hot lemon water.

I think it helped. When there are so many variables shifting in your life at once, it's hard to say definitively what helped and what didn't. It's not like the powers that be issue you some homunculi you can run through other potential scenarios, so you can assess your best move. You are one, and you are all you've got, so you have to trial-and-error it, people, you have to trial-and-error it.

Winging it was my only methodology.

Chaya is the woman who took me for a massage — the second massage I had received since Alice died. It was helpful. I had no idea how much tension I was holding until the gal started working on me. But I was able to release some armor during the massage. I felt so much different after the treatment. Chaya and I had a wonderful talk over tea afterward. She also asked me how I did it, or something to that affect. I can only remember staring blankly, thinking, "I have no idea. Am I 'doing it'? I mean, I don't know if what I'm doing could actually be considered 'it.'"

I still very much felt like I was surfing a wave the best I could, with as little effort as possible. I didn't have it in me then to exert much effort.

Chaya helped me so much, in so many ways. She was one of the folks who referred me to Southern California Counseling Center (SCCC), the sliding-scale counseling center where we sought family therapy, which would turn out to be an enormous contributor to my healing.

Dealing with the physical symptoms of PTSD is as important as dealing with your mental and emotional symptoms, and though I was doing yoga, I had not received much bodywork. Chaya clearly knew this, and she led me to something I considered a luxury, which allowed me to realize it was anything but. For me, bodywork was — and is — crucial. I also fully realize that not everyone has access to affordable, quality bodywork like we do in Los Angeles.

FOR PEOPLE who do not have access to bodywork, I recommend stretching, hugging a pet, tapping, or receiving any sort of caring touch from a trusted friend. I believe trauma treatment requires a somatic component, but more on that later.

THE PEOPLE who helped me fulfill my commitment to self-care allowed my daughter to continue to have a whole mother. A broken-hearted mother, yes, but a whole mother. I can look back now and know that although I was clearly not my best, Grace still had her whole mommy, thank God. And she had a real version of her mommy. And that's all any of us can hope for, because none of us are perfect.

Later that night, after the massage, I noticed I had not experienced a blepharospasm since I had the massage. That was noteworthy, because my eyelid had been in constant spasm for seven weeks.

WITH ONE EXCEPTION, my eyelid has never gone into spasm again.

THOUGH I HADN'T LISTENED to music at all since Alice died, I somehow got stuck on Big Star one day that week. I've been a repeat-ad-nauseum music listener my entire life, but I hadn't listened to music since Alice died. And this was worth noting too because I am an enormous music fan. I suppose I needed silence. I guess my brain, heart, and soul were so busy processing what had happened that I could not take in much external stimuli unless I deemed it essential to my healing and/or functioning.

But on this day, I found myself listening to Big Star's melancholy "Thirteen" repeatedly. I call this practice "going inside the melancholy to purge the melancholy." Purge has "urge" inside it, after all. "Thirteen" seemed like a safe choice because it's melancholy, but it's not about kids dying or anything. Nor is it the kind of song that makes you tear up by the third chord (F you, "Landslide"). But if your kid just died, the lyrics to "Thirteen" suddenly take on a whole new meaning. It kinda tricked me into purging, which was fine. I allowed myself to feel the music and my own feelings deeply. I wept and swayed and wept some more.

After an hour or so, I felt the quiet glimmer of relief and unexpected accomplishment I often felt at the end of such listening sessions in the past. It is a passive yet triumphant feeling. It is as if diving into the melancholy allows its transformation into a new emotional state. Radiohead is also good for this, but Radiohead was too much for me at that time. Big Star is more stripped down.

IN RETROSPECT, *I know this signified I was probably going to be able to avoid slipping into a deep depression. With clinical depression, one often loses interest in things one used to love. I'd dipped my toes back into my passion for music. This was far more significant than I realized at the time. Again, I was just winging it then. But in retrospect, my shock-induced instinct was in good shape. Perhaps this was another lesson in not overthinking things so damn much.*

MONTHS BEFORE ALICE DIED, we had planned an apple-picking trip with my mom and my sweet stepmonster for this particular weekend. I decided we would still go. It was a tradition, and as I have said before, I didn't want Grace to lose all her established traditions after her sister died. Nor did I want to hide my grief from her. I needed to balance grieving Alice with going forward in life. I wanted Grace to see the real me — tears and heartache and all — but I also wanted her to see I was going to do my damnedest to ensure she still had some fun traditions. So I grieved, but I moved. I moved, and I grieved. I wasn't sure what else to do.

I love going to Oak Glen, California, for apple picking in the fall. I love fall and apples and mountains and dirt roads and farmers and bluegrass music, and the whole shebang. And so do/did my kids. The first year we did it, I decided it would be an annual tradition. Oak Glen has several pristine apple farms on a six-mile stretch of mountain road. All the orchards decorate and host activities for the autumn celebrations. In addition to apple picking, there are horse-drawn carriage rides through the orchards, petting zoos, music, make-your-own-cider stands, hay mazes, jumpy houses, and all manner of fun for kids. I adore it. I knew my mom would love it, so we had planned a visit around apple-picking.

In packing for our trip, I realized I did not have to stop myself from packing the diaper bag. This gutted me. Prior to this, there were several times I unconsciously went to grab diapers, wipes, sippy cups, diaper bags or the like. But I didn't need any of those things any longer, and every time I realized this anew, I developed a sinking feeling in my gut and water would literally shoot from my eyes.

That Alice missed this trip caused a huge sinking hole in my gut. She would have been old enough to actually pick apples this year. Regret: Oh, God, regret is one of the more painful emotions in our human experience. I try to avoid it as much as I can, but this regret was unavoidable. Regret is a relentless, cold-hearted bitch. I knew I couldn't go too far into it, for I had just endured possibly the largest source of regret — the loss of a child. There is so much to regret: "I should have done X while she was living, I should have spent more time with her," and on and on and on.

I attempted to redirect my thoughts to a less self-punishing form of mourning. We do not live in a culture that presents us many authentic options, do we? We feel as if we are in uncharted territory, without a compass, a guide, or instructions. We have to figure it out for ourselves and hope for the best.

Once we arrived at the orchard, I felt literally torn in two; I was excited to take Grace and my parents, but I had a heaviness of heart that was impossible to describe. I felt like my head was dragging my body through the mountains I love so much. It was healing to be among them, but the knowledge that this trip had been planned with Alice in mind, but that Alice was not here and never would be again, was so omnipresent it could not be ignored. My head pressed on, but my body knew what my mind was trying to ignore:

ALICE SHOULD BE HERE. *But she is not. And she never will be again.*

I NEVER KNEW how people survived the loss of a child before I lost a child, and I had trouble figuring it out once I had no choice. But I went at it. One foot in front of the other, through the mountains and apple orchards and even the activating bouncy house. The beautiful orchards and mountains seemed like a set. I once again had that feeling I wasn't a part of my surroundings. I felt *The Truman Show* effect again.

ONE OF MY *apples was walking through the trees with me and one had fallen back to the earth.*

ODDLY, I had the unmistakable feeling my body was "waking up" later in the day. It's as if I became aware of my body that day but hadn't noticed we'd been separated. I felt like, "Oh! Hi! There you are! I hadn't noticed you were gone, but now that I think of it, I knew something was off! Welcome back!"

This is mainly of note because I had always been hyper-aware of my body. I have danced since I was two. I've done yoga, and qigong, and tumbling, and Pilates, and all manner of activities that require a strong mind-body connection for my entire life. Yet, in my state of shock, I hadn't noticed that mind and body had become disconnected. I'm not exactly sure what prompted the returned awareness of my body. Was it the massage? Was it just a matter of time? Was it the mountain air? Was it everything? In the end, what matters is this: I had a glimpse of my body again, and I knew this was a good sign.

That sign was good timing too, for I believe the newfound awareness of my body helped negate some of the hopelessness I felt.

It was an act of grace, perhaps.

The skies were quite ominous that day. I recall thinking it looked like tornado weather, which was curious because tornadoes are not a big concern in Southern California. Earthquakes, yes; tornadoes, not so much. I found the ominous skies to be somewhat soothing, to be honest. Finally, the skies reflected my feelings. It felt validating although I knew, of course, the skies didn't give a rip about reflecting my feelings. I'm just saying, when you are going through an existential crisis and every day is sunny, warm, cloudless, and perfect, it gets friggin' annoying.

I wanted the sky to cry with me. I wanted to see Alice's death impacted the very heavens. On this day, the sky matched my feelings, which made me feel at ease, thus transforming my feelings of hopelessness. Thank you, Sky.

Yes, it is enormously selfish, immature — and perhaps even ignorant — to want the skies to match your feelings, but that was the truth of my feelings at that time.

Monday, we went back to the city. Back to school. Back to work. My parents went back to their home. It was harder than usual to say goodbye to my parents this time. It was one of the first days I felt alone. I don't often feel that way because I enjoy being alone at times. I guess even as adults, sometimes we just need our mommy.

When writing this, I saw I began a sea change during week seven. I read this, and saw the following words: *autopilot, winging it, emptiness, hollow, low, sad,* and *down.* The weeks prior were tinged more with pure shock, and what psychologists call a "hyper-vigilant" state that can happen post-trauma.

But I also see words that indicate I was undergoing changes that would help me stave off a deep depression: the reawakening of my body awareness, the release of body armoring, and the return of my interest in music.

It seems I was in limbo at this point. There was diminishing shock, allowing for rising grief, and I was in the state between, like purgatory for those grieving an unexpected loss. From what I hear, you can be in purgatory a helluva long time (pun intended, I couldn't refuse) — just hanging out, stagnant, unchanging. At least something happened in hell; purgatory always sounded worse to me. To be forever trapped in limbo — that's hell to me.

Prior to writing this, if someone would have asked me to identify which week I began to shift from mostly shock to mostly grief, I would have said that the shift started near the beginning of November and was basically complete by Thanksgiving.

But in reading this, I see words that belie an earlier shift. Although I was still in shock, I was becoming unstuck. It's as if the Band-Aid of shock was slowly peeled away, not only exposing the fresh, raw grief and sadness just below its surface, but also allowing the fresh air of awareness and music in there to heal the wound.

WEEK 8: THE LOW BAR

5:30 a.m. I cried my eyes out and wished to God I could have the privilege of waking up with Alice at 5:30 a.m. and felt intense pain and guilt for all the days I lay there praying she would go back to sleep so I could get through the day without sleep deprivation. She went to sleep, all right. She went to sleep so well she never woke up. Clearly, her death was all my fault for praying she'd go back to sleep so I could have a shot at not being a tired, grumpy bitch for a day.

When I told Tommy that I was regularly waking up at that time, unable to go back to sleep, he simply said, "It's Alice telling you to get up and at 'em because you still have a lot to offer the world." I felt a shock go through me.

I wanted to be mad at him, but I couldn't, because I knew he was right. And because he is too kind to be the target of any misdirected anger. And because it helped to hear it, even though it was not what I wanted to hear. I wanted to hear, "You are waking up at 5:30 a.m. because you get a second chance at waking up with Alice," but no one could tell me that because it wasn't possible.

In any event, rather than descend into darkness, I decided to remain grateful for his support. Tommy had demonstrated the courage not to promise me something that wasn't possible.

175

Eventually I decided to let the 5:30 stirrings be a comfort instead of a curse. I do believe it was Alice waking me at 5:30 a.m. God knows it wasn't me, myself, and I: that is truly not my jam. I do believe it was her way of communicating to me from the Great Beyond. But I had to arrive at this decision on my own. I had to go through the terrible feelings of loss and regret and guilt to get to the other side.

The only way through it is through it, and "it" is not all sugar and spice and everything nice.

It was a Tuesday. Alice was born on a beautiful Tuesday morning and died on an otherwise gorgeous Tuesday afternoon. My brain was not consciously thinking of this, but my body remembered all too well. Images of her face as I pulled her out of the crib would occasionally consume me while I made dinner, leaving me breathless. The mind-body connection is a wonder, and what happens when a trauma severs that connection is *no joke.*

On this Tuesday, I thought I would try to trick my nervous system into submission. I decided to meditate around the time Alice died to activate my parasympathetic nervous system (rest and digest), thus inhibiting my sympathetic nervous system (fight or flight). It wasn't a bad idea; it's just not as easy as that, as it turns out. I decided to accept my sweet friend Jeanne's kind offer to come to the house to guide me in a meditation that Tuesday afternoon.

As we started, I realized I lay down exactly where I had performed CPR on Alice. My body started to panic and my heart started to race once I realized the connection. I remained committed to my experiment on myself, however, so I refused to move. Why? I guess it was part of the "dive right in" approach I found myself undertaking. At the time, I didn't consider why I'd picked that place, but now that I understand PTSD on a deeper level, I get it. I thought, "I have a meditation teacher here. Let's see if we can get me back on track without avoidance."

The meditation helped tremendously. I still became hyper-aroused that day, but it was nowhere near the panic attack levels of weeks past. Later, when I felt my heart rate increase, I got in the tub, which also helped. I thought I was on track to gaining stability, and on my way to a panic attack-free life.

Tommy checked in on me via text again this day and reiterated an open invite to be "an ear, at any time." Some people say this, and you both know they can't really do it. But every once in a while, someone says that and you *know* they truly mean it. And you know they will enthusiastically make the time for you without resentment. You know they are going to listen to you on the bad days and the good days. You know they aren't going to pressure you into turning a bad day good — and as a result, the bad day will indeed turn around. You know they aren't going to judge you. You know that they "get it."

Although Tommy offered to talk on the phone, I was still having a difficult time speaking and on this particular day I simply ran out of words. It seemed a Herculean feat to get words out of my face without feeling completely spent. I thought of learning sign language.

Before bed that night, four-year-old Grace went into a twenty-minute loop of "Are you going to die? Is Grandma going to die? Is everyone we know going to die? If we are all dead, do the builders come and take down our buildings? If everyone dies, who will be left in the city? Will there just be a bunch of empty buildings?" It went on and on. She was basically asking, "If we all disappear like Alice, the evidence of our collective agreed-upon reality will remain standing like a world-sized graveyard, and who in the hell is going to deal with that?" My thought bubble read, "That's an excellent question, Grace. A bit macabre, but excellent. I wish I could answer you, but once again, you have me stymied."

Verbally, I tried to explain we don't die all at once, so there will be people here for the foreseeable future, but this only seemed to spawn more questions. Even as I said it, I thought, "Actually, I don't know this for sure. My kid died for no reason; anything can happen. I guess a major catastrophe could take us all down at once. Am I lying to her? Do I tell her the truth?" I decided to keep the possibility of a global catastrophe to myself to get her to sleep, but I also felt like I was lying to her. It was simultaneously heartbreaking, amusing, awe-inspiring, and exhausting.

That night, I slept.

On Saturday of that week, Grace was sick and my (ancient) computer crashed. This was extremely worrisome, as all my photos of the girls were on there. Most were backed up, but my brain hadn't been normal for the last two months so I couldn't be sure I'd done anything in a technically correct way. I'm no tech wiz in my best mind, and I was very aware I was not in my best mind. I was anxious about the potential loss of photos but tried my best to not spiral into the Darkness. Fortunately, my friend Tony is an Apple Genius (for real) and came by save the day. He brought his lovely girlfriend Missie and we ended up having a nice visit while several yellow swallowtail butterflies flew around us. I took it as a sign Alice was near and keeping watch on me — and our computer.

To this day, I still regularly see yellow swallowtails, regardless of where in the world I am. I also see a lot of monarch butterflies. I savor the magic of every single sighting and allow the experience to uplift me. Every time I see one, I say, "Hi, Alice!" And because I have the best family and friends on earth, they send me photos every time they see one.

Years later, I found a text I'd sent to a friend that difficult Saturday. "This event has created a profound change in me. Not sure what it is exactly yet. It feels huge and like I am supposed to do something to help people in its wake. Haven't sorted out what it is yet, but the feeling is there. I don't know how else to describe it." My friend assured me events like this are larger than us, are humbling, and make us better people. "Not that you need improvement," he clarified. He assured me I was strong, that I had what it took to become a whole person — albeit one with a broken heart — and that he had no doubt I would help many others during my life.

It helps, so much, to hear people say you're capable and strong. I didn't believe them, mind you, but it helps to hear it. I can't lie, I never wanted to find out if I was this strong. "If it's true that God only gives us what we can handle, I wish God would go back to thinking I'm a loser who can't handle a parking ticket," I wrote in "Thank You, Alice." No one wants to find out if they are strong enough to outlive one's child. It's difficult not to wonder if you could trade in your alleged strength for your daughter's life.

You can't, though, so you will take the alleged strength as an undesired consolation prize.

To CLARIFY: *Telling someone to* be strong *is not the same as telling someone they* are *strong. It implies you do not feel your friend is living up to your definition of "strong." It also betrays the fact you have no idea what strength it takes to survive a tragedy. Telling someone they* are *strong conveys you see strength in them when they may not feel strong at all. It also implies you do not confuse their temporary devastation with weakness.*

THAT NIGHT, I went to the Hollywood Bowl at my friend Sarah's invitation. I had not been out much, so I wasn't exactly sure how it would go. I started to have a panic attack upon leaving. This was unusual because, up to this point, I'd only had the attacks on Tuesdays. It suddenly dawned on me it might be because I was leaving my sick child at home and the last time there was a child with the common cold in my home, she left in a hearse. I thought about staying home with Grace, but too many other people involved in the plan were already in action, and I didn't want to cause anyone an inconvenience. And in my heart, I knew she was going to be fine. But my nervous system was, well, nervous.

I don't recall exactly how I pulled myself out of that panic attack, but I did. I did pace the entrance to the Hollywood Bowl for quite a while, however. When Sarah walked up to me, I apologized for my antsy behavior. "Are you kidding?" she quipped. "I am surprised you aren't in bed with a needle hanging out of your arm."

I laughed. It felt good to laugh.

That exchange reminded me people still had a low bar of expectation for me in the wake of losing Alice. "I wish I would have thought of lowering the bar before this," I quipped to Sarah. "It never occurred to me how relaxing it could be."

That low bar was incredibly freeing, and was perhaps one of the greatest gifts I was given after Alice died. It made me feel safe to have bad days. It made me feel safe to emote in front of other people. Both of which are necessary to evolve past a titanic loss like this. It gave me the space to go through what I had to go through — and that is exactly what got me through it. The only way through it is through it. It also bonded me closer to my friends, which is key because the support is crucial.

Another great perk to the low bar is, it allowed me to feel like I was functioning "above the bar," whether or not it was true, and this alone began to repair my completely destroyed self-confidence. Confidence building was/is another crucial part of healing, because, though I didn't realize it at this point, my self-confidence was FUBAR.

We sat in a box for four, just the two of us. There was a lot of space around me, so I didn't get buggy the way I can sometimes get in crowds. I enjoyed the show, but I was still feeling separate from the reality of others — an almost dreamlike state. And it was a dreamy night with gorgeous weather. I felt anonymous and invisible, like a specter who could see but could not be seen.

I went home feeling otherworldly and checked on Grace as she slept.

After work the next day, I came back to a house that was not as full as it used to be. After a while, Grace came up to me, and said, "Mama, I don't know what it feels like to not have a sister." And then, with giant tears in her eyes, she said, "I miss Alice."

My heart froze, then shattered.

I had my own giant grief, and then I was jolted into seeing my living child's grief — a feeling she could not so easily express because she was four years old. I wondered if I had missed signs of her grief in the haze of my own. I tried not to spiral into guilt. I tried to answer questions to the best of my untrained capabilities. And then I grieved for the fact my living child had any reason to grieve, for the deceased child I never thought I'd lose, and for the life I once had, which was no longer.

Grace asked for privacy in the bath that night, which was a first. "I need privery (sic), please." So, I let her have some "privery," but I stood near the door. All I needed was for my only remaining child to drown in four inches of water. While standing there, I heard her playing in the bath as if Alice was there. She was chatting with her sister and having a great time. I stood there, smiling, tears running down my face, my heart simultaneously swelling and exploding. God, I love my girls.

Of the Western working mom, some people say, "She has it all!" But I did not have it all. I never did have it all. And now one of my "alls" was no longer.

I found myself resenting having to participate in any portion of the rat race that is modern Western civilization. I did not want to waste four hours at the DMV so I could drive a car, because I didn't want to drive in the first place. I didn't want to waste four hours on anything — I wanted to stroll ... slowly. I found myself resenting every piece of paperwork I had to fill out, every invoice I had to write. It seemed to me the powers that be absolutely bury us in paperwork until we can barely live. I wanted to spend my day in contemplation and meditation and reading and pondering philosophical and spiritual matters, healing my bereaved trauma-struck body-mind-soul, researching healing methods, writing thank you cards, tending Alice's altar, thinking about happy memories, documenting her life, adjusting to life without her, and creating beautiful memories with my living child. But I couldn't ... because I "had it all."

I fully realize I was, and am, better off than most people on earth, and that compared to those people, I do indeed have it all. This was simply a time in my life where "She has it all!" was difficult to embrace, because half of my all was never going to be mine again, and the whole experience led me to ponder whether my "all" — my girls — were ever "mine" in the first place. I also wondered how I got sucked up into the collective delusion that any person can — and, according to our society, should — "have it all."

Not long A.A.D., I found my brain flooded with images of priest-esses and warriors and *Mists of Avalon*-type scenes. I did not have the slightest clue why this was happening, but I kinda liked it. I hadn't summoned these images and nothing in my external world seemed to be reminiscent of such topics. I felt as if they were being downloaded into my consciousness, and at great speed. I remember thinking it was strange at the time, but I also found the images comforting so I didn't do much to stop them; I was in dire need of comfort and any port in a storm, I suppose. I kept hearing the terms "divine feminine" and "hieros gamos" (Greek for "sacred marriage") in my head and felt consumed by nudges to investigate those topics. I guess some part of me knew this was odd, because I told only one person, but I didn't feel bad about it whatsoever. I somehow knew these "downloads" came in peace.

For reasons unknown, I was also consumed by pondering gender roles and polarity, division of labor through the ages, and how this related to sexuality now and in the ancient past. Though I had abso-lutely no idea why this was happening, I didn't question it much, which was unlike me. While reading up on these topics and choosing meditations based on these nudges, I started to realize I wanted to be able to be softer and have a hell of a lot less on my plate.

I suppose, in the wake of this experience, not only was I emotion-ally and physically scrambled and reconstituted, I was also under-going a massive spiritual sea change. Instead of rolling along with "women should work while barefoot and pregnant ... and plan parties ... and write thank you notes ... and itemize invoices ... and sing lulla-bies," I was called to investigate big-picture stuff: How did we get here? Is this new paradigm really working? If not, what can we improve and how can we improve it?

But I had established a life around current social paradigms — "You can have it all!" — and wasn't quite sure how to abandon that while keeping a roof over our head.

Why didn't I discuss this with many people? First, I was still having trouble talking without becoming exhausted. Second, I have always been a person who processes silently in the beginning of any large upheaval. Third, I have always been somewhat private about my spiritual research, journeys, and evolution, probably because, as a child, I began my investigations in secret. Fourth, I suppose I thought if I told anyone, they might institutionalize me. As a bereaved mother, I was well aware that everyone was watching to see if I would go off the deep end. I was determined not to go off the deep end; I didn't trust anyone to properly care for Grace and me if I did. And I sure as shit didn't want to be considered a victim for the rest of my life.

What I'm trying to say is sometimes having control issues comes in handy.

Mostly, at this point, I didn't have the bandwidth to evaluate why I was drawn to these topics. I was simply processing these things, doing so privately, and not analyzing why. As a lifelong overthinker, this in and of itself was miraculous, and I was determined to enjoy any miracle in this Darkness.

Besides, "Why?" questions are a slippery slope when one doesn't know why their perfect child died. From the start, I knew "Why?" wasn't a train headed to a real station. No one knew "Why?" so hopping on that train of thought was a sure way to torture myself on a hellish ride to nowhere.

In any event, a large chunk of my days was spent pondering current relationship dynamics and gender roles and how this affected sexuality, mental health, and individual growth. I learned I was wired differently than I had been raised or encouraged to be. I felt peaceful and at home during this research; I felt both intellectually stimulated and psychologically soothed, so I kept at it. I could tell it temporarily quelled the hypervigilance of PTSD; I began to feel softer — and softer felt better to me. I figured if I was crazy to suddenly be consumed by these investigations, it didn't matter; they seemed to help me get through the day, so how bad could they be? I wasn't hurting anyone. I was helping myself.

I continued.

I CONTINUE TO THIS DAY.

. . .

MY NEXT BLOG PIECE, "WHAT HAPPENED?" was finished that week. My dear friend Beth was talented and kind enough to edit for me. For the most part, it seemingly poured out of my fingers as if I had nothing to do with it; it wrote itself. I felt nudged by something much bigger than me to write it. I don't often feel this way, but when I do, experience has demonstrated I'm better off obeying these nudges.

The only way through it is through it, and writing about it helped/helps me through it. Writing was the only time I felt as if I had a fully functioning brain. Virtually every therapist I saw said that writing was one of the best things I could do because writing helps one form a narrative around the tragic event.

Writing helped me find meaning when I had no explanations and connected me to something bigger than me. And that is probably the key to the entire healing thing.

So I wrote, and I cried. I cried, and I wrote.

During this time, I noticed I had further adapted to Alice's not being here. Realizing I was not lighting the candles near her picture every night, realizing I no longer had to remind myself I didn't need to make Alice's beloved homemade food, etc., hit me in the heart and gut like a missile.

I think some part of me assumed it would be years before a semblance of acceptance started to peek through the haze of grief. The realization that acceptance was developing sooner than expected sent me into a serious wave of grief.

The acceptance was healthy, but the realization that acceptance of Alice's death was on the rise was petrifying. Maternal instinct fights this acceptance fiercely. I could witness that fight in my brain as if I were watching it on TV. It was the damnedest thing. The acceptance felt like a betrayal of Alice though I knew it was not; it was, in fact, necessary to my mental health. I knew I could not betray my mental health, so I told myself to take it easy that week. I decided to let my brain finish that internal war, allow myself to grieve my baby as well as the fact I had unwittingly, incomprehensibly, somehow come to accept this titanic loss.

That week, I moved slowly, though I did keep moving. I didn't take on anything not necessary to survival. I didn't think much. I felt … and softened … and felt some more. I let it all pour out while I worked, cooked, self-cared, parented, and rested. I took on no other obligations.

It remains one of the saddest, most incomprehensible, most life-altering weeks of my life.

At this point in the Aftermath, I was still just spitballing. I knew I was winging it. In retrospect, I know expecting much more then would have been pointless. This allowed me to heal authentically, without comparing myself to others or carrying unrealistic expectations of myself. For some reason, I knew I couldn't do that. I knew it would ruin me. You can't think your way through it. You gots to feel your way through it. You gots to feel your way under a very low bar.

SEASONS

THE FREE FALL

$\mathcal{I}$ knew it was autumn because the stores started carrying pumpkin-flavored everything. My favorite season was here, but one of the two people with whom I wanted to share it was not.

After the eighth week, I could not seem to write weekly pieces.

At first, this frustrated me. Documenting my thoughts and feelings had been helpful. Posting them to my blog as fast as I could write them was a way to connect without having to cry in people's faces or manage their fear of crying in mine.

In retrospect, I realize a convergence of factors pressed *Pause* on my writing. My brain wasn't processing every tiny detail the way it had been. The tension at home regarding differing grief responses was escalating, which made it difficult to find time to write. Mostly, the number of weeks since I'd last held a living Alice was becoming a number I just couldn't see in print.

My dear friends Mike and Nancy arranged for their landlord to give us her cabin in Big Bear for a weekend getaway. I love me some mountains, so I gratefully accepted and invited our friends Todd and Stacy — who dropped everything to help us those first few days after

Alice died — to join us. It felt nice to be able to do something for them in return.

Although it was not planned this way, I ended up having five hours of alone time in Big Bear before Grace and the others arrived.

It had been so long since I'd had any alone time of any kind or spent any time in the mountains I love so dearly.

While walking around the property alone, I felt a giant rush of relief. I felt lighter. I noticed I was smiling to myself. This was a good sign, I noted. "I might be able to pull out of this hell if I can manage to smile alone at times," I thought.

There I was, smiling, singing, and dancing around the mountain cabin. I was moving more freely than I had in years. I felt as if my body had been freed from an armor I did not realize I was wearing. And then I started having creative thoughts. *"OMG,"* I said aloud, *"I had an original thought!"* It had been so long since that happened, I forgot I wanted or needed it. Like so many other mothers, I had not had the time nor space for creative thoughts. Even before Alice died, life was so chaotic I told a friend I felt like an amoeba — a single-celled organism whose sole purpose was to respond to outside threats or external stimuli. *That* was a depressing thing to realize. At one especially trying point before Alice died, I realized I no longer had dreams for the future.

Once I realized I felt like an amoeba, I had a moment of hope because only once something is identified can it be rectified. The miracle is the awareness, for once you have that, you can enact measures to improve and the methods for doing so are often surprisingly clear and the payout, enormous.

But the fires kept coming, so I kept putting them out, going to work, feeding kids, and happy to do all of it but feeling very much like I was only living out a sliver of my potential.

But at that particular point in my life, I was hard-pressed to figure out how to get out of that rut. Like every other mother and worker in the world, so many people depended on me, I had lost my own needs in the process. Work-family balance is not easy in the best of situations. The demands on my time were so overwhelming, I simply could not see how I would find the time to help myself by spending a few moments alone, in silence. Hundreds of millions of people were — and are — worse off, but I had never been more acutely aware of not living up to my potential.

AFTER THIS EXPERIENCE in the mountains, I began to prioritize quiet time, particularly in my home. The foundation of my world had been ripped open in an instant, and I needed to just be sometimes. I'd ignored my soul's pleas for quiet because I thought I had to plow ahead, solve problems. Now, I no longer could. Peace and quiet were no longer luxuries; they were necessities. Sometimes you need to do absolutely nothing but pay attention to your innards to be more outwardly productive. I have learned to plan my self-care time, and I have to honor that time. When I do, I am happier, I am more focused, I am healthier, I am more productive, I have more energy, but most importantly, I don't feel like an amoeba, a robot, or like the life is being sucked out of me.

THAT WEEKEND, I rode an alpine sled with Grace, a first for both of us. It was exhilarating. I was relieved to find I could still have fun. I felt a little guilty having fun without Alice, but the look on my precious Grace's face was enough to keep me in the moment; The Guilt drifted away in the flood of Grace's joy. There is a wonderful picture of this moment. It is perhaps the first picture of me truly smiling *from within* A.A.D. I know full well how I was feeling at that time: I wondered how I would find joy again, and the thought of doing so still seemed like a betrayal of Alice. Even then I knew it was not a betrayal, but that thought kept going through my head. I call this one of the Dark Thoughts: thoughts I recognized as self-sabotaging and self-harming.

I knew I had to reckon with them before they destroyed me.

Dark Thoughts are extremely seductive. We all have them. I knew what they were, I knew they were not helpful, I knew the Dark Thoughts were not true, and I knew they were not me. "If I enjoy life without Alice, I am betraying her memory ... I should have stood next to her during her nap to protect her from whatever the hell took her ... I should have been a stay-at-home mom ..." Those were a few of the Dark Thoughts that circled my brain. It requires time and energy to deal with the Dark Thoughts, but not dealing with them takes all your time and energy and ruins your entire life, so there's good incentive to stay on task. Each time I had a Dark Thought — and it was often — I had to make a concentrated effort to acknowledge it, examine it, reckon with it, and discard it. Once emptied of the Dark Thought, I noticed what naturally bubbled forth. Inevitably, what came up was gratitude. I'd sit in that feeling for as long as I could.

I was grateful I was their mother. I was grateful for my supportive friends and family. I was grateful Alice didn't suffer. I was grateful she didn't endure a lengthy and painful illness. I was grateful I had tools and resources around me to help me deal with this loss. I even became grateful for the pain. The pain was born from the love of her. I had to be grateful for the pain but decide not to live there.

It was a more or less constant battle with Dark Thoughts in those early days and years. I didn't spend a lot of time judging them or wishing I didn't have to deal with them or talking about them. I simply spent a moment or two nipping them in the bud every time one came up.

Years later, Dark Thoughts happen far less often but still pop up, especially if I am overwhelmed or sleep-deprived. Sleep deprivation leads me to insomnia, which leads to more sleep deprivation, which increases Dark Thoughts. It's a vicious circle and one I recognized fairly early on. I had to make sleep a priority.

IN THIS CRAZY world that practically canonizes sleep deprivation, overwork, and overwhelmedness, I had to simply say to myself and others, "Sleep is not optional for me. I start circling the drain far too fast if I do not get enough quality sleep. If I have more than two nights of inadequate sleep, I become activated, which means I start having increasingly disrupted sleep, become overly sensitive and irritable, become consumed with crippling guilt, and so consumed with Dark Thoughts I can no longer tackle them one by one. They quickly outnumber me."

Because sleep deprivation is both an early symptom and an exacerbator of PTSD, it's a vicious cycle and the time between noticing PTSD symptoms emerging and their fully taking hold is brief. I know if I have two nights in a row of little sleep, sleep must become the priority. I work, I care for Grace, but everything else goes out the window. I nap if I need to. I take a bath if necessary. I swim if a pool is available. If my symptoms present with body pain (and they often do), I do yoga, get a massage if it's in the budget, or both if the pain is relentless. Because once I'm fully activated, it is impossible to do anything except simply try to talk myself through making toast. I have only had a few periods that bad, and I never want to have to crawl out of a period like that again. In my experience, the key to that is prioritizing sleep, peace, and the things I need to do to maintain that sleep and peace.

My experience with sleep and sleep deprivation has made me somewhat of a sleep evangelist. The things I experienced are explained by science; sleep deprivation has ill effects on everyone, not only on PTSD patients.

Folks grow accustomed to how they feel, however, and think it's not "that bad" until something happens to make it worse. I hear patients and friends complain of tiredness, lack of focus, depression, anxiety, weight gain, high blood pressure, scatterbrain syndrome, being consumed by their own Dark Thoughts, et al., all of which can either be caused or exacerbated by sleep deprivation. Yet so few people want to change their lives to get more sleep. Sleep, my friends. It's fun, it's free, and you will be healthier and happier than you ever thought you could be.

As we drove home from our lovely time in the mountains, Grace told me Alice was sitting next to me in the front seat "like a big girl" and she was so excited to be near me. She told me Alice gave me a kiss. At that precise moment, a small rainbow appeared in the only cloud in the entire sky. My face rained but a smile pierced the storm.

I took that rainbow as a sign because I needed a sign.

Once home, I wondered what to do about all the activities that

season. I didn't want Grace to miss the joys of her childhood traditions because her sister died, so I soldiered on.

On our trip to the pumpkin patch that autumn, I noticed I had to
concentrate on staying in my body. Doing something I loved to do
with the kids, minus a kid who would never go again, made my soul
want to leave my body, I suppose. I had to remember to breathe. I had
that sense of heaviness yet floating. In the end, I enjoyed watching
Grace's joy, but I longed for Alice.

A few days later, I harvested the pumpkins I had planted with the
girls. Alice's perfect pumpkin was ready to pick, but Alice was not
here to pick it for she was harvested much sooner than I expected.
This filled me with awe. I stared and stared at that pumpkin as if it
could provide the answers no human could provide. How could the
seed Alice planted grow into a pumpkin though she would never
grow to hold it? As I stared at that pumpkin, in my head I heard the
words, "She ripened perfectly." This was not what I wanted to hear at
all, yet I found it simultaneously reassuring and gut-wrenching.

At the time, those three words comforted me. No one, and I mean
no other human, could have said this to me with good results. This is
the kind of revelation a person needs to experience for themselves
when they are in their dark night of the soul.

Ten weeks A.A.D., I threw our annual Halloween party for eighty
people. I saw the wisdom in making it a potluck that year; I'm not a
complete moron, as it turns out. I didn't want Grace to feel like Alice's
death killed our life as she knew it. At one point, I remembered Alice
was a newborn her first Halloween and that last year — her second —
she was ill and missed it. I remember I thought, "There's always next
year!"

But there wasn't a next year. And there never would be again. Alice
would never truly be part of our family Halloween party tradition. My
stomach churned, and my eyes welled up.

And then I took a deep breath and resumed hosting the party.
Grace was happy, which was all that mattered in that particular "right
now."

The aftermath of losing a child is an incredibly murky place; often it is not obvious what would be best in any given situation. I felt like shit and frequently had no idea what to do about that, so my thinking was, "What is best for Grace?" And then I would do that. This is what I do to this day. Grace was, and remains, my North Star.

Around this time, my marriage started to crack, but divorce was not yet on the table. Bad news and tragedies were relentless for weeks. I was clearly becoming maxed out on struggle. Yet I recognized then, as I still do today, there are many people in the world with situations worse than mine. This knowledge gave me the strength to keep going. If the refugee mother could still go on as her child starved to death, then I'd better bless my food and shelter and keep going just like she does.

I'm sure you've heard the saying, "Everybody grieves differently." I would add: every individual grieves different losses differently. Sure, there may be some through-lines, but for the most part, individuals don't have the same grief reaction to every death, so of course you cannot expect two individuals to grieve the same death in the same way at the same time. Two people grieve differently, at different times, and it's not like either one of you have any control over the manner in which the grief bubbles forth. Sometimes the disparate grief reactions make it difficult to remain in close quarters. All you can do is notice what comes up and deal with it however you can.

Bubba's husband Rey took me to see the movie *Gravity* one week that autumn. I was thrown by the child-loss storyline, but what really kicked me in the gut was the theme of isolation, which was evident long before we discovered Sandra Bullock's character had lost a child. Her character felt isolated and perhaps found comfort in isolation. I found myself jealous of the Bullock character, to be honest; I was surprised to find the idea of becoming untethered in space sounded like bliss to me.

I thought about it for weeks.

It's simply exhausting to force yourself to live on Earth day after day when one of your children is no longer bound by its gravity.

But Grace was my gravity. I could not escape to outer space. I had to stay here, bound by Earth's gravity to Grace and all the other people who cared about me.

That's the thing: I had the honor of people sitting with me with their open hearts while my heart was torn open. People have always opened their hearts to me, but it was coming from a whole 'nother level now. I had the opportunity to witness people at their best, their most compassionate, vulnerable, and helpful. It is a stunning thing to witness, and a true miracle to be the recipient of that much open heart. There was more love than you can imagine. This is life. This is what creates meaningful friendships. For those afraid to tend to the grieving, for those who scroll right past the posts of friends who are dying or have experienced loss, know this: It is an honor and a privilege to tend to the vulnerable and allow yourself to be vulnerable in the process.

Consider this not a chore but the most precious of gifts, for both parties. You can run but you cannot hide; we will all experience great loss and we will all eventually lift off this mortal coil. If other people's losses make you uncomfortable, it is not their problem; it is yours. If I have learned anything, it is that you cannot truly live well unless you accept death and our lack of control in that process.

Around this time, I experienced panic attacks three days in a row. In retrospect, I realized this was perhaps because not only was Alice gone, but also because all hints of her daily life were disappearing as well. I donated her diapers. Her crib was long gone. Her car seat was no longer in the car. I no longer bought her special milk or beloved puffs. The diaper bag was still there but had not been touched since August 5. Her toys were not all over the floor. I no longer had a reason to go to her school. Her death was the main thing, but the reminders of her presence in our lives were slowly disappearing as well. I began to feel as if she had been only a beautiful dream, a feeling that brought me to my knees.

I knew that was not sustainable and I wanted to avoid medication, so it was an enormous relief when Southern California Counseling Center (SCCC) called and said they had matched me with an experienced EMDR therapist. EMDR, or Eye Movement Desensitization and Reprocessing, is a highly effective form of trauma therapy that I had requested a few weeks prior. I would try EMDR and if that didn't work, I would try medication.

I began the EMDR therapy on Halloween in 2013, and not a moment too soon.

The first two sessions are one hour each and are basically preparation for the real work ahead. We identified my sources of activation as well as situations that seemed to exacerbate and alleviate my symptoms. We also identified the specific intrusive images (seeing her blue face come out of the crib, knowing firemen were pronouncing her dead though I could not hear their words, seeing red liquid come out of her mouth while I did CPR) that haunted me as well as my primary negative emotion, which was The Guilt. There was not much discussion about these topics. We merely labeled and identified the problem areas.

We also selected the bilateral stimulus I wanted to use once we began reprocessing. In EMDR, you are exposed to bilateral stimulus as you recall the trauma. You can choose auditory, visual, or tactile stimulus. Although I was sure I'd select the visual cues because I had keen awareness of my eyes darting around after the firemen arrived that terrible day, I tried each stimulus before making my choice. The auditory cues come from earphones that beep in one ear, then the other, in a slow, rhythmic fashion. I hated those; they made it difficult for me to concentrate. The tactile stimuli came in the form of hand-held buzzers that alternately buzz one hand, then the other. I rather liked them. Lastly, we tried the visual stimuli, in which your eyes follow a cue to track right, then left, right, then left, as you recall the trauma. Although there are machines that provide a moving ball for you to track, SCCC did not have one so the therapist moved her fingers back and forth.

I had two issues with the finger-tracking. The first was I realized the therapist was going to have to move her fingers back and forth for two hours on the first session and I felt bad for her. I also had trouble accessing the past — which is the entire point of EMDR — while doing the visual finger-tracking, so it was simply not going to work. It is likely I had trouble accessing the past because I felt bad for her having to move her fingers back and forth in the present. So I decided on the hand buzzers. We then tried different frequencies and intensities for the buzzing, and she noted my preferences. I could feel my brain respond as we determined my settings. Trippy. I found them quite soothing.

Speaking of finding different frequencies: a few days later, I had my appointment with the medium. I never thought I'd go to a medium, but I also never thought my two-year-old daughter would die for no apparent reason.

Though it had only been three months since Alice died, it felt simultaneously like a decade ago, a second ago, and like she'd never existed anywhere but in my imagination. What I wanted to know from the medium, but which I did not tell her, was this:

IS ALICE OK?

WAS IT MY FAULT?

HOW THE HELL *can I raise one child while memorializing the other?*

I FOUND the experience more helpful than I thought, primarily because the first thing Alice communicated after her name was "It wasn't your fault, Mama."

I sobbed.

Fleur, the medium, went on: "It feels to me like Alice's body just stopped working and there was no lead-up to it — that's the feeling I get. She feels like a lively, smart girl. Talkative. Knee-height. She gives me here the sense that it is still unexplained. That doctors aren't able to figure it out or give you a definite reason; do you understand that? You still don't have closure on what happened; do you understand that as well? That makes me want to recognize there was nothing that could have been done or been changed. As traumatic and disastrous and heart-wrenching as it was, it was simply her time to go. That's the feeling I get."

At this point, I was sobbing uncontrollably and blurted out, "Did she suffer?"

"No," answered Fleur, "she keeps showing me she was sleeping. No, I don't believe she suffered at all, that's the feeling I get. I feel her soul was prepared to leave her body at that time so I don't feel there was any suffering there, I really don't. And I also feel she really hasn't left your side since the moment her soul left her physical body. I feel like it happens very, very quickly. And I feel as well, she wants you to know you were very, very attentive; there's no feeling it's your fault. She's flourishing and wants you to as well."

I almost dissolved into a puddle of relief when she said that. I knew even if this was one hundred percent horseshit, it was worth every penny to have someone who didn't know me, or the situation, say it wasn't my fault and have a break from the relentless guilt.

While writing this book, I listened again to the tapes. It was quite an exercise going through that session and transcribing it. I had another experience of feeling immense compassion for the lady quietly sobbing, only to realize that lady was me. I have had a few of those moments; they surprise me every time.

A couple of weeks later, I had my third EMDR session, which was the two-hour session. This was where the real work began. It was *intense*, perhaps the most intense thing I have ever willingly done. For the first time since Alice died, those feelings from that terrible day came rushing back with the same intensity. I did not cry. I wailed. I was *right there*.

Through breathless sobs and fountains of tears, I discussed every detail of that horrific afternoon. It was as if I were in real time again, only I was not as calm as I had been that day. Not that I was calm that day, but I had extended periods of catatonia. And on *the* day, there was still hope for a spell. That day, the fresh shock numbed me for a while. On November 14, 2013, I told the story, but I already knew the ending. Therefore, on November 14, 2013, the story was told through a lens of immense grief, guilt, horror, and trauma stemming from the story's end. I no longer had the grace of shock to absorb the intense loss and associated feelings. I had to take breaks at times. I did not beat myself up for taking breaks, which was notable. When I needed to break, my therapist brought me back to the grounding or nurturing image I had previously selected, and then we "went back in" once I calmed down some. Oddly, it did not take long to calm myself — only a minute or two.

I found the buzzers as soothing as my grounding image. I grew to wish I could walk around being comforted by those buzzers all damn day.

I remember being very determined to get through this work. I remember being one hundred percent committed to its process because I was one hundred percent committed to not becoming a victim in the story of my life. I went all in, took breaks when overwhelmed, and then went right back in with total commitment and determination. There was no negative self-talk. None. There was absolutely no questioning of my ins and outs. Why I cannot seem to do this reliably in real life is anyone's guess, but for whatever reason, I was able to do this in EMDR. I suppose I knew my life depended on it, or, at the very least, my quality of life absolutely depended on it.

I remember thinking I'd spent too much of my life engaged in negative self-talk and that part of my inner dialogue could take a long walk off a short pier.

After the session, I was whooped and felt dazed so I thought it best to walk before I drove.

IF YOU EVER DO EMDR, I would recommend arranging a ride from your first two-hour session, just in case.

WHEN I ARRIVED HOME, I sat on the couch to return emails and ended up passing out sitting up. I do not sleep sitting up. I couldn't fall asleep on a plane if you paid me one meeeeeeeellion dollars. But on that day, I passed out cold for two hours, sitting in the corner of my couch.

The next day, I was profoundly exhausted, and my entire body ached, but I felt quantifiably different emotionally and psychologically. When I say my body ached, I mean I felt like I had my ass kicked by a throng of bodybuilders in an alley and was left unconscious for hours on the concrete. There was not a single inch of my body that was not sore or aching, from my scalp to my throat to my toes. But the emotional and psychological improvements were quite clear. I could literally feel my brain cells firing; it felt like popcorn was popping in my brain and in the process releasing guilt and body armor. I do not know why or how, and I did not question it, but I definitely noticed it. It was as if I were aware of my own neuronal firing.

After my fourth EMDR session, I scheduled an acupuncture session with my friend Romeo (yes, really), which seemed to spare me the body pain I'd experienced after the previous session. I was slowly beginning to find what nourished and anchored me so I wouldn't fall into a depression, wishing to be free of gravity.

THE HELLIDAZE

*T*hanksgrieving was a meal served with endless courses of
silent tears and blessed with heartfelt gratitude to everyone
who waited on me throughout my undesirable feast.

These tears were marked by an eerie calmness. These were not
hysterical tears; this was water pouring out of my stoic face. I noticed
the tears streaming down my face more than I felt them. I felt
deflated, as if I had hit bottom, surrendered, and was no longer
attempting to claw my way out. The emptiness was unmistakable but
no longer unpalatable; there were hints of acceptance in this grief
bouquet. This new grief palate inconveniently started *on* Thanksgiving, at Bubba and Rey's gathering. I was shocked to find myself in that
state, but I knew with certainty I could not stop it so I simply ducked
into empty corners when the tears hit. I didn't want to ruin anyone
else's Thanksgiving. I didn't want it to become about me. I already
knew that many of the other guests had not seen me since Alice died
and were unsure how to behave around me, and I didn't want to make
it worse.

I have always preferred to cry alone anyway.

. . .

No, really. I'm not just saying that to make you feel better.

I WASN'T sure why Thanksgiving hit me so hard. We did not have any major family traditions on that day; traditions bring any absences into focus.

In retrospect, I realize what I was feeling was surrender to something to which one would never want to admit defeat. No one wants to accept the Grim Reaper, much less the death of a child.

We fight and fling ourselves against it with all our might until we are exhausted and have no might left. I first felt deflation and lethargy, then I noticed the tears, and only then did I notice the pure, unadulterated sadness behind the tears. I was experiencing the emotions, but I was also somehow witnessing them as if they were happening to someone else.

It was such a silent, serene sadness. I realized all previous sadness was diluted with other emotions such as anger, defiance, guilt, shock, judgment, or betrayal. Maybe I had never experienced pure, unadulterated sadness before this?

It was around Thanksgrieving I realized I had not suffered guilt or intrusive images since the third EMDR session. I had spent several intense hours releasing The Guilt and only noticed its absence when sadness and lethargy seemed to bubble forth in its wake.

I wrote on a napkin, "With the space left by the receding guilt and intrusive memories, the dawning of acceptance and the resulting grief can come forth, I suppose."

I had not gone gently into my dark night. My body, ravaged by the psycho-physiological effects of trauma, had railed, railed against the dawning of the light of acceptance.

Once acceptance dawns, one can begin to deal with the crux of the pain, I suppose. And you know what? It isn't as bad as the shenanigans your body and mind pull to avoid it. In my experience, the sadness was/is not nearly as difficult to handle as either the PTSD or the unconscious self-inflicted torture we utilize to avoid acceptance. Honestly, I found the sadness to be almost a relief.

I remember thinking, *"Thank God* I'm older. The sadness *feels* bottomless, but I know it will not be. I'm not sure a younger Melissa would be so sure of this."

It wasn't until years later I realized the EMDR and the visit to the medium occurred so close in time because my sense of time was so ... capsular ... in the early days A.A.D. In a matter of two days, I released immense amounts of guilt to two vastly different types of healers. I realized days still did not feel connected to each other at this point in the Aftermath. Moments felt like individual capsules, but they also felt like one large never-ending capsule, and none of it felt linear whatsoever. I had no concept of time in the way we have agreed to mark time.

It seemed to me we rarely experience the pure present. We experience the present as it exists on a continuum — aware of the past that led us to a particular "now" while holding expectations that the law of cause and effect will lead us to a relatively predictable future. But that perspective had been annihilated for me after finding Alice dead. In those early days A.A.D, it was if I were floating in the present stunned by a traumatic past, which made a future of any kind inconceivable.

For months, even years A.A.D., I had to set alerts on my phone to keep appointments or perform routine tasks, something I'd never had to do in my entire life. All I could manage to say was, "Time feels like bullshit."

God, I missed Alice.

I still do.

The day after Thanksgrieving, Grace and I went to Phoenix to visit my wonderful friend Teresa and her family. Grace and Teresa's son Nate met in gymnastics as toddlers and our families became friends.

They'd moved to Phoenix not long after Alice was born, so we hadn't seen them much and were excited to reconnect.

During a dinner at Teresa's neighbor's house, tears started coming down my face and I couldn't stop them. Nothing in particular had triggered them; it was as if someone poked a hole in me and all my energy and eye fluids leaked out. I was trying to be social, but I was truly struggling and didn't want to ruin everyone's evening or make myself the center of attention. Teresa was unfazed by my facial leaking, which helped the tears pass faster, but I still didn't want to be a buzzkill. I was so grateful to have company who did not judge me or look at me like, *"Shit! What do I say to her?"* Everything about Teresa's expression and body language read, "Yup. Of course, you are crying. That is a completely normal response to a horrific event. Need a tissue?" That created a low-pressure environment in which to release the high-pressure emotions within me.

Although I had to set alerts to go to the grocery store, I could still remember basic physics, for reasons unknown.

The grief wave that started on Thanksgiving lasted several days. These days, a wave rarely lasts that long; it's more like a brief storm rolling through. It might last a few hours, tops, then just blows away completely. I occasionally have weeks where there are multiple storms, but I have rarely had a storm that lasted as long as the Thanksgrieving wave.

In retrospect, I realized part of what I was experiencing was a "coming down" of sorts from the heightened state of PTSD.

After Thanksgiving, during my fifth EMDR session, while holding the buzzers, my therapist asked me to come up with an image of what the grief looked like and felt like.

I told her I felt as if I were at the base of a giant wave, looking up at it. It was frozen. I was not necessarily scared; more awestruck — and awe-*stuck*. I couldn't move. The wave couldn't move. Nothing moved.

She asked what would happen if I let the wave come down. I

thought about this while the buzzers did their thing silently. I had to try to force it down with my mind, which was frustrating. I verbalized this. She asked what happened if I forced it.

I'M SUDDENLY LOST in the wave though I never saw it come down. I cannot find the top. I do not seem alarmed by this. I am simply limp and being tossed around. I am oddly relaxed although I am unsure if I will surface. It's like I don't care if I drown. In this image, I seem like I could take it or leave it, as if I could handle any outcome.

UTTERING that sentence unleashed a tsunami of tears.

NOW I SURFACED, and my image-self is floating.

SHE ASKED how I felt about this.

WELL, shit. I surfaced. Now what? I do not know what to do next or how I will get back to shore, but I also do not seem to be overly concerned about it. I am simply floating. It seems I am too tired to fight the wave and too tired to try to get myself to known safety. Too tired to live and too alive to die.

SHE ASKED what would help me get to land.

I SEE A HUGE STRONG MAN. He is silent. He swims out to me and supports my head on his shoulder. We stay there awhile. Eventually he begins swimming back to shore while supporting my head. Once he can touch bottom, he scoops me up, my head still on his chest, his other arm under the crook of my knees. He walks, carrying me, well past the shoreline into a clearing in a grove of trees near a tree stump and then sits with me, still holding me. There is nothing sexual about this. There is no desire, no lust; just care. Once he sits down, he clasps me more tightly and I start crying, water pouring forth effortlessly from my eyes.

I get the impression he is strong, so I do not have to be the conventional notion of the word "strong" in that moment. It was an indescribable relief to be given the opportunity to be not strong.

I WAS A LITTLE SURPRISED, and annoyed, that I had such a typical damsel-in-distress-type image. I'm a grown woman who can handle her own shit, after all! But it was the image I had so I went with it, however unpalatable. Although irritatingly romance novel-esque in nature, it was an intensely clear image for me.

I found it fascinating to observe where the mind would go if given a push but no directions. Later, I remembered one dream theory is that we are all the characters in our dreams. Maybe my strong side just needed to sit down, shut up, and nurture my soft side for a spell?

During my sixth session EMDR the following week, my therapist asked me to continue with the images from the previous week. This time, I did not have to force the wave down: the wave came down of its own volition. I popped up faster this time. I also experienced less stress and disorientation before it came crashing down. I floated on my back. It was sunny. I was alone, but I didn't mind. I don't remember much else from the session, just that the entire wave sequence occurred effortlessly.

A week or two later, in an effort to give myself more alone time in real life, I went away.

I went to Las Vegas not to gamble (which I loathe) or drink (which was largely unappealing at the time) but to just rest, alone, in a discounted resort room where other people cooked and cleaned. I hadn't done anything like this for decades, if ever. The morning I left, I woke up with a cold and was not feeling very well. I drove off anyway. I figured it was a sign I should go rest alone. Every mother knows how difficult it is to recover from the flu when you have babies to nurse and toddlers to tame. I was being handed a fantasy come true: if I had to be sick, I could do so without anyone needing me *not* to be sick. You may think I have a low bar for bliss (and you may be correct), but this was bliss. I ordered soup and slept and took steam showers and lay in bed while I wrote.

Two days after my return, Alice's medical examiner called with the final findings. My heart started pounding when I saw the number.

I'd just walked out of a yoga class. My heart truly felt like it was fighting its way out of my chest.

I sat on the curb between parked cars to take the call.

I clutched my yoga mat in my arm and used that hand to plug my ear with my finger. I was terrified he was going to say it was something preventable, but I also welcomed the chance to know one way or the other for the months-long purgatory of not knowing was as close to hell on earth as I have ever experienced.

He. Was. Speaking. Very. Slowly. And. In. An. Extremely. Measured. Pace. Throughout. The. Entire. Conversation.

I WON'T TYPE it that way because that would be super annoying. Just know everything I'm about to write was spoken in that extremely measured cadence.

I COULD TELL he was fighting his emotions. I could tell he'd prefer to not be emotional in front of a "patient's" family, but obviously he felt some sense of duty to be the one to tell me anyway. I will never forget his bravery or generosity in that moment.

He began by expressing his extreme sympathy for our situation. He spent some time discussing how difficult these types of cases were for him. He said he could tell Alice was well loved and cared for — at which point I felt a sense of indescribable relief, as if someone let two thousand pounds per square inch of pressure out of my upper body because that statement alone let me know they did not think her death was my fault. Guilt began to evaporate as soon as he said that, enabling me to truly hear the information he was about to provide.

He went on to discuss the temporary tattoos Grace and Alice had applied all over Alice — "Tah-toos!" Alice exclaimed — how much that touched him, and how difficult it made his job. He was not obligated to tell me these things; I am sure his life would have been much easier had he not. Perhaps he did so because he imagined it is what he would want to hear if it were his child.

He went over every detail of the findings slowly.

For the most part I do not recall what exactly he said, because in the end, the findings were as everyone suspected: there was absolutely nothing wrong with her. She had nothing wrong with her heart, her brain, or any other organ. She did not suffocate. Toxicology was normal. She had a mild case of the common cold, but he did not feel that contributed to her death in any way. There was some bruising around her thymus caused by post-mortem CPR attempts. After five months of endless testing, they found no cause of death, therefore it was classified as SUDC: Sudden Unexplained Death in Childhood.

He explained they would keep certain samples of Alice's cells in case we ever wanted to have them tested. Theories may develop in the future, at which time having tissue samples to test may be beneficial.

He assured me they would be mailing me a copy of the findings, but he wanted to explain to me personally, because those findings could be difficult to see. He said I could call him at any time if I had questions, which was extremely generous.

That man wanted to be human for me. I was touched he took the time to call me himself. I still stand in awe and deep gratitude for his humanity in a job where that must be incredibly difficult to navigate. In the coming years, I would learn that many SUDC families were not so lucky.

I sat there on the curb, between cars, hearing some of the most important and difficult news I would ever receive. I have no doubt the relief I experienced was partly due to the compassionate delivery of the information itself.

. . .

IT WAS NOT MY FAULT. It was not my fault. It was not my fault. It was not my fault.

I LET that thought wash over me repeatedly for some time after.

Eventually, I contacted family members to let them know, and then got dressed and went to work to treat patients. I wanted to stay home and meditate and write, but that was not an option. During this time of my life, I would experience something as intense as a call from the medical examiner, process it for a few minutes, and then go back to work.

I was strangely relieved nothing was found. If nothing was found, there was nothing I could have done to prevent her death; therefore, I could begin to stop the endless guilt trip I was on, which I knew was incredibly destructive. Anything they would have found, I would have found a way to make my fault. And if it were confirmed I could have done something to prevent her death, I am certain I would not have survived that guilt.

So, in the end, not knowing her cause of death in those early days A.A.D. saved mine. I'm not saying I would have died by suicide, but a lifelong paralyzing guilt will kill slowly.

SHE SIMPLY SAILED ON. Or, as my friend Charlie said, "She just split, man."

AS PUMPKINS ROTTED and poinsettias turned up in their place, I began to seriously struggle. The absence of Alice and the unspeakable tension at home, combined with the ubiquitous holiday music, created a dichotomy my brain could not endure.

Although I generally love all the pre-Christmas festivities, I couldn't do most of them in 2013. Strangely, I didn't feel guilty about it; I knew my limits. If not for Grace, I would have foregone Christmas entirely that year. But I was going through the motions. I had to force it. I hoped Grace would not notice. Decorating the tree was one thing I managed to do. It is generally a highlight for me, but this year I had knots in my stomach as we soldiered forth. I became relieved as we finished everything but the star. As we did, Grace said, "Remember last year we did this with Alice? She had fun. I wish she were here. I wish we could still give her a present."

POW.

Because we still didn't know why Alice died and because Long QT syndrome — an inherited heart problem that affects how the heart beats — is one of the suspected causes of SUDC, Grace had to go see a cardiologist that same week to rule out any sort of electrical issues in her heart. I had to go on autopilot to navigate the stress of that; I was able to function, but I had to consciously decide not to obsessively worry about these tests. In the end, she was given a clean bill of health and I was given the longest exhale in my history — the best Christmas gift of all. At the time, I didn't realize the medical examiner call and the cardiologist visit were so close together. I find it curious how often I was confounded by time in the early days A.A.D.

Christmas itself was a nightmare of Tim Burton proportions. I had low expectations going in, but it was far more difficult than I could have imagined.

Not only was this our first Christmas without Alice, my marriage was also hanging by a thread and we travelled to see family, so we weren't in Alice's house on Christmas. Because I did not have a homunculus I could run through various options, I have no idea if being away from home made Christmas easier or harder. I only know it felt more *The Nightmare Before Christmas* than *It's a Wonderful Life.*

ALICE'S NAME *was still on her stocking. Do we hang it? This gift tag I planned to recycle from last year has her name on it. Do I use it? Do I buy her a present to help Grace adjust? Would it even help? Here is the photo of the girls in their vintage dresses after Christmas last year. Do I use this photo for our Christmas card? Here is a Santa picture from last year, but her dress fell out of the bag on the way there so the girls aren't wearing their adorable matching outfits. I'd flippantly thought, "Damn. Oh, well. There's always next year!" Except there wasn't a next year for Alice. And why did I even care if they wore matching photos in a Santa picture? What a ridiculous thing to concern oneself with for even one second.*

Every one of these meaningless material reminders of Alice was the Universe screaming in my ear, "Evidence of Alice abounds but there is no more Alice." All the while, traditional holiday songs still played in stores and people still hung lights and families still made cookies together like nothing had changed. I didn't expect the world to stop for me. I just couldn't sort out how to keep spinning on the earth below me when the world within me was frozen.

WHILE NERVOUS ABOUT being away from our home that Christmas, I wasn't convinced I'd feel any better being home than not home, so I followed the crowd on this decision. I tried to focus on being grateful I had a home at all — and a surviving daughter. While reading in the busy airport, I came across a quote by Charles Dickens, whose daughter Dora died suddenly and unexpectedly at eight months old:

AND IT CAN BE that in a world so full and busy, the loss of one creature makes a void so wide and deep that nothing but the width and depth of eternity can fill it up.

IN THAT AIRPORT full of Christmas travelers, I was emotionally validated by a man who'd died ninety-nine years before I walked the earth. Thank you, Universe.

Christmas Eve has always been one of my favorite days of the year, but in 2013 I had to force myself to move through the day. My brain kept telling itself it was just another day, but my body wasn't having it. Fortunately, I had the opportunity to swim that day — as I did most days during our visit — which took the edge off for a spell, but otherwise I was overwhelmed with paralyzing dread. I had to try to make some joy for Grace's sake.

We tried to take her for a Santa photo, but Grace wasn't having it, which was a first, so we took her to "Mikeldonalds," at her request. I am not a mom who frequents 'Mikeldonalds," but I was a mom eager to do anything to try to make Christmas fun for my daughter even though I was in a decidedly not-fun mood.

Out of nowhere Grace said, "Mama, I'm sad Alice isn't going to grow up like me. Do you miss her every day so much?"

Through tears I responded, "Yes, Grace. I will always miss her, every day, more than I can say with words. A mama always loves her children." And then Grace sighed: "I remember when I used to have a happy family."

I felt like I ran into a cement pylon going 120 mph, but somehow managed to (mainly) remain intact. But as soon as we returned to our accommodations, I went to my room and had a whopper of a pre-dinner cry. When I made my way downstairs, my soon-to-be-brother-in-law was making cocktails for everyone. "Single or double?" he asked. "Have you heard about my year?" I replied. "Right. Triple coming right up," he offered.

The martini helped some, but not as much as his compassion. I made it through dinner.

Before bed that night, Grace asked, "Remember Alice got a rocking horse from Santa last year? I wish she could be at home riding it." She then asked if Santa would bring something for Alice.

So, Sad Santa got her ass out of bed and did just that.

Christmas morning felt like actual torture from the moment I opened my eyes. I wanted it to go away, but I had to get up and face the caroling music. I had to focus on every movement of my body.

"GET OUT OF BED. Put your shoes on. Open the door. Breathe. Hold the railing. Go down the stairs. Don't fall — oh, my God, that's all anyone needs right now."

And so forth.

.   .   .

I WAS DAZED and truly going numb and had no idea what to do about it. The numbness seemed like something which should be addressed, but as it wasn't common for me, I had no clue how to navigate it. Suddenly Grace shouted, "Santa got me just what I wanted!" Her joy snapped me back to "reality." I made a conscious decision to attempt to stay focused on my breathing and her joy to get through the day.

Later that afternoon, Grace suddenly ran downstairs, threw herself around me and said, "Mama, I'm sorry your baby died. Mamas shouldn't have babies die, right, Mama? Mama, I'm sorry you miss Alice and I know you are happy I'm alive."

"Grace, you have *no idea* how happy I am you are alive."

A few days later, Grace lived long enough to add another year to her age. I was able to celebrate, though keenly aware her little sister would never have that chance. Immediately, something in my head said, "Alice is in bliss beyond birthdays," and I chose to believe that because I needed to believe that.

My hero brother and his family drove to see us for a couple of days, which was a huge help and basically saved me. Still, I was struggling. Grace was so very excited to see her cousins, Tucker and Zeke. It brought me so much joy to see them bond, but it broke my heart Alice was not there to join in; Alice and her cousins had taken their relationship as far as it would ever go. At one point Grace asked, "Are my cousins sleeping here? Will they still be my cousins when we grow up?"

My heart broke, because most five-year-olds don't realize that timelines don't always proceed as expected or that they might be meaningless.

With Thanksgrieving, Christmas, and Grace's birthday behind me, I counted the days to January 2, 2014. I was eager to escape the numbing purgatory of the first Hellidaze A.A.D.

YEARS

THE CALENDAR READ 2014: THE JUGGLING OF BOULDERS WHILE WALKING ON SAND

"There are days or weeks in life where so much happens that it can take months, even years to sort out all that has taken place."
—*Jonathan Carroll*

*N*ew Year's is not my favorite holiday. It seems an excuse for people to become unapologetic a-holes. Aside from the heartache of watching the calendar turn to a year that would never hear Alice's laugh, my marriage was crumbling at an exponential pace. Home was not a sanctuary; home was a pressure cooker. There was nowhere to catch a breath. The intense pressure began to manifest physically: I was losing my hair, my stomach hurt, and I couldn't sleep. Despite telling myself that calendar years don't contain actual life, my body did not want it to be a year in which Alice didn't exist.

But I was functioning.

Everyone thinks you are *OK* if you are functioning. They think you are *strong* if you are highly functioning. I was highly functioning, but I was not *OK*. But I did not let being not-*OK* stop me. I decided that functioning while not-*OK* was just the way it was going to have to be for the moment. None of this made me superior to someone who cannot fully function after their child dies. I had/have no idea why I could function, so I can't take any credit for it. In truth, I was perhaps over-functioning, which ain't ideal either. I often wondered if I might collapse once life settled; it seemed probable.

The next day, I told Tommy that although I was functioning, my insides felt like I was being ripped apart. I have felt ripped open before, but those were mere fractures compared to this total disintegration. In previous episodes, I had a sense I was reassembling in an improved fashion even as I fell apart. This time, I only felt the shattering. Perhaps it was because there were so many simultaneous transitions. Perhaps my sense of time was so annihilated I had no idea which future required my reassembly. Perhaps A.A.D., I simply had to endure total obliteration before restructuring could begin. In the end, I realized the "why" didn't matter, nor did the "how," "when," or "where." The only thing I knew for sure was I was disintegrating. I decided to let that be and hope the answers would come forth from the rubble.

I told Tommy I had no idea what to do except constantly say this to myself: "Keep breathing into your core and keep walking toward the love and peace, so you can remember who you are."

Tommy listened quietly, then calmly responded, "You're Melissa Motherfucking Monroe."

I gasped. I felt like someone turned on all my lights and shot me into a new dimension. It wasn't what I expected him to say but it left me feeling empowered — and just in time.

The 4th of January started off sweet. Grace and I had one of our "special days," going for haircuts and then — after months of begging — she had her ears pierced. She was so excited and proud. Afterward at lunch, I delighted in listening to her chatter about all her passions and ideas. I would never get another special girls' day with Alice, so I was determined to make the most of those I was able to share with Grace. As we drove home, she exclaimed, *This was the best day of my whole life!*

My heart soared, and a smile spread across my face. I was relieved and thrilled I'd been able to provide such a monumental day for her. But it also brought tears to my eyes because I knew the second part of the day might not be so great and my innocent daughter had no idea. I willed the tears to dry up, and continued to enjoy Grace's excitement, because one must enjoy the simple pleasures as they come.

Later that day, during an intense couple's counseling session, my husband and I separated.

"Everybody grieves differently" seems like a tight, tidy, and true cliché. Living it, I discovered it to be true, but it is anything but tight and tidy. In a perfect world, everybody can grieve differently and support each other in close quarters and live happily ever after. But this is not a perfect world and sometimes one person's grief can make the other uncomfortable because they have not arrived at that stage yet. Or maybe they've already gone through it and cannot bear to be near it again because that particular wound is healing and susceptible to re-opening.

Sometimes the most loving thing you can do for each other is give each other the space to heal. Sometimes having two parents healing in different places is better for a kid than two parents unintentionally hurting one another while trying to heal in one place. Sometimes decisions have to be made in the child's best interest, though the solution may not seem ideal to outsiders. What matters is this: I have a living, exuberant daughter to raise who has two parents who love her to infinity and beyond.

The five-month period after A.A.D. wasn't for the faint of heart, and I knew adjusting to all that titanic change meant the next months and years weren't going to be a cakewalk either. None of these changes were the type that could be tidied up in a day or two or even a year or two. I left therapy dazed and shaking as I pondered this.

We had no idea who was going to live where or where the second "where" might be. I was supposed to go to my friends Nancy and Mike's house that night anyway, so I asked if I could crash on their couch. I ended up having a rich conversation with Mike and Nancy about everything under the sun. We sat outside and cried and laughed and drank vodka because I like vodka and Mike was Russian so, yeah, they had vodka.

The moment I opened my eyes the next morning, a sigh escaped my lips as tears leaked from my eyes. I didn't intend this; it was a simple release. I realized it was the first time since Alice died I hadn't awakened in a tension-filled house. Although I was devastated about Alice and the state of my marriage, I was so grateful to have a moment to cry in peace.

And then I got up, wiped my tears, went to work, and tried to figure out the logistics of a separation.

Of the top ten life stressors, I had six out of ten, including the top three. No one was going to sell me life insurance right then, if you know what I mean. I felt like Paul Newman in that scene in *Cool Hand Luke* where he keeps getting up only to get clobbered again. I wondered if my friends wished I'd stay down and sleep it off for a spell.

As I paced one particularly intense night during the separation, I looked up at the sky and said, "Hey. Remember me?" (God and I are frank with one another. Saves time. I value efficiency.) "Surely you must. I know there are people worse off than I am, but I'm getting kinda maxed out here because I'm not as strong as you seem to think I am. If you want me to continue to help people, I'm going to need a second to catch my breath."

So, of course, the following day I was rear-ended at a red light by someone going 25 mph. I was diagnosed with a concussion and whiplash and was advised to take a week off work. This was inconvenient timing since we had *just* separated and were doing the "nest" thing where Grace stayed in the house with the parent in charge while the other parent stayed elsewhere. I wasn't in great shape to couch-surf, I didn't want to have to ask to change the custody arrangements two days into a separation, and I couldn't afford the time off work.

Apparently, it is ill-advised to tell the Universe you've reached maximum capacity. It will respond with, "Oh, really? You want some cheese with that whine?"

Oh, I get it! *I am not in charge of anything.* I am at the bottom, dismantled into atom-sized pieces. I realized I was going to have to sit in the muck and take a breath. I guess I was waiting to take a breath until I was out of the muck. (That's cute. It doesn't work, FYI.) Once I took that breath while sitting in the shit, I realized I was more relaxed because, duh, I was no longer wasting energy trying to prevent further disaster.

And after that breath, I knew I must look up toward the light.

"I must deal with the crap and I must look for the love and peace where I can find them, and I must appreciate them when they offer themselves to me." This was my mantra.

Two days later, I finished my course of EMDR therapy. The intrusive images never returned and the guilt around Alice's death seemed resolved. If anyone would have told me EMDR could be that effective, that thorough, that quickly, I would have laughed in their face. But it did, and thank God, because the bulk of the PTSD was managed in time for me to process the dissolution of my marriage.

News of a missing plane was on the TV in the hospital when I went to meet Bubba and Rey's twins that March. I stared and stared. And then I realized I hadn't watched the news since Alice died. For nine months, I hadn't done something I had done most days for years. I never intended to stop watching the news; I just didn't. I found that fascinating. I realized I was able to be present at work and present with Grace, but every second I was alone — mostly in the car — found my mind filled with the same existential fare that had been circling my brain since Alice died. Every night, I searched through books and papers trying to find something that matched and fueled the feelings brought forth by the spontaneous visions, and desperately wished I had enough time to immerse myself in these pursuits.

Everything else felt like trivial bullshit.

I was never much for small talk before Alice died, but I had zero tolerance for it at this point. Fortunately, there was no small talk in my inner circle, not even from Grace.

"Mama, I love that picture of you and me and Alice where we are all laughing. One day, when I get old and die, I'm going to take it to

Alice. I can't wait to see her after I'm old and die. Do you think I will get old before I die? Will she know what I look like when I am old?"

Everything was existential 24/7 up in here, which was fine. Being expected to engage in small talk made me feel as if I were going to internally combust and dissolve into a pile of ash. I became extremely discerning about how and with whom I spent my time.

Navigating moving in and out of the house every week while making sure Grace had everything she needed and I had what I needed to run my life was a challenge — but not as challenging as the previous situation, so I forged ahead. It was a metric shit-ton of minutiae to juggle when I was freshly bereaved, and my executive functioning skills were not a hundred percent. I was profoundly exhausted. I told my friend Nancy I felt like I was juggling boulders while walking on sand.

While pacing one night that week, I realized the eleven-day period between Alice's birthday and death day was likely to be challenging. I wanted to immerse myself in something positive, in Alice's honor, to help navigate that time. I thought about how grateful I was to SCCC for the EMDR work that enabled me to remain a functional human who could give back to society.

My girls and I love music and have many friends in the business, so the idea to host a memorial concert around Alice's birthday to benefit SCCC was born that night as I paced, five months A.A.D. The next day, I asked the center if the funds could be earmarked to help their trauma training program so more therapists could be trained in trauma modalities, therefore enabling them to treat more patients, and treat them sooner. They were thrilled to have the help.

My dear friend Kim Grant, a music publicist, jumped on the idea and booked the event for the day after Alice's birthday at The Echo, a club on the hip east side of town. I asked Ramsay if he would come in from Austin to play the show with his old LA band, Waynesboro, and booked four other acts. I had the entire event scheduled in less than forty-eight hours. "Meant to be," I thought.

While home alone one day, it occurred to me we'd eventually have to divide the girls' things. I had the gutting realization I would have to eventually divide Alice's ashes.

The thought of this sent me spiraling into a pit of horror and anxiety. I knew anxiety could lead me to redevelop PTSD symptoms. I *never, ever* wanted to have to recover from PTSD symptoms again because it was the most difficult thing I'd ever done. So I took a deep breath and reminded myself I had some time and space to do it little by little. I reminded myself not to anticipate difficulties, to stay here and now, to do what I could when I could do it.

A few days later, I tried to go through Alice's clothes while Grace was at preschool. I thought I'd start with one thing at a time. Just her clothes.

It didn't go well. I found myself in a heap on the floor of the girls' tiny closet. I cried until I had nothing left and determined I was not quite ready to go through Alice's clothes.

Then I picked myself up, picked up Grace from school, and made dinner.

At dinner she said to me, "I'm going to be good for you, Mama. I am going to be calm. Because your baby died and I'm sorry for you and I want us to have fun!"

She somehow knew I was struggling that day though she wasn't home for the worst part. I didn't want her to have to comfort an adult, and I began to feel guilty about that. I was, however, relieved that my child possessed compassion. I smiled and hugged her and reminded her I loved her at all times, forever.

Three days later, I tried going through Alice's clothes again. I have no idea why I thought it would go better three days later. I think it speaks to how disconnected I was from time. Holding up everything she ever wore and deciding what to do with it was BRUTAL.

"Keep this one? Donate it? What to do with the ones I keep? Make a quilt with them? Keep them in a box for Grace to have? I remember when she last wore this. I remember her sauntering into school with that hoodie over her head. She never grew into the shoes Aunt Mandy bought her. She had her

*first feeding in this onesie. She wore that on her first day to preschool. I
remember the moment she created this stain; the stain is here but she is not."*

AS THE YEARS PASSED, this is how I managed to release anything Alice
may have touched — little by little over long periods of time, like
radioactive decay of the heart.

That night, Grace suddenly said, "Mama, you're lucky you picked
two girls, so you still have one after Alice died. I'm glad I'm still alive
for you. I like being alive." And then, "Mama, you made me so happy
today." And then she handed me an envelope and said, "Can you send
letters to heaven? Then will you please send this one to Alice? Make
sure it goes to the right heaven that Alice is in, OK?"

My heart simultaneously burst apart and filled with love as tears
shot out of my eyes.

In retrospect, I suppose I was still in shellshock, walking through
life like a stoic, broken-hearted ninja, tossing away obstacles without
breaking stride — and then going home and crying in the fetal position in a decidedly non-ninja-like manner. I have no idea why I could
do that then. I sure as hell can't do it as efficiently anymore. But it was
a blessing at the time. I suspected it might catch up to me later. I knew
it was unsustainable because my insides were gasping for air.

You know the Golden Buddha, that giant statue in Thailand? I saw
it once, on my way to India. I found myself fantasizing about lying in
the fetal position in the giant hand of that Buddha. In my daydream,
the giant Buddha wasn't stationary; he was walking around while I
slept peacefully in his palm. I have no idea why I fantasized that
soothing image, but I did, and still do on occasion.

*YEARS LATER, I recognize I felt vulnerable, unprotected, and exhausted during
that time; therefore, I fantasized quiet strength for handling shit while I
rested and restored.*

A girl can dream ... and then make those dreams reality within herself.

. . .

221

LORD, I was tired.

As Mother's Day 2014 approached, I became anxious but tried not to focus on it. I didn't want to create what I feared. Maybe it wouldn't be so bad. (Ha!) I had no idea what to do that day. My friend Catie was kind enough to invite Grace and me to breakfast with her and her daughter, so I picked up Grace and joined them downtown.

It was not our usual Mother's Day and I was seriously struggling, but I vowed to enjoy as much as I could. It was lovely for those two to spend the day with us, but I kept thinking about the previous year with my two girls and the photo that captured that day. It is my favorite photo ever. I'm kneeling while holding both girls and we're all laughing. It was my second, and last, Mother's Day with both of my girls and it seemed impossible there would never be another. Later that night, I closed my eyes and tried to take myself back in time, into the day that photo was created. Eventually, I slept until it was no longer Mother's Day.

By the end of May, my friend Kathy took a five-month job in Atlanta and offered me her place while she was gone. It was a massive relief to have one solid place to stay on my days away from Grace that summer.

But summer meant Alice wasn't going to turn three and would be dead a whole year: something I could barely process. One day, out of the blue, Grace walked up to me and said, "You know what I have been thinking about, Mama? I have been wondering what Alice would have looked like if she grew up to be a kid. Can I tell you something? I think she would have had long hair. Why was her hair light-colored? I kind of miss having babies around the house. Do you miss having babies around the house? My poor little Mama had her baby die. You are lucky I didn't die too, right, or you would have no children and you would be sad, right, Mama? Can I tell you something? When I grow up and get a phone, I am going to send messages to Alice in heaven. Do you think she still knows her name? You are sure? Is she still a baby up there? Has she grown? I know she knew her name here, but does she still know it? You can sit with me and tell me how to spell the big words, Mama, then I'll send the message, and Mama, what do you think the Easter Bunny's phone looks like? I think it has a handle ..."

I was too awestruck by her curiosity, compassion, courage, and clarity to be heartbroken by the questions. Her questions were like kintsugi, filling every crack of my broken heart with an exquisite golden love. Like the gold-filled cracks in those Japanese ceramic bowls, Grace's words made me view the breaking and mending of my heart as part of its history to be honored, rather than disguised.

A few days later, seven weeks before the one-year anniversary of Alice's death, the coroner's report finally arrived. One never thinks one is going to receive one's child's coroner's report. May none of you ever have to read such a thing.

I stared and possibly didn't exhale for minutes. My funny, sweet, spunky daughter's name was on a coroner's report and not a school report card. I did not cry. Eventually I opened it. I read all the words but like a speed-reader. I mainly read to see if there was anything I didn't already know. There wasn't. After months of tests, no one knew why she died. I knew we would probably never know why Alice died. I knew I would have to accept that to live fully. I knew it didn't matter whether acceptance was palatable; it was essential.

"Where does one keep one's child's coroner's report?" I wondered.

The rest of the day was rather solemn. There is nothing, and I mean nothing, that can prepare you for receiving your child's coroner's report. I needed a little time to just be in that experience. I had little interest in anything else anyway. Everything else seemed so trivial.

Alice's birthday, death anniversary, and memorial concert were fast approaching. For months I had been planning the Agastock concert (named for her beloved pacifier, which she called "Aga"). Focusing on an event that would honor Alice *and* help others helped me stay sane during that time.

A week or so before Alice's birthday, I was at Kathy's non-air-conditioned apartment. I woke up feeling despondent and panicky. It was 102° and unusually humid. I am not my best self when it's hot and humid, and I was already a hot mess. I could not stop crying. I could barely move. "Is this a breakdown? Am I sinking into depression?" I could not afford to have a breakdown or major depression right now. I had to expand my business. I had to raise Grace. I was moving in and out of the house once or twice a week. I had to sort out permanent housing. Alice's concert was in a week and there was so much to do. In the eleven months A.A.D., there was not one day I felt completely immobilized, so I was worried this was a new phase. I became worried it would become permanent. When Tommy called, I was sobbing and had zero ability to hide it. "I don't know why I can't move or stop crying! Why *now*?"

He took a breath and said, "Melissa. Some people who haven't been through a tenth of what you have sometimes take a day to sit on the couch and watch *Iron Chef* all day. Just take the day. Write off today. It will feel better tomorrow. The problems will still be there, but you'll have a clearer head with which to tackle them."

I didn't know if I believed him, but I didn't have a choice. I felt as if I were strapped to the bed.

I wondered if I'd gone crazy. I wondered if I should just say, "Eff it, I'm going to go crazy." No one would blame me, but if you go crazy, other people make your decisions, and I'm not down with that. In the end, it didn't matter because this was quite clearly all I could muster on this day.

I surrendered.

Surrender on that day looked like me lying on the bed, with tears silently falling from my eyes while I stared at a ceiling fan.

Eventually my mind went blank for a while, which was an unexpectedly pleasurable phenomenon.

Eventually I did the meditation my yoga teacher taught me, fell asleep, had dreams of flying for the first time in years, and woke up feeling exhilarated, free, and ready to tackle my problems. Tommy was right.

About a week later I realized I'd experienced a massive grief wave likely brought on by Alice's impending birthday and death day. I suppose it hadn't occurred to me I might tank prior to, rather than *on* her "big dates."

Eventually, Alice's third birthday arrived without her. Grace wanted to throw her a party and I desperately needed Alice to be remembered, so that's what happened. Lynn — my "other mother" — sent the bubble artist Alice had enjoyed at Lynn's grandson's party. I served Goldfish crackers, watermelon, and lemonade: Alice's favorites. At one point, Grace said, "I wish I could see what Alice was going to look like when she was three."

Me, too, kiddo. But I couldn't picture Alice as a three-year-old. I could only envision her as a two-year-old — something true to this very day. Trying to imagine her otherwise seemed like a painful exercise in futility. I couldn't do it, and there didn't seem much reason to do so when the exercise only brought pain.

The following day, the first annual Agastock Concert benefitting SCCC in Alice's memory was held. I was so busy I didn't sit down all day, but I was blown away by the immense show of support from all the bands, attendees, and folks who donated money or items to the silent auction.

Ramsay flew in to headline and ended the show with "I Saw the Light" at my request. It felt like church — with $10 beers and a sticky floor.

The concert truly anchored me that first year and raised $6,000 for SCCC. It provided purpose and focus as well as overwhelming support for a cause that would help more folks gain access to effective, accessible mental health care. Additionally, organizing the details kept my executive functioning on track. It also eased my fear Alice would be forgotten. So I made it through her birthday.

August 6 was met with a plan to treat myself gently because this was the shittiest anniversary of all time. As I walked from my car to yoga, a yellow swallowtail butterfly followed me halfway to class, which I gratefully took as a sign. "Hi, Alice! I'm trying!"

Later, my wonderful friend Pam met me at the Peace Awareness Labyrinth & Gardens near my house. I found it when I researched "meditation gardens near me." It's a gorgeous old estate where we meditated with butterflies, walked the labyrinth, dined, and listened to the history of the building. I learned the original owners of the home lost four of their five children, who are immortalized as angels in the painting on the ballroom ceiling. I unwittingly chose the right place to reflect on my daughter, it seemed. I felt Alice all around me that day, which was a comfort.

Afterward, my friend Elizabeth C. and her daughter Darla, Alice's friend, picked up Grace from school and stayed for a visit. Other friends visited and were in and out all night, bringing food, flowers, and hugs, thus making a difficult date into something beautiful. You know how I know it was a good night? The following morning, a grumpy Grace adjusted her attitude when she looked in the kitchen to see all the food and love we had been gifted the night before. "Mama, last night was really great. It was fun, and it is great to have so many friends to love."

Later that summer, my "other mother" Lynn sent us to her beach house for a couple of wonderful days. One day, while we walked the boardwalk, Grace asked me point-blank what we did with Alice's body. There was no way around it. I took a deep breath and told her when someone dies you can either bury their body in the ground or you can make it small, so you could always keep them with you. I wanted Alice to be with us so we did that.

I crossed my fingers.

"How do they make it small?"

Shit. I should have known I couldn't get away with that answer, but it was worth a shot.

"Well, they get the body very hot and then it becomes ashes that you can keep with you."

"You *burned* Alice?"

"Well, *I* didn't. There are people who do that for you because it would be too hard for people to do that to their loved ones. But the other way, when you bury the body, the body begins to fall apart and it's in the dirt, and you can't have the body with you. I wanted her with us, so this way — it's called cremation — seemed better for us though burial is better for others."

I somehow managed not to cry while I explained why we cremated her sister's body. I bawled alone later. I would not wish that conversation on the vilest of humans.

The following day, Grace asked to see the ashes. She furrowed her brow and asked, *"That is Alice?"* and "What are the white pieces?"

"Um, those are parts of her bones."

"Those are her *bones?*"

It was not an easy way to greet the morning. A full year out, things like that could still sneak up and slam me to the floor. There was no one to whom I could throw a sidelong glance that asked, "Dear God, am I doing this adequately?" There was no one to give me an understanding look, a knowing pat on the back, or a hug. Just me and Grace and a huge ocean and time to answer the unanswerable.

It wasn't what I thought I was going to do with that day, but if the question had to come, I am glad it came when I had the time and space to answer it. Thank God it did not come as I rushed her to school or tried to fax invoices.

It was a good question deserving a thoughtful, relaxed response. And a hug. And ice cream. This was definitely a job for ice cream.

Grace started kindergarten that autumn. We worked to open that school for two kids, but now only one would ever attend. I had a sinking feeling in my gut, but I remained upbeat for Grace, who was a little nervous. It broke my heart to see her marching into a whole new experience all by her five-year-old self. I wondered if she realized this routine would be hers for the next thirteen years, God willing. At this point, I realized I miraculously did not live in fear of Grace dying.

I also thought, "If Alice were still alive, I'd have to hurry to get her to her preschool across town."

But Alice doesn't live here anymore.

I got in the car and cried all the way to work. And then I treated eight patients who had no idea I'd had to patch together my broken heart sixty seconds before greeting them.

On October 1, I was able to move back into my house full-time. Grace and I had until April of 2015, thanks to the generosity of so many friends who saw how unhinged I was becoming at the prospect of moving and made sure I got some time in that house alone. I did not want to leave the only house Alice ever lived in.

My first hour in the house alone, I did something dear to me I had not done in a long time: I turned on some music and I danced. It was not a celebratory dance nor was it a dance of sadness. I suppose I felt like I could finally completely inhabit my space and my body. I realized I had barely listened to music since Alice died. The first year after A.A.D., silence was the main soundtrack of my life.

After dancing that night, I went to sleep and had a dream:

I WAS LIVING in what appeared to be a campsite, hanging out with a bunch of friends, a ton of kids, as well as Oprah, Jeff Tweedy, and that dude who hosts Survivor. That's weird. In the dream, it was all very normal that Oprah was camping, which was how I knew it was a dream even in the dream. Apparently, in the dream, I could make water come out of my fingertips at will. I filled up buckets with my bare hands. Folks in the dream seemed to think this was cool, but no cooler than being able to tie a cherry stem with your tongue. They seemed to think it was a novel but not earth-shattering skill I had mastered. This skill did, however, make me somewhat popular during the dream drought. And super rich. But apparently being rich didn't stop my love for camping. Anyway, I could literally make it rain!

I HAD no idea what the dream meant and frankly, I didn't care because I woke up laughing instead of panicked for the first time in fourteen months.

Thanksgiving rolled around. We spent it with my stepsister Sarah and her husband Jeff. Again, I had an enormous sense of deflation. Quiet tears fell down an exhausted body. It was hard to explain to my hosts, but they were patient and understanding, which was a relief because the tears are extra difficult if I am a guest or have guests. You can't always shuffle off and hide until it passes. You have to explain. There are questions. There are often suggestions. The suggestions never help and can be annoying because unless the person has lost a kid, they have no credibility on the issue.

As Christmas approached, my heart went out to those who would be sad and alone on Christmas. I hate not having a full house on Christmas, so I extended an open invitation to those who had nowhere to go on Christmas Eve. A few people ended up coming, so I cooked and entertained, which made me — and Grace — so very happy.

Somehow, I made it through Christmas morning as well and had a nice time at Janet and Mark's later. There were moments of sadness, but I believe focusing on making Grace and my friends happy enabled me to feel like I could carry my boulders in a backpack as I walked across solid ground.

The New Year was a different story.

OUT OF SEQUENCE

THE WHOLE LOVE

*O*n Christmas Eve 2014, a dear friend found out that his friends' young daughter had hanged herself. Her dad performed CPR on her for twenty minutes. Hearing this sparked intrusive images in my mind of me doing CPR on Alice. It sparked feelings of shock, panic, guilt, hopelessness, and yes, inadequacy, that I could not love her back from death. I heard many tragedies in the wake of losing Alice — after you lose a kid, people feel obligated to tell you every story of every dead child — but none of those stories activated me.

I wondered why this one did. My friend could tell that this story had sparked my intrusive images before I did and felt horrible. But you can't activate something that isn't there. Some part of me still had work to do. If there was more work to be done, sooner was better than later because this shit doesn't get easier all by itself. The only way through it is through the shit and the panic and the mud and the activations and the tears.

So it was a gift that I was activated.

A gift that left me crying in the fetal position for hours and days on end, but a gift nonetheless. I had to deal with it whether I wanted to or not. I deal with it every single day, but sometimes it hits bigger, brighter, and faster than the speed of light. And like light, it comes in waves (or particles, depending on the circumstances).

The day after Christmas, I woke up feeling annihilated and physically sore on every square millimeter of my body. I wasn't sure *why*, but I felt utterly deflated and rapidly descended from there. I spent more time in bed between December 26 and January 5 than I have in decades. I experienced multiple panic attacks punctuated by paralyzing lethargy and endless tears.

My family doesn't live locally and most of my support was out of town for the holidays. For the first and only time in my life, I called my therapist for an emergency session because I realized the seriousness of my state and was scared. We scheduled sessions with my EMDR therapist.

In the meantime, I religiously did my self-care, but it was no match for this week.

I signed up for a late-night yoga workshop on New Year's Eve. It was a lovely event and it felt good to move my body, though I did not have my usual energy level. I silently cried periodically throughout the three-hour class.

But I wailed in the car on the way home. I found myself repeatedly crying, "I miss my baby." I screamed, *"She didn't deserve that!"* at the top of my lungs. I have no idea why I was suddenly so angry, but I released quite a fury in the car. That yoga class really shook loose the inevitable "anger phase."

It was tempting to isolate at this time, but I reached out to several friends for help. The most generous and helpful thing anyone has ever done for me was to simply sit with me while I collapsed. Without judgment. Without advice. Without commentary. With only love. I was, and am, so fortunate to have people in my life who saw me at my worst and love me anyway.

Because, as I keep saying, the only way through it is through it. Sometimes you have to do things outside of your "normal" order to get through something like this. Sometimes, you have to honor what's happening at the moment and that requires some changes. Sometimes, you need to abandon what you think you should do and do what you have to do. For all those reasons, this chapter, like Alice's death, is out of sequence.

If there is one thing I have learned, it is you cannot die of a broken heart. There are times it hurts so badly you wish it could release you from this life. But it can't. If it could, I would be long since gone.

I have also come to realize I no longer fear death. I do, however, have some healthy, and maybe not so healthy, fears about life. I can't lie: in some moments, death seems like a relief. But since I am clearly meant to be here without Alice, I try to make the most of life. This is sometimes surprisingly easy. Sometimes hard. Sometimes scary as hell. This chapter is about my scary-as-hell period.

Beyond the grief, sadness, shock, regret, and overall devastation, the loss of a child is utterly disorienting. It is, hands down, the most disorienting experience of my life. It feels like you are on really, really bad drugs 24/7 and you can't come down. In some moments, it might be more precise to say, "You can't come up." I can't put my finger on exactly what makes it so disorienting because, hey, I just said the experience is disorienting, and disoriented people can't put their finger on shit.

Perhaps one aspect of the disorientation is I have one child here and one child elsewhere. I can't see, touch, taste, hear, or smell Alice. I have, at times, felt her. I desperately wanted those moments to freeze so I could savor them. I obviously have Grace here, who needs my care and attention. One could assert Alice no longer needs my care and attention. But do I know that for sure? Your maternal instinct does not conveniently shut down after your child dies.

That reminds me of a video I saw of a dog caring for her dead pup. Or that whale who tended to her dead calf for seventeen days. I *completely* understood that whale. The urge to care for your deceased child is all-encompassing, except there is no child "here" to care for. Therefore, I do my best to care for her memory and create her legacy.

The feelings of failure I was experiencing due to not being able to resurrect Alice were somewhat interesting, because though guilt was a serious problem A.A.D., I did not feel guilt specifically because CPR had failed. I realized I was like that dog trying to nurse her dead pup.

Around this time, I dreamt of her, which rarely happens. In the dream, I was doing simple stuff, like putting her straw in her juice box, but I was so happy to be doing so despite the doomsday-like appearance of the dream world. I have prayed many times to see her in my dreams, and ninety-nine percent of nights, I do not. When I finally did, I was simply and happily caring for her.

You must balance the instinct to mother the child no longer here with the instinct to mother the child who is very much here. You walk between worlds like a broken-hearted, untrained shaman. The world where Alice now resides is completely unknown to me, so that has inherent problems. I know the world where Grace lives, but in the aftermath of losing Alice, I find myself wondering how much I know about this world. Both worlds seem foreign. Sound disorienting? It is. It also left me feeling somewhat inadequate to do any mothering at all. I think most parents feel inadequate at times but losing a kid to an unknown cause will absolutely inflame feelings of parental inadequacy.

GOOD THING *I wrote during my healing because I didn't realize I was suffering from feelings of inadequacy until I saw myself write it.*

JUST HOURS A.A.D., I was told "grief is not linear." This is true. The nonlinear nature doesn't bother me. Each new level of understanding you obtain, every tweak in your perspective, requires time to integrate into your consciousness. If grief were linear, there would be no resting place to integrate, process, and self-discover. So many revelations of self, life, relationships, society, and the Universe unfold after a child dies. All the while you still have to deal with all the details of regular life, and sometimes you just need a damn minute.

The fact that grief comes in waves allowed me to rest and to assimilate the new feelings and resulting titanic shifts in perspective. The trouble comes when you aren't expecting the next wave, or when a wave's amplitude is suddenly much bigger than the one before, or the frequency of the waves increases, leaving you overwhelmed.

For me, grief waves are generally not initiated by thoughts. Before I lost a child — and even right after — I would have bet my paycheck I would spend a lot of time thinking, "If she were here, she would be doing XYZ," before dissolving into tears, but after the first month or so, I didn't. I have no idea why. She was two years old. I spend very little time extrapolating beyond that. Therefore, it is not always easy to know what initiated a wave.

It is as if I harbor this being called "grief" inside me and though I know it's there, mostly it allows me to function normally. But every once in a while, it pops up and knocks me flat on my ass. I can't see it coming because it resides *within.* For me, a grief wave begins as purely physical, then becomes emotional, and may or may not become mental.

When a wave of grief comes, my first clue is a pit in my stomach and a hole in my chest. Then the emotions spill. There are rarely "sad thoughts." Therefore, thinking my way out of it doesn't work. Talking doesn't work either — in fact, it can make it worse for me. I can become easily teary. I feel an emptiness sometimes. Sometimes, I feel physical tension and soreness, like a struck bell. I become easily over-whelmed. I can become forgetful. I had a great memory before, but I lost my keys and left the car lights on so many times in the seventeen months A.A.D., I'm surprised my AAA card was not revoked. Some waves leave me feeling as breathless as I felt right after she died. Sometimes I experience anxiety among crowds.

All that leads to a place where I must fight the urge to isolate and hide.

In the beginning, I didn't give two hoots who judged me, so I was not sure if the return of that fear was progress or not. I didn't spend a lot of time fretting about who may be judging me, but occasionally, I noticed. I was always shocked, because folks I discovered were harshly judging me were uniformly the same people who went on eighty-comment Face-book tirades about bad service at a restaurant or who had complained about a toxic relationship for years. Flummoxed, I thought, "You can't handle bad service at a restaurant or losing your favorite sweater. You have cried for years over someone who treated you like shit. You think you are going to rock the loss of a child?" It's laughable, really. But, in my weaker moments, I'll admit: It hurts. And in early 2015, it made me angry.

The anger phase was bound to unfurl eventually, I suppose.

So I turned my focus to caring for myself and sought solace with more supportive friends.

In the beginning, it was impossible to isolate. So much support was pouring in, it was nearly overwhelming, though necessary and deeply appreciated. But when the support is not pouring in and people get used to you doing "well … considering," you learn to ask for support when necessary. In the seventeen months A.A.D., many people said to me, "You are so strong. You are doing great." Not one person, other than my therapist, said, "You are allowing yourself to be vulnerable. That is brave and strong."

As a society, we have maintained a notion of emotional strength that often does not allow for vulnerability: keep your head up, chin up, stiff upper lip, etc. I learned to not hide when vulnerable, but it ain't for the faint of heart. I learned I am strongest when I am vulnerable. But it was a new skill, and I wasn't yet completely confident in it.

When I finally began a second round of EMDR, I again chose the hand buzzers as my dual stimulation, which keeps one rooted in the present while recalling the past. This encourages reprocessing of the trauma by allowing the higher brain centers to be utilized during recall. In trauma, it is believed (by some) the higher brain centers close down, thereby leaving traumatic events partially unprocessed by the higher centers and "pocketed" in the lower brain centers and physical body.

During the first session, my therapist directed me to choose some imagery to ground me when reliving the memories became too intense. I never know what I am going to choose until I hear it come out of my mouth. Once I chose an image, we would turn on the buzzers while I thought of it, aka "tapping it in."

She asked me to come with a calming image.

· · ·

I AM SEATED in a meadow in tall grass, facing north. There are mountains to the north and west, and a stream directly in front of me, nine or ten feet away. I can't see the stream because the grass is so high, but I know it's there. I can hear it babbling sweetly past me to the southeast. There are little pink flowers on various blades of grass that look like bluebonnets, except they are pink. Alice is there, directly ahead of me, playing in the grass, happily plodding along and not paying much attention to me. I am smiling, watching her play.

MY THERAPIST, Hilary, asked if I thought it might be problematic to have Alice involved in my calming image because our focus would involve traumatic images of Alice. I thought it would be fine but would rethink it if necessary. I could tell she didn't think it was a good idea, but we tapped in that image anyway.

Next, she asked me to form a nurturing image.

THIS IMAGE IS the same as above, except I am leaning back against a man's chest, his arms around me in a strong, loving, relaxed fashion. I am completely at ease as we watch Alice play. I cannot see his face, but I know I've known him forever.

NEXT, the protective image.

THE SAME SCENE, except the man rises up from behind me and calmly walks in front of me, his giant sword drawn. It is only then I see a gang of about fifteen men coming toward us. My man raises his sword to his left and sweeps right, beheading fifteen men in one fell swoop. I am not alarmed in the image. Nor is he. He just calmly walked over and beheaded fifteen people without breaking a sweat, as you do, before taking me in his arms again. Alice walks toward us, also calmly.

. . .

237

I REALIZE this is one helluva an image, but it is the one that came to me so I stuck with it. As with the first round of EMDR sessions, I was somewhat annoyed my image was so romance novel-esque, but it was clear, so I kept it.

Next, I was to formulate a wise person image.

I SEE TWO PEOPLE: a man and a woman. Is that OK? I still feel a little like a pain in the ass because I cannot seem to follow simple instructions when it comes to imagery formulation. I guess I need a wise couple.

LASTLY, I was to formulate an *image of putting my intrusive and disturbing thoughts regarding Alice into a container,* so I could take them out when I needed to deal with them but they were not with me all of the time, so I could function. I found this challenging, which was frustrating because the other images came so immediately. I saw a big dark leather chest. We were in some sort of hut. I had trouble placing memories in the chest and locking them up. I had trouble leaving it alone, all of which I conveyed to Hilary, who suggested I try putting the chest in a closet or something to see if that helped me walk away. I thought it did.

But when I returned the second week, I couldn't make the chest image work. I realized shoving aside any memory of Alice, even a traumatic one, felt like I was betraying her. I conveyed this to Hilary through wet eyes. She asked what might help me feel OK about setting the traumatic images aside. I erupted into tears: "I just don't think I can. It feels like such a massive betrayal of her, and it goes against every motherly cell of my body." I became inconsolable; I was doubled over crying. Hilary asked, "What about a column of light? You can put the traumatic memories in there, and get in there with them, and bring Alice too if you like?"

I liked that, so we tapped that in. I felt better.

During the second session, I asked Hilary why my entire body became so damn sore when activated. We discussed that as well as

Peter A. Levin's book *In an Unspoken Voice: How the Body Releases Trauma and Restores Goodness* and Bessel van der Kolk's *The Body Keeps the Score.* She asked what my body felt like during the trauma. I realized I had no awareness of my body whatsoever until the moment I was pulled away, so the paramedics could have access to Alice. I was pulled back about five feet from Alice, but I recall my body was slanted forward as if I were lying face down in a cone. It was the first moment I was "away" from her since finding her. Hilary said it sounded as if I were being pulled in two directions. *Yes. Exactly.* I hadn't thought of that before. I told her I felt as if I were in that carnival ride with centrifugal force, where you get sucked back to the wall and the floor drops, except my face was to the wall. Try as I might, I couldn't lean away from the wall. And, I suppose, finding your child dead will most certainly feel like the floor dropping out from under you.

Hilary asked which part of the traumatic event seemed to be troubling me most, so we could start there. She turned on the buzzers. In response to a therapist's questions, you can internally process or speak aloud. I prefer to talk, because I have sometimes found I don't know that I know something until I hear myself say it. She suggested we start at the CPR, since that is what activated me.

Now, I dive right in during EMDR. I do not hold back. I do not dip my toe in. I go in there all the way and let it rip. I do not fear "going there." Instead, I fear living the rest of my life crippled by *not* going there. I guess I figure, "I'm here, I have this amazing person willing to do this for me, I can't live in the state I've been in, so I'm going to dive right in." I suppose I've always been the kind of gal to dive right into my emotions anyway. We started the buzzers. I took a deep breath and went back in time.

I RECALL DOING CPR on Alice. On my baby. Thirty thrusts, then two breaths, at the tempo of the Bee Gees disco hit "Staying Alive," the suggested pace. Can I just say whoever had the idea to tie that song to CPR has never done CPR on their child? It's so fucked up I can barely think about it. It made me angry as I did it. But I did it.

I grew Alice in my belly for nine months, then I fed her with my breasts for a year, and now I was trying to use my breath to bring her back to life. Belly to the breast to the breath. "I can do this. I can do this," I thought. But this was not how I thought I was going to spend my Tuesday. This was not how I thought I was going to spend any day of my life. I did chest-thrusts and internally counted 1-2-3-4 because by now 911 was on speakerphone and my neighbor was here, and they were both talking. Thin, red, watery stuff started coming out of Alice's nose and mouth. I screamed to the person on the other end of the phone this was happening as I counted out chest thrusts ... 25-26-27... They screamed at me to keep going ... 29-30. I gave her two breaths. She had changed color by now; she was no longer blue. There were wheezing sounds. Could it be working? I did not think it would really work when I started, but she was my beloved child so I had to try, and it seemed like it might possibly be working ... 11-12-13-14... She'll surely have brain damage if she does survive. The chances of finding her blue and stiff and surviving without brain damage were very low, I reasoned ... 18-19-20 ... More stuff leaked out of her face. I screamed this out loud as I counted internally. Was it the watermelon she had for breakfast, the only food she'd take that day? Had she been dead for so long autolysis had started? Were her cells decomposing? Oh, shit, was this decomposing cellular matter from my child? 24-25-26-27 ... The emergency operator screamed to keep going. I kept going. I have studied anatomy and physiology. I have taught anatomy and physiology. I have witnessed hundreds if not thousands of surgical procedures, but I had no idea what the hell was coming out of Alice's face. Should I be doing this? Am I making it worse? 29-30-breath-breath. I have never been so focused in my life as I was in those moments when I was doing CPR on my child. I have never been so "in the moment."

I was hysterically crying as I recounted this scene. I went in so far, it was like I was there again. But the buzzers let me know: "You are not there. You are here, now." I soldiered on.

. . .

I LOOKED up and saw two firemen coming up my steps. I saw their expressions change entirely when they saw my face. I could tell they went from thinking it was a garden-variety situation into realizing it was a very serious situation. I cried something at them but didn't stop doing CPR. I didn't stop. I had no choice. I had to try. If I hadn't tried CPR on my darling daughter, I could have never lived with myself.

Someone told me to stand back. I did. I remember feeling pulled back, but I am not sure an actual human pulled me back; it felt like an unknown force. It is possible a fireman pulled me back; I have no recollection of how I arrived there. Odd, because everything else about that time is so clear and emblazoned in my mind. No one told me where to stand but, like a child in elementary school, I found a line on the floor under the arch and stood there, toes on the imaginary line. I felt as if I were lying face-down in a narrow cone but pulled back at the same time. Once I was still, I noticed my eyes were darting all around, like prey.

I purposefully refocused my eyes on Alice, on my beautiful daughter. There were two firemen. One to the left of Alice had gear, the one to the right was assessing the situation. I saw the gear-guy hand an oxygen mask to the Alice-guy. I thought, "Oh, my God, there is hope. Is there hope? Really?" The Alice-guy took the oxygen mask very slowly. "Why so slowly? If there is hope, go faster, dammit!" I thought. The Alice-guy stared at the gear-guy as he half-heartedly placed the mask over Alice's tiny face. "If you are going to do it, do it right!" I thought. They spoke no words, but I knew what the look meant. "Are we really going to do this? Are we really going to give hope to this poor mother?" And then the Alice-guy looked up at me with a face full of dread and empathy and said something that ended with ... "I'm so sorry."

I collapsed on the floor in a heap as I released an inhuman cry. I was shocked I was capable of such a sound. I heard myself make the sound and wondered how I produced it even as I was making it. Was this me? It was like I was both me and an observer of me. I may or may not have hit the ground with my fists. (I am fairly certain I hit the ground with my fists.) I immediately thought, "Why are you so upset, Melissa? You knew. You knew. You knew, but you needed them to tell you for certain, because you hoped. You hoped. You hoped."

. . .

WELL, Melissa, you were upset because your daughter just fucking died for no apparent reason and without warning.

SHE DIED? *She's dead? She's dead.*

WHAT THE HELL?!

WHAT. *The. Hell?!?!*

I WAS IN HYSTERICS, but I continued.

I WAS on the floor under the archway, which still proudly bore her birthday banner from her party only ten days earlier. "But it was just her birthday!" I screamed. I guess, in my state of shock, I thought she couldn't die if she'd just celebrated her birthday. She couldn't die if her birthday banner was still up. If her birthday cards were still all over the piano. If her birthday dinosaurs were still at the dinosaur lake chatting up the tiny princesses in toy cars. These should have protected her from death, my shocked brain thought.

MAGICAL THINKING, that's what that was. It's part of the grieving deal. It's so annoying to discover you have some predictable responses to tragedy. Why? Mainly because you never think this will happen to *you* in the first place, so having any predictable response is further evidence you are not beyond the hands of fate, I suppose.

WHEN I STARTED SCREAMING that it was her birthday, I saw a fireman, about six-foot-four, with his face in the corner, shoulders shaking. He was not just crying, he was sobbing. "Oh, my God," I thought. "This is really bad. Some-

thing so bad happened in my house that this giant man, who sees terrible shit every day, is in my corner crying." Of course, I already knew Alice being dead was very, very bad, but for some reason seeing a giant fireman crying drove that home in an unpredictable way.

WHEN I STEPPED on that line, it was the first time I had stepped back from the situation, both literally and figuratively. I was completely *in* it ... and then I was five feet back. Part of me wanted to stay in it, stay with her — I am her mother, after all. The other part knew I had to step back so they could do their job.

The moment I went to the line on the floor was the moment I ceded control over the situation and just prior to realizing I didn't have any control over a damn thing in this entire world.

I continued.

I RECALL SITTING OUTSIDE ALONE, late at night, after she died. The two men inside the house were sleeping. I knew I wasn't going to sleep. I was more awake than I had ever been in my life. But I was a zombie. I sat and stared and tried to take in what had happened. It was so quiet after all that horrific hubbub. I felt literally empty, as if my body were hollow, formless. I felt as if I consisted of a giant, heavy head slumped over a stake that ran through the area where my abdomen would be if I still had a body. I could see my limbs moving, but I had no consciousness of moving them, nor did I perceive they were attached to what I knew as "me." I thought, "Am I making my arms move? How? Why? And why can't I feel them?" I had no awareness of sending the commands to my arms to move. My body felt like a faint, wispy outline. I felt vaster, but not solid, as if I were made of light and air.

Later, I noticed I felt as if I had a hole in my chest, replacing my heart. You hear people talk of this and it all sounds like sappy bullshit, but there I was feeling it. When I drew my attention to where my heart should be, I saw a black cavern with crazy neon lights blasting through it. The lights were similar in color to the colors used in the old Lite-Brite toys. I saw mainly neon pinks, greens, yellows and blues streaming through like electrons. For reasons unknown, I thought, "That's love."

I realized I had become an observer of myself, my experience, my feelings, and wondered if this is what "they" are talking about when they tell you what to aim for during meditation: to become an observer of your experience. If so, why did I pick such a shitty moment to achieve this? Why couldn't I have done this in India, or in meditation class where there are pretty pillows, nice incense, and a teacher with a mellifluous voice? "What the fuck is wrong with me that I didn't learn my lesson in a less costly way? What the fuck is wrong with me that my daughter had to die before I got it?"

I WAS DOUBLED over crying as I cried these words.

Hilary calmly asked me what my wise people would have to say to these questions of mine. I asked if I could lie down. She said yes, so I quickly reclined on the short couch, with my legs bent over the far arm.

I reclined and tried to get quiet, so I could hear my wise people. The woman was on my left and looked somewhat like a 1970s version of a woman, but in blue medieval attire. The man, looking somewhat wizardly, was on the right. They smiled compassionately at me.

As they spoke, I spoke aloud to Hilary.

"THAT ISN'T how it works, and you know it. You have the order wrong. It is not that you chose not to learn your lesson, so she died. It is that she died and now you can choose to learn a lesson, or not. You can choose to love, or not. You can choose to live, or not. She did not die because of anything you did or did not do. She died. And the only choice you have in the matter is about how you are going to live."

AS SOON AS I uttered those words aloud, I felt as if a hand I never realized was there released its grip on my neck. I then felt and saw a thick, heavy blanket of black goo being peeled off my chest. My entire body relaxed noticeably after this. I felt so relaxed my head dropped over to the left, because of the placement on the crappy therapy couch cushions. I relayed these feelings to Hilary (minus the harsh judgment of the crappiness of the couch).

She asked me to go to my nurturing scene.

I RELEASE BACK into the man's chest and arms, relaxed, content, and at peace. We are watching Alice play in the meadow. I am aware of how it feels to lean back into the man. I completely let go. I'm going to enjoy that in silence for a moment, OK?

Now I see and feel Alice crawl up onto my chest and nuzzle her head into my neck and right shoulder — the place she nestled in every night at bedtime. All I can see is Alice's head, but I can feel her little body on mine, and my body against the larger body behind me. Alice whispers, "I love you, Mama."

We sat there for some time.

Whole. I felt whole.

I REALIZED my entire struggle A.A.D. stemmed from the nanosecond where I was separated from my daughter. The nanosecond I stepped away from her, I ceded control over the situation — or, more accurately, the illusion of control over the situation. In that nanosecond, I saw the situation from the outside for the first time. In that nanosecond, I was no longer holding my daughter. I was no longer "in it." But most importantly, in that split nanosecond, I clearly assumed full responsibility for her death. In that split nanosecond, I felt torn between feeling like I needed to step back to let them do their job and feeling like I needed to go to her, to do *something*, because I am her mother. In the next nanosecond, it was confirmed she was dead. In that next nanosecond, I discovered we were not only separated by five feet of floor space, but also by space, time, and possibly other dimensions.

The separation. *That* was the problem. The separation from Alice — physically and spiritually. The separation of myself — simultaneously torn between wanting to actively help her and knowing I had to yield control to the professionals. The separation of my psyche — feeling I should have control over the situation, yet knowing I had no control over anything. Feeling that, as her mother, I was existentially responsible for her death, yet knowing sometimes no amount of motherly love can save a child.

It's the separation, stupid.

All of these layers of separation manifested in my body, which reenacted the struggle of feeling simultaneously pulled forward and backward, thus causing my full-body physical symptoms.

The mind-body connection is no freakin' joke.

As I sat there in my nurturing scene relaxing with Alice and the man behind me, I felt myself begin to smile and spontaneously recalled happy memories of Alice. She was so friendly to everyone — but didn't want to be touched — so we called her "The Mayor." I recalled what an easy baby she was, so easy to care for, so easy to love. Alice was almost entirely devoid of strife. And now, I miraculously felt at ease as well.

Never before had I smiled in EMDR, so I felt like I was onto something and kept at it.

I wondered aloud if Alice had any idea of all the love that had been shared in her absence.

Does she know how much love poured through our home in the days and months after her death? Does she know how deeply I love her, then and now? Does she have any idea how much more deeply I can love now after this awful experience, and how I wish to God I could have learned to love more deeply in any other way? Does she have any idea how many people loved her? Does she have any idea how many notes I get from friends and total strangers telling me they love Alice, me, and Grace? Does she know she was basically a little harbinger of love?

. . .

As soon as I said that, I felt Alice crawl up higher onto my chest. She whispered in my ear, "I know, Mama."

I felt like I exploded into stars.

I cried, but this time it was happy tears, *sans* physical tension.

I felt whole. And relaxed. And a peaceful happiness that defied description.

It was the separation. I mean, duh. It was the reason my subconscious mind placed her in the calming scene, despite my therapist not thinking it was a good idea and despite being a person who likes to "get it right" for my mentors. It was why I couldn't put the traumatic images of her away in a box or hide the box. It was why I felt psychologically stuck at the moment I was pulled away from her after performing CPR. It was why, when I finally stopped blaming myself and accepted that I did not kill her by "not learning my lesson," I felt my vulnerable side relax into a steadier part of myself and then she *came to me.*

When I accepted the separation without guilt or blame, she came to me. We were no longer separated. We were never separated, except by my own self-flagellation.

It was the mental construct of separation that caused the separation. Alice, and my love of Alice, was always there for me to access whenever I could stop punishing myself.

It may seem obvious to you in the retelling, but you don't "get it" until you get it. You can get it with your head, but you don't get it until you have an *aha* moment with your entire body, mind, and soul. Even your pinkie finger gets it in an *aha* moment. Even your red blood cells get it in an *aha* moment.

All of that psychological torture stemmed from *one nanosecond.* Life really can change in an instant, and our ability to reframe it can also change in a nanosecond. We have to hope life can improve in a nanosecond and we aren't too clueless to notice when that happens.

After my EMDR session, I was relaxed all day. I was as placid as I was after receiving a Watsu massage — which is one of the top five best things that has ever happened to me — except now I was calm *and* going about my business. I am fairly certain I have never been productive at the level of relaxation I enjoyed that day. I had not slept for more than four-hour chunks in weeks, but I *knew* I was going to sleep that night.

I slept seven hours straight for the first time in ten weeks that night.

It was perhaps the most therapeutic hour of my life. The first time I did EMDR, it was a game-changer. This session of EMDR was a life-changer.

I can't stop thinking about what my wise people told me: *Now you can choose to learn a lesson, or not. You can choose to love, or not. You can choose to live, or not.*

I choose to learn my lessons. I choose to live. And I choose to love and be loved as deeply as humanly possible as a way to honor both my daughters. And I know in my bones the only thing that can separate me from myself — and my girls — is my own self-blame, guilt, and negativity. When I love and am loved in return, my girls are present with me. Always.

The whole love.

EPILOGUE

I realize people want stories wrapped up with a pretty bow. I can give closure with a bow to no one, for I cannot provide you with something I do not have myself. Nor can I provide advice, for everyone has a different set of internal and external variables with which to work.

I have learned not to wait to step forward into the future until I get a bow on the past, because we may never be present enough to craft our future if we focus on hope for a tidy past. The past is often not tidy, and our insistence that it should be causes us to bring the past into the present and project it into the future. This creates a lot of problems. Alice died: that is my closure. It's not the closure I wanted, but death is about as "closure" as it gets.

So it's the end of the book but not the end of the love story, because grief doesn't end. I've learned to embrace this because if this story doesn't have an ending, it means our love endures. I will love Alice until I die; therefore, I am aware I will grieve her until I die. I'm finally OK knowing the rest of my history will involve grief; I don't fight it.

I'm not OK with PTSD, however, so I do fight that. I have never again experienced an intrusive image or a guilt spiral since doing

EMDR. Occasionally, I can tell I am at risk for activation of other PTSD symptoms, but I now know what to do. After my second round of EMDR, I was prescribed — and accepted — an anti-anxiety medication to have on hand when activated. I have found it helpful when I sense a PTSD spiral developing.

I am operating in our mutually agreed-upon time more often these days. Hysterical memories have become historical memories; I recall everything, but it rarely brings me to my knees anymore. I'm sure it makes it easier to interact with me, but I can't say I prefer it. Although painful beyond description, there was a liberation in those early weeks of shock, those weeks of past-present-future all jumbled together.

In later years, I realized that most of the work I found truly healing involved identifying the nanosecond my brain made up a story about an external event, understanding the damage that caused, and deciding to form a new — inner and outer — response in similar situations. All of which required extreme focus and slowing down time to the nanosecond. The trauma of finding Alice allowed me to experience the entire emotional landscape entrenched in a nanosecond, but it also kept me stuck at certain traumatic nanoseconds. In fact, I largely continued to experience life as an endless string of potentially dangerous, seemingly unrelated and directionless nanoseconds. The vastness of perspective I held before Alice died seemed inaccessible A.A.D. I couldn't see how an action now may lead to a certain future because I knew all too well that future could be destroyed by something as banal as sleep. EMDR allowed me to slow down time enough to change my perspective in those problematic nanoseconds — and also to regain some of the vast perspective I'd enjoyed before that trauma.

Later, I realized that the tools I'd learned in EMDR can help me change just about any behavior that seemed habituated or was associated with automatic responses. I just had to focus, observe my thoughts, and slow time down to the nanosecond. I could choose a different thought, a different response. It's not easy. But it's not impossible. And it becomes easier with practice.

Shortly after the timeframe documented here, I delved into PTSD studies. I recalled the "timekeeper" part of our brain is offlined in the wake of a trauma. That was certainly my experience. It was an interesting exercise to study the academics of PTSD after observing and documenting my raw experience for a spell. I did so in the hopes I could better assist others because, for me, helping others in Alice's name makes life worth living.

Obviously, I still have the urge to be Alice's historian. But I am the historian for a hero's journey that ends in the first instead of the final chapter. It's a shitty gig, but it's the gig I got.

Speaking of gigs, in subsequent years, I did — and do — my best to help others gain access to the tools that helped me. I did my best to raise money and awareness for trauma therapy, SUDC, the Southern California Counseling Center (SCCC), and other organizations that serve underserved communities. I continue to raise money for SCCC via my Agastock concerts and other fundraisers as well as speaking at their gala, taping a PSA for them, and writing about them as much as possible.

In 2016, I was contacted to start an acupuncture and meditation program at a hospital and a clinic in South Central Los Angeles, which was rewarding both professionally and personally. Lotus Seminars reached out to me to teach continuing education classes for acupuncturists on grief and PTSD, which not only helped me to help others who help others, but also helped me see my own experience from an objective perspective, which was incredibly healing. Lastly, I finally joined the SUDC Foundation. There is still no known cause(s). Therefore, there are no treatments, screenings, or opportunities for early intervention. Though it is the fifth leading cause of death in toddlers, many medical professionals have never heard of SUDC because most medical and nursing schools don't address it. For the sake of other parents, I hope this changes as soon as possible. Within the SUDC community, I have met some great friends, and found my prediction to be true:

Beautiful people, shit club.

After much searching and researching, I finally figured out my urges toward the divine feminine, etc., were trying to nudge me to surrender and acceptance, which turned out to be a blessing. We all have masculine and feminine aspects. Undeniably, the modern world demands more of our masculine. Furthermore, trauma leaves one stuck in hyper-vigilance, which is a more masculine state. My inner nudges steered me toward developing and nurturing my feminine side — surrendering and accepting. When so much is stripped away so quickly, one often steels oneself against tides of change. Those nudges helped me to remember to soften into the stripping away and to nourish myself rather than waste energy fighting an invisible, unconquerable beast: the wish to go back in time and change things. When I softened into what was taken, I found so many blessings in the rubble — none of which will replace Alice, mind you, but any port in a storm. I am grateful I listened to those nudges, knew where to look for information, and found such amazing guides and teachers along the way. I continue this inner work to this very day. These experiences have helped me find inner balance as a working mother.

I'D STILL GIVE anything to have had more time with both girls when they were little.

I CAN'T PROVIDE you with closure to this story, but I do hope to provide something. If even one other person is able to find comfort, validation, support, or resources in this story, I will be happy.

Mostly, what I hope I provided was hope itself. Hope that you can move through the roughest waters in your personal Sea of Life. Hope that you can grow, learn, and survive situations that are far from desirable. Hope that you will eventually not only survive but also thrive. Hope that communities can band together and make a significant impact on a person's ability and willingness to live. Hope that there is help out there — and in there. Hope that you can access the phoenix within you when the flames get hot, so you can ascend while making meaning of the beautiful toast of life.

RESOURCES

*S*OUTHERN CALIFORNIA COUNSELING CENTER
Providing effective, affordable counseling in Southern California as well as counselor training.

HTTPS://WWW.SCCC-LA.ORG/

HTTPS://SCCC-LA.ORG/ALICE-FERGUSON/

SUDC FOUNDATION: **Sudden Unexplained Death in Childhood**
For families who have lost children 1-18 to SUDC or other sudden, unexplained causes.

HTTPS://SUDC.ORG/

HTTPS://SUDC.ORG/ALICE-FERGUSON/

. . .

COMPASSIONATE FRIENDS: Supporting Family After a Child Dies
For families who have lost a child.

HTTPS://WWW.COMPASSIONATEFRIENDS.ORG/

OUR HOUSE GRIEF Support Center
Los Angeles-based grief support with many national resources

HTTPS://WWW.OURHOUSE-GRIEF.ORG/

GREEN BURIAL COUNCIL
For green burial locations, providers, education, and more.

HTTPS://WWW.GREENBURIALCOUNCIL.ORG/INTERACTIVE-MAPS.HTML

TRAUMA THERAPIST LOCATOR (select your country at top of site)

HTTPS://WWW.PSYCHOLOGYTODAY.COM/US/THERAPISTS/TRAUMA-AND-PTSD

USA SUICIDE HOTLINE
Call 988

READING LIST

This is not a complete list. These are the books referenced in this book or that I read during this timeframe.

Survival of the Soul by Lisa Williams

The Body Keeps the Score by Bessel van der Kolk, M.D.

Waking the Tiger by Peter A. Levine, Ph.D.

In an Unspoken Voice by Peter A. Levine, Ph.D.

Behold the Spirit by Alan Watts

The Tao of Physics by Fritjof Capra

On Grief & Grieving by Elisabeth Kübler-Ross, M.D. and David Kessler

When Things Fall Apart Pema Chödrön

The Joy of Feeling by Iona Marsaa Teeguarden

Tao Te Ching by Lao Tzu

The Gospel of Mary Magdalene translated and interpreted by Jean-Yves Leloup

Mists of Avalon by Marion Zimmer Bradley

ENDNOTES

3. WEDNESDAY: THE AFTERMATH

1. Byron, Lord George Gordon. *Childe Harold's Pilgrimage: Canto the Third.* (London: printed for John Murray, 1816.)

ACKNOWLEDGMENTS

If I individually thanked everyone who helped me navigate life A.A.D., this book would be (and was!) seven hundred pages long. No one wants a bereaved parent's *War and Peace*, so these acknowledgments will be for those who helped this book be born. Still, I vividly remember every act of kindness from every person. I will spend my life attempting to pay it forward.

Beth Figuls tenderly edited the *Mothering in Memoriam* blogs. Without that blog, this book would not exist. Beth and her husband Mo — the Figulses! — also served as beta readers for the book. They have my deepest love and gratitude.

After years of nudging me to write a book, the fabulous Teresa Strasser eventually led me by the typewriter to complete this book. This book would not exist without her guidance. I could not have asked for a better developmental editor or friend. Her feedback made me laugh and cry, but mostly, it made me a better writer. Love you, T.

A huge thanks to Kriss Light, Dan Koeppel, Liz Friedlander, Candace Cahill, and Jocelyn Cox, who also read early versions. Additionally, Kriss recorded a song, "Alice Ferguson," for which I am deeply grateful. Tommy Doyle, Sam Martinuzzi, and Meleva Steiert also provided "other eyes" on the manuscript. Without the last three, I would be crazier than a shithouse rat, and no one would understand me. Massive love to all of you.

Bliss Bowen, who supported my writing and fundraising from Day One, provided a final proof before formatting. You are a truly lovely human and friend.

Thank you to Laura Martin Pierre for being the very last pair of eyes on this manuscript and for some of the best years of my life. I began secretly writing in our Belmont apartment in the nineties. I would not be who I am today without her and those halcyon days.

Suzanne O'Keeffe is my brilliant webmaster, dear friend, and has the patience of Job. Love to you.

Rachel Thompson has been an indispensable resource on book publishing. You are everything good about humans and social media.

Rachel and I met on #WomenWriters of Twitter, organized by Megan Aronson and Abby Alten Schwartz, from whom I have learned so much. Big thanks to all of the #WomenWriters.

Alexandria Szeman deserves endless thanks for being my "other eyes" and my fabulous co-host on our podcast *This Club Suuucks: Grief Support for Parents After the Lasagnas Are Long Gone*. Love to you.

Endless thanks to Kim Grant and Pam Moore for helping me figure out how to get this book into the world and for being wonderful friends through good times and bad. I love you.

Huge thanks to Shane August for tech — and other! — support while writing this book and creating my podcast. Big love to you.

Michael (Bubba) McDonald, I can never repay you. You and Rey Herrera have provided shoulders to cry on as well as the most epic laughs of my life. I love you and your children like family. Clara Magyar, Jon Armstrong, and the Kemps (the Britalians!), you too, are family and the finest of friends. Additional thanks to Jon for the beautiful image of me and Alice.

I literally would not be here without my parents: Pat and Sandy Monroe, and Linda and Terry Gramlich. My mom was my first editor and my dad was my first photographer. All four of my parents have supported me and my girls through thick and thin. I love you all with all my heart.

I couldn't ask for a better bother, Steve. You have raised two wonderful young men: my amazing nephews, Tucker and Zeke. I am so proud of you three. Thanks to all my stepsiblings: Darin, Mandy, Jon, Josh, and Sarah. I really lucked out in the stepsibling department; I actually truly like you all! My cousin Tonja Williams has been incredibly supportive despite fighting cancer for years. I love you, warrior. My extended family has also gone above and beyond to support me through the hard times, but listing them all would require another book. And then there is my sister-from-another-mister, Gwen Mercer, who keeps me laughing through every shitstorm. Huge love to you all.

Most importantly, my brilliant, beautiful, hilarious, creative Saving Grace. Sweet girl, you inspire and encourage me every day. You are my world. I am so proud of you. I can't wait to continue to watch you change the world. Like Alice, "I love you infinity." This book, like everything, is for you.

ABOUT THE AUTHOR

Melissa M. Monroe is a mom, acupuncturist, author of the blog *Mothering in Memoriam,* and host of the podcast *This Club Suuucks: Grief Support for Parents After the Lasagnas Are Long Gone.* She lives in Los Angeles with her daughter and dog but heads to the mountains whenever possible.

For more, visit www.melissamariemonroe.com

Made in the USA
Las Vegas, NV
12 May 2023

71940031R00163